# CORPORATE EXCELLENCE

# CORPORATE EXCELLENCE

**Manu Agarwal**

KALPAZ PUBLICATIONS
DELHI - 110052

**Corporate Excellence**

Rs. 690

ISBN : 81-7835-357-1



Published in 2005 in India by
Kalpaz Publications
C-30, Satyawati Nagar,
Delhi - 110052
e-mail : kalpaz@hotmail.com

Laser Typeset at : Hansa Graphics, Delhi
Printed at : Mehra Offset Press, Delhi

# Contents

# List of Tables

# Foreword

Writing foreword of a book written by a student who is no more with us is indeed a very difficult task. A lot of emotions, old remembrances come into the way, but the last wish of the departed soul has to be fulfilled. Therefore, it gives me great honour putting forward this book to you, the readers.

The present book is a revised version of his Ph.D. thesis where he had tried to analyze as to whether the various factors contributing to corporate excellence discriminate among each other, that is, one factor may be more important that the other. He used multi-discriminant analysis for this purpose.

This is a pioneering work where multi-discriminant analysis has been used to test as to whether some ratios are more important than the others towards contributing to corporate excellence. The results are illuminating and I am sure it would be useful for managers and researchers. I wish the departed soul rests in peace and his work in the form of this book enlivens him forever.

October 19, 2004

(Prof. J.N. Shukla)
Retd. Professor
Department of Commerce
Lucknow University
Lucknow

# Preface

It is a well-established fact that the object of every company is to achieve excellence in its operations. But the big question is 'How to measure excellence?'. This poses a major problem before the researchers and analysts. Several studies have been made in this respect and the present study is also an attempt in this direction. In this study, the attempt is made to find out as to whether the financial ratios of the companies discriminate among excellent and not so excellent companies and to test if some ratios are more discriminating than others.

A number of studies have been made on the prediction of company failure or bankruptcy. The most prominent among these studies is the study done by Edward Altman. He gave a model for prediction of bankruptcy of a company. He used the technique of discriminant analysis for his study. This study also uses the same technique to find out whether discriminant analysis can be used for measuring excellence of a company and hence, this study seeks to classify companies into two categories: excellent companies and not-so-excellent companies.

This study also tries to explain which ratios are relatively more important from the point of view of measuring corporate excellence. The findings of this study may be helpful to the investors and other analysts to find out which ratios should be analyzed to assess the excellence of the company. The study may also help the companies to judge their own performance in the light of the findings of this study.

The study has been divided into seven chapters. Chapter 1 is related to the introduction of different concepts. It explains the meaning of terms like corporate excellence. It also brings forward the important features of corporate excellence and the methods of becoming excellent. This chapter also includes cases of some companies, which were earlier considered to be excellent but they failed due to various reasons.

Chapter 2 deals with some latest developments related to the field of corporate excellence. This chapter provides an insight into some latest concepts related to corporate excellence like EVA and MVA, which have been recently developed and are now widely used.

Chapter 3 deals with the review of the literature available on the related topics. This chapter discusses a number of studies where ratios were used to assess the performance of the company. This chapter summarizes many of these studies and based on these studies it attempts to find out the ratios that are most commonly used in similar studies.

Chapter 4 is related to the research methodology and research design. It explains the methodology adopted in performing this research. This chapter tries to explain how the sample was selected and the sources from where data was collected. It also gives an idea about what discriminant analysis is.

Chapter 5 deals with discussion of various measures, which can be used for measuring corporate excellence. It also describes the meaning and importance of the ratios selected for our analysis and also explains the meaning of each ratio as is used in this study.

Chapter 6 deals with the analysis and interpretation of data. In this chapter, use of discriminant analysis in corporate excellence is analyzed. It analyses the data collected year wise, industry wise and size wise. This chapter includes the discriminant functions, which can be used for different industries, companies of different size. It also provides a discriminant function that can be generally used for assessing corporate excellence of a company. This chapter also tries to explain the effect of outliers and correlation among different variables. It also explains which ratios are more important in discriminating companies between excellent and not-so-excellent companies.

Chapter 7 deals with the findings, conclusions and areas for future research. It discusses the various findings and conclusions of the study and gives an idea regarding the areas in which research can be performed on related topic in the future.

In the preparation of this thesis, I have received encouragement and support from various quarters. I am thankful to all my teachers and friends, who provided me all the support in completing this study. I am really grateful to Prof. Sidharth Sinha, Prof. Rajesh Agarwal, Prof. Ramesh Bhat and Prof. Rajendra Patel of Indian Institute of Management, Ahmedabad for providing me an insight into the topic of study.

I feel deep gratitude to Prof. J.N. Shukla for supervising this study and giving me invaluable advices on the study.

I am also obliged to the librarians of Indian Institute of Management, Ahmedabad; Indian Institute of Management, Lucknow and Tagore Library, Lucknow University for providing me all the resources I needed to complete this study.

I am also thankful to my parents for giving me all the encouragement required for completing the study.

Finally, I would be failing in my duty if I do not acknowledge the deep debt of gratitude that I owe to various writers whose writings have provided me an insight into this topic. However, the views presented in this study are my own.

**Dr. Manu Agarwal**

# 1

# Corporate Excellence : An Introduction

**Concept of Excellence :** The word 'excellence' comes originally from the Greek word *arête* meaning the sum of good values that makes up character. Thus it is clear that excellence means something good. Excellence means surpassing or outstanding achievement. Excellence is important for the society because everyone wants to be excellent. Excellence works as a benchmark for what is above standard. Thus, excellence is something above mediocrity. According to Blake and Mouton, "Excellence is seen as the single most valid and most risk-free path to profitability. An excellent corporation is by definition a profitable one. It is one that is able to compete, to solve its operational problems, to lead, to innovate, to live by a rigorous code of ethical responsibility, to evolve, to be profitable year after year, decade after decade. An excellent corporation is a smart corporation; one that is able to get the lead and to keep it in a competitive free enterprise system."[1] Excellence is the result of continuous improvement. Improving on one's past performance on a continuous basis leads to excellence. In other words, if we want to be excellent we have to improve on past in the present and we will have to go on improving on present in the future. Thus, excellence is related to performance. According to Ronnie Lessem, "Excellence, or outstanding performance, is acquired in cumulative stages. Unless a business realizes potential of each stage, it cannot fully excel. To excel, overall, is a progressive process."[2] Thus. excellence is a continuous, never ending and ever-expanding quest for perfection, and in that sense it is an ever-evolving target. Excellence refers to a surpassing quality or merit and an outstanding performance in one's field of work. A vital force for growth, it sets an example or a standard of behavior and galvanizes people into doing something remarkable. It can act as bedrock of renaissance in developing countries. The varied forms of excellence can be seen in competitions, inventions and innovations. Breaking one's own past record, succeeding at an extremely difficult-task, doing some unique or pioneering work, developing one's multi-dimensional potentials, rendering selfless service and pursuing self-enlightenment, etc., are a few others. Excellence involves immense mental and physical effort, which must be recognized and suitably rewarded. It flourishes in the nurseries of corporations, but is noticeably absent in corporations which are hotbeds of politics and cold-blooded commercialism. It requires both individual and team efforts.

**Corporate Excellence :** As stated above, everyone wants to be excellent; it is the case with companies. Every company, whether a manufacturing concern, a trading body or a service sector unit; whether a public or a private sector unit; and irrespective of size of operations performed by it, wants to be excellent. According to A.K.Jain, "Organizational excellence is a continuous process and not a one-time act either of investment or innovation. Organizational excellence is defined as the ability of an organization to continuously renew itself."[3] This excellence may take various forms. Continuously renewing itself and adapting to the dynamic and competitive business world of today is just one form of excellence. In an excellent organization management devotes attention to the external environment and determining issues like corporate positioning, product mix, organizational architecture and culture, budgeting and information systems, and management control systems. In excellent companies, the distinguishing factor is the possessive passion with which employees owned corporate decisions and targets. Continuously giving good financial results along with performing its social responsibility is another form of excellence. According to Blake and Mouton, "An excellent organization is able to achieve and sustain an outstandingly high return on investment over long periods of time. Its managers have learned how to identify and create new opportunities while meeting present responsibilities. They plan for the future in the face of stiffening competition and rising costs."[4] To satisfy all the interest groups is another form of excellence. According to Pradeep Khandwalla, "Excellence means surpassing or outstanding achievement. Excellence is important to society because it sets an example, a standard of behavior that is socially useful."[5]

Excellence may be of different forms. It may be human excellence, natural excellence, or organizational excellence. Being the best in one's own field is the best form of human excellence. Take the examples of Mother Teresa, Sachin Tendulkar or Amitabh Bachchan; all of them have achieved excellence in their respective fields. According to Ronnie Lessem, "Excellence is related to seven attributes which everyone of us has, in varying degrees, and in differing combinations. These are- physical prowess, social ability, intellectual skill, willpower, analytical ability, intuitive awareness, and creative imagination."[6] According to Pradeep Khandwalla, "Human excellence comes in many forms. Being the best amongst competitors is one form. Doing much better than what one could do in the past is another form of excellence. Performing far better than the general standard in a field is a third form of excellence. Persisting and succeeding at a difficult task that can be accomplished only after a long haul is also a form of excellence. Doing something unique, something no one has done before, is still another form of excellence. Pioneering is a related form of excellence. Invention or innovation is still another form of excellence."[7] Here, our main concern is organizational excellence. Organizational excellence may also take various forms and all of them have their own significance. There are different operations performed in any organization, which are related to marketing, finance, manufacturing, personnel, or R&D. Each operation will have its own excellence like marketing excellence, financial excellence, etc. Organizational excellence indicates sustained commitment and quest of the organizational members to individually excel in their chosen area of work. Thus, specialization is a form of excellence. Also, there are a number of interest groups in any organization like shareholders, customers, creditors, employees, financial institutions, government, etc. and also society as a whole. All of them have their own interests and they want their interests to be satisfied. Generally, these interests are of a conflicting nature. Hence, it is essential to bring a balance among the interests of all the interest groups. Satisfying interests of all of them is one form of organizational excellence. Being the best among the competitors is another form of excellence. Continuously renewing itself and adapting to the dynamic and competitive business world of today is one form of excellence. Continuously giving good financial results along with performing its social responsibility is another form of excellence. Remaining profitable not only in short term but also in long term is another form of excellence. Thus there are many different forms of corporate excellence. Thus we can say that excellence in organizations results from the way managements harmonize their valuable resources. The style of getting the best out of these resources varies from one organization to another. But one thing is common among all the excellent organizations that all of them identify their areas of strengths and weaknesses and they plan accordingly. For this purpose they perform SWOT analysis. The leading companies of the world like Microsoft, Wal-Mart, Compaq etc. all have one thing in common that all of them innovate. They all seem to create a corporate theme, a philosophy of managing people and weave their HR processes around that basic core philosophy.

**Features of Corrorate Excellence :** From the above definitions of corporate excellence, we can say that the important features of corporate excellence are as follows:

1. Organizational (corporate) excellence is defined as the ability

of an organization to continuously renew itself. Thus, excellence is a continuous process.

2. An excellent organization is able to achieve and sustain an outstandingly high rate of return on investment over long periods of time.
3. An excellent organization always tries to enrich the capacities of its members and pays attention on the development of its employees.
4. An excellent organization tries to utilize the full capacity of individuals effectively and efficiently.
5. An excellent organization tries to fulfill expectations of all the interest groups.
6. An excellent organization is able to rake quick and correct decisions.
7. An excellent organization has good labor management relationship. It does not have problems like frequent strikes, lockouts, labor turnover, absenteeism, etc.
8. An excellent organization maximizes the value of its shareholders.
9. An excellent organization has good relationship with its customers, creditors, borrowers, etc.
10. An excellent organization is able to pay back its liabilities as and when they become due and also to utilize its assets optimally.

Thus, in an excellent organization, all the departments work effectively, be it finance or marketing, personnel or production, everything is always right. All the interest groups are always satisfied.

The patterns to be followed by truly excellent companies are as follows:

1. They have a single, integrated improvement strategy.
2. They do not fall prey to fads.
3. They have a conscious focus on using a set of fundamental principles of management to guide behavior in their organization.
4. They actively manage performance.
5. They link rewards for all employees to organizational performance.
6. They benchmark themselves against other leading companies and set corresponding stretch goals.
7. Most importantly, they link together the elements of strategy, actions and operations, performance and rewards in powerful, sensible ways.

An organization is excellent is no guarantee that it will remain excellent and profitable in the long run also. There are a number of cases where companies considered excellent could not face tough times and that resulted in their downfall. The reasons of their downfall may be different. Some examples of such companies are Uptron, Murphy, HMV, etc. The most important reasons for their decline were labor problems and fast changing technologies.

Case of HMV: About 30 years ago, HMV was the market leader in gramophone records. But the company could not keep pace with the fast changing technologies in its industry. As the time passed, gramophones were replaced by tape recorders, music systems, and most recently by audio CD players. In old days, people used to listen music on gramophone but with the coming up of new technologies and new products in the form of tape recorders and audio CD players, use of gramophone has ceased. Thus, HMV, which was the leader at the time when gramophones were popular, could not remain on top after coming up of new technology. New companies like T-Series and Venus came up with good quality audiocassettes at a lower price and so the market of HMV was reduced sufficiently. Recently HMV has come up with dance remixes of a number of old songs and collections of famous singers of their time like Mukesh, Mohd. Rafi, Kishore Kumar, Lata Mangeshkar etc. and is expecting to regain its old position in the music industry. Even the management at HMV accepts this. In words of one of them, "It started in the mid-eighties when music wasn't of the quality of the melodious late 50's and 60's. The music market wasn't exactly booming. That was when Gulshan Kumar decided to step in with Super Cassettes and cash in on the rich repertoire of film music. He came up with recordings of golden oldies in the voices of struggling singers like Kumar Sanu and Sonu Nigam who were only too willing to sing them. These recorded versions were then packaged with say Kishore Kumar's face prominently displayed below the title 'Hits of Kishore Kumar'. Never mind the actual singer's name printed in inconspicuous letters in an equally inconspicuous corner. The low priced cassettes sold well. These version recordings came to be known as cover versions.

Interestingly, while all music companies, starting with T-series, Venus and Tips, made a killing out of cover versions, HMV, to whom the rights of the repertoire belonged, took a passive stand. Recently, T-Series had a field day releasing the 'tribute' series of Anuradha Paudwal, which had a rich collection of evergreen songs composed by greats like Madan Mohan, SD Burman, Roshan and RD Burman. HMV seemed to suddenly wake up sometime ago, and released a compilation of Mohammed Rafi's great hits.

But, unfortunately, they were a few months too late. T-Series sponsored PhiRafi, which contained the same Rafi classics in Sonu Nigam's voice had already done the damage. Interestingly, Rafi's original couldn't stand against Sonu's 'cover'. Dealers attribute this to better recording quality and good promotion. "The sound quality of the original was not up to the mark. Besides, HMV didn't promote their album as well as Super Cassettes. Cover versions sell better in interiors and consumers there don't care who is singing as long as he gets good quality of music," says a music dealer. But Sonu's PhiRafi and Anuradha's 'tribute' series sold well with the urban consumers too. Mehmood Curmally of Rhythm House says, "Anuradha Paudwal and Sonu Nigam are good singers and T-Series had wisely picked up the best of the all-time favourite songs."

There is no doubt however, that HMV has been very slow on the uptake. Its effort to gain lost ground by bringing out three original remix versions, Mere Sapnon Ki Rani, Yeh Mera Dil and The Greatest Dance Mix Collection did not amount to much. Why has HMV been sleeping over a phenomenon, which has led others to steal a march over it? "

Case of UPTRON and BALCO: Both UPTRON and BALCO had a considerable market share in their products. Even if they were not on the top, they were amongst the leaders in their industries. But continuous labor problems, frequent strikes, lockouts and increased absenteeism have led to a situation where they are nowhere near the tops in the respective industries. Thus these companies could not retain their positions in the industry due to poor handling of labor problems.

UPTRON: UPTRON was established in March 1979 at Lucknow for the production of Aluminium electrolytic capacitors. In the same year another unit was established at Allahabad for the production of televisions. Very soon, it had a handsome market share in both the products. By the year 1986, it was one of the leaders of both industries. From then onwards, it continuously shifted its offices from one place to another both at Lucknow and Allahabad. Due to these, its market share started coming down and finally the division for television was soon suffering from heavy losses. In 2000, UPTRON tried to revive itself through diversification into information technology by setting up an InfoTech mart in Lucknow. But with the recent strikes and lockouts at UPTRON the revival could not come through.

BALCO: BALCO was incorporated in 1965 and since then, it has been a major player in the aluminium industry. It also played a major role in development of the nation's Intermediate Range Ballistic Missile (IRBM) Agni and surface missile Prithvi by developing and supplying special aluminium alloys. Till recently, it was one of the most prominent companies of the Chhattisgarh state. But the decision to disinvest 51 percent of the government share in BALCO has brought storms in the company, which was running normally. Chhattisgarh government strongly opposed the move of the Central Government and it led to a tussle between the two. As a result of this conflict, production ceased for almost two months and it resulted into heavy losses. Recently, on 11th December 2001, Supreme Court gave its decision endorsing the Centre's decision of disinvestments. Analyzing the financial statements of the company, it can be easily observed that although both assets and liabilities of the company have increased but the liabilities have gone up at a much faster rate than those of assets, thus resulting in loss of capital. Also, the position is clear by government rating of BALCO. It was excellent for the year 1993-94 which declined to very good for years from 1994-95 to 1998-99 and declined further to good in the year 1999-2000.

Case of Murphy: Murphy was considered to be one of the best companies for electronics products. But it could not keep pace with the fast changing technology in the industry. It continued to manufacture radios when transistors replaced the entire radio market. Thus to remain excellent it is not only important to be excellent in own product but also it has to keep continuous watch on the external environment whether some new technology is coming and also to adapt itself to that new technology. This is where the concept of excellence, that a company, which can adapt itself to the outside environment fast, is excellent, comes into picture. This also shows that being excellent is one thing and remaining excellent is another. A company, to be truly excellent, should have both of them.

Case of Hero Cycles: In the bicycle industry, Hero was on the top. But, with the increasing competition it could not sustain its top position. A number of competitors emerged like Atlas, etc. Then Hero shifted to manufacture of two-wheelers like motorcycles (Hero Honda) and mopeds (Hero Puch).

There are a number of other examples (like Hmt, Ece, Weston, etc.) where a company considered being excellent could not maintain its position and failed. Though, the reasons of their failure may be diverse. They may range from labor problems to increased competition, from changing technology to coming up of substitute products. But one thing is clear that to remain excellent is a different aspect from being excellent. It is said that being on top is difficult but staying on top is even more difficult.

**Achieving Corporate Excellence :** One of the most important forms of corporate excellence is continuous success. According to John S. Oakland, "The key to success is to align the employees of the business, their roles and responsibilities with the organization and its processes. Some of the obstacles to achieving total organizational excellence are that it can be seen as time-consuming, bureaucratic, formalistic, rigid, impersonal, and/or the property of a specialist group. These may be overcome through education, communication, participation, involvement, facilitation, and support."[8] He adds, "There are 10 principles which may not lead directly to excellence, but they certainly can be found in those organizations which aspire to become world-class. These are:

1. The organization needs long-term commitment to constant improvement.
2. Adopt the philosophy of zero errors/defects to change the culture to right first time.
3. Educate people to understand the customer-supplier relationships.
4. Do not but products or services on price alone- look at the total cost.
5. Recognize the improvement of the systems needs to be managed.
6. Adopt modern methods of supervision and training – eliminate fear.
7. Eliminate barriers between departments by managing the processes- improve communications and teamwork.
8. Eliminate:
   (a) arbitrary goals without methods
   (b) all standards based only on numbers
   (c) barriers to pride of workmanship
   (d) fiction, get facts by using the correct tools
9. Constantly educate and retrain- develop the experts in the business
10. Develop a systematic approach to organizational excellence."[9]

In summary, we can say to achieve excellence, identify customer- supplier relationships, manage processes, change the culture, improve communication, and show commitment.

According to David Bradford and Allan Cohen, "For excellence, all the members of the organization share a commitment to making the unit extraordinarily successful in accomplishing agreed-on organizational objectives. The concern for task accomplishment includes a strong emphasis on quality- of products, services, and members themselves."[10] According to M.K. Raju, "For achieving excellence in management, an integrated approach is required. You must have a goal to achieve in order to show a result-oriented performance."[11] He further adds, "Some of the core beliefs for sustained success are: excellence in quality; service to the customer; sustained growth with profits; welfare of the employees and service to the shareholders."[12]

According to Arun Kumar Jain, "In excellent organizations, the distinguishing factor was the possessive passion with which employees owned corporate decisions and targets."[13] Thus, employee participation is a key to excellence.

According to Ronnie Lessem, "Excellence, or outstanding performance, is acquired in cumulative stages. Unless a business realizes the potential of each stage it cannot fully excel. To excel, overall, is a progressive process."[14] He adds, "Excellence is a layered set of qualities as follows:

| ***Stage*** | ***Pioneering*** | ***Managed Organisation*** | ***Developing Corporation*** |
|---|---|---|---|
| *Quality* | Person centered | Product centered | Environment centered |
| *Physical* | Hard work | Hands-on, value-driven | Physical/ human energy |
| *Social* | Personal contact | Productivity through people | Community of interests |
| *Mental* | Mental agility | Flexible structures | Enabling change |
| *Emotional* | Entrepreneurial Flair | Autonomy & entrepreneurship | Spirit of enterprise |
| *Conceptual* | Simple form, lean Staff | Loose-tight properties | Complex form |
| *Aesthetic* | Hunch and intuition | Design for wholeness | Conscious evolution |
| *Creative* | Personal imagination | Corporate mission | Industrial transformation |

Thus, excellence is achieved in different stages from *pioneering* through *managed organization* to *developing corporation."*[15]

According to E.B. Knauft, Renee A. Burger & Sandra T. Gray, "The four hallmarks of excellence are- mission as the guiding force, presence of a true leader, existence of a dynamic board, and the ability to attract resources."[16]

According to Kenneth E. Ebel, "Excellence requires a systematic approach to developing a Total Quality culture and building Total Quality into the fabric of the organization, including:

- Transforming the attitudes of the people in the organization
- Developing an integrated set of improvement mechanisms

which provide for a never-ending organization-wide effort

- Controlling the quality of products, services and activities
- Gearing up for strategic quality management."[17]

Ebel adds further, "Leadership is the key to excellence. The aim of management must be to help people to perform and improve their job."[18]

Thus, if every individual in the organization fully knows what he/she has to do and how to do it, this will lead to excellence on individual level and if each and every individual performs its work with excellence, the organization will become excellent.

"Business World magazine has identified following criteria for excellence:

1. Quality of management
2. Quality of products
3. Innovativeness
4. Financial soundness
5. Quality of personnel
6. Responsibility to community
7. Profitability
8. Company to work for (related to work environment)"[19]

Thus, if a company is sound on all these attributes, it is moving towards achieving excellence.

**Importance of Corporate Excellence :** From the above discussion, it is clear that in the present competitive environment, it is essential for an organization to keep pace with the rapidly changing business world. Today's economic environment is highly dynamic in nature. If an organization is not able to adapt itself to changes in the environment fast, it cannot succeed. Also, no organization can think of success if different groups related to business are not satisfied. It has to satisfy customers by providing them quality products at reasonable price. The shareholders want maximum return in the form of dividend. The creditors (suppliers as well as financial institutions) want their money back on time with interest. The employees want higher salaries, bonus and other benefits. The management wants maximum profits. The government wants tax and duties to be paid in time. Every organization has to satisfy all these requirements in order to grow. Most of the times, these interests are of a conflicting nature. An excellent organization is able to make a proper balance among these conflicting interests. Thus, corporate excellence is important to satisfy the diverse interest groups and hence, to run the organization smoothly and effectively.

It is said that a team is as good as its members. An organization has to work like a team of employees. So it is important to develop each employee individually. Only then an organization will be excellent. Thus corporate excellence is also related to organizational development. This will also provide the employees great satisfaction.

Corporate excellence also helps in raising funds, which is the major requirement to run any organization properly (also described as life blood of an organization, i.e., as playing the same role in an organization as played by blood in human body). An organization, which has achieved corporate excellence, has very good reputation in the market. Due to its reputation, the investors readily invest in the shares of these companies. Lenders and financial institutions also provide them funds more easily at lower rate of interests as they are more assured of getting the amount back. The suppliers of raw materials also provide credit to such companies more easily than they do it to a company with no reputation. Thus, corporate excellence also helps in raising the funds from the market.

Also, an excellent organization is able to recruit better and more talented personnel than their non-excellent counterparts. Everybody wants to work for an organization of repute. Thus, corporate excellence also helps in getting services of more talented and experienced personnel.

**Objective of Study :** It is said that numbers are easier to understand and interpret. Here, we have to compare different companies on the basis of excellence achieved by them and also to classify the companies into excellent and not-so-excellent companies. So comparison is made easy by representing the excellence in terms of numbers. The objective of this study is to find out a set of financial ratios which can be used to find out the excellence of a company; and then using discriminant analysis, finding out a discriminant function to discriminate between excellent and not-so-excellent companies. Till now, discriminant analysis is generally used to predict bankruptcy of a company. A number of studies have been conducted to use discriminant analysis for prediction of bankruptcy by a number of writers. All of them have used different sets of ratios for this purpose. The most prominent among such management thinkers is Edward Altman who gave a model of Z-score for predicting the bankruptcy of a company.

The objective of this study is to use discriminant analysis technique for assessing the excellence of the companies. Here our objective would be to analyze different ratios on the basis of their discriminating power between excellent and non-excellent companies and then to develop a multiple discriminant model based on ratios, which could easily discriminate between the two groups i.e. excellent and non-excellent companies.

This study is also aimed at finding out the relative importance of different ratios in measuring the corporate excellence of a company. Thus it will help in finding the ratios, which are relatively more important than other ratios for assessing excellence of a company. This study will be advantageous to both investors and the management of the company. Investors like to invest in the companies that provide adequate returns to them. This study will help them in tracing such companies. From the management point of view this study will help them in analyzing the performance of the company and will also let them know where the company stands on the basis of its performance.

## References

1. Blake, R.R. & Mouton, J. S. (1968): *Corporate Excellence Diagnosis;* Austin, Texas; Scientific Methods Inc.; p. 1.
2. Lessem, R. (1985): *The Roots of Excellence*; London; Fontana; p. 31
3. Jain, A.K. (1998): *Corporate Excellence;* New Delhi; Excel Books ; p. 35
4. Blake, R. & Mouton, J. (1974): *Corporate Excellence through Grid Organisational Development;* Houston; Gulf Publication ; p. 2.
5. Khandwalla, P.N. (1995): *Organisational Designs for Excellence*; New Delhi; Tata McGraw Hill ; p. 42.
6. Lessem, R. (1985): *The Roots of Excellence;* London; Fontana; p. 15.
7. Khandwalla, P.N. (1995): *Organisational Designs for Excellence;* New Delhi; Tata McGraw Hill ; p. 42.
8. Oakland, J.S. (1999): *Total Organisational Excellence;* Oxford; Butterworth- Heinemann; pp., 22-23.
9. Oakland, J.S. (1999): *Total Organisational Excellence;* Oxford; Butterworth- Heinemann; pp., 16-18.
10. Bradford, D.L & Cohen, A.R. (1984): *Managing for Excellence: The Guide to Developing High Performance in Contemporary Organizations;* New York; John Wiley; pp., 6-7.
11. Raju, M.K. (1995): *Managerial Success;* Hyderabad; Hyderabad University; p. 109.
12. Raju, M.K. (1995): *Managerial Success;* Hyderabad; Hyderabad University; pp., 109-111.
13. Jain, A.K. (1998): *Corporate Excellence;* New Delhi; Excel Books; p. 38.
14. Lessem, R. (1985): *The Roots of Excellence;* London; Fontana; p. 31

15. Lessem, R. (1985): *The Roots of Excellence;* London; Fontana; p. 37.
16. Knauft, E.B., Burger, R.A. & Gray, S.T. (1991): *Profiles of Excellence;* San Fransisco; Jossey Bass Publication; p. 150.
17. Ebel, K.E. (1991): *Achieving Excellence in Business;* Milwaukee; ASQC Quality Press; p. 2.
18. Ebel, K.E. (1991): *Achieving Excellence in Business;* Milwaukee; ASQC Quality Press; p. 12.
19. *Business World;* 28 March – 10 April 1990; p. 74.

# 2

# Corporate Excellence : Some Recent Developments

**Recent Developments in the Concept of Corporate Excellence :** The shareholders are the owners of the company. Hence, their interests cannot be ignored. The aim of every business entity should be to maximize shareholders wealth and all the activities of the firm should be directed to achieve this objective. Investors measure overall performance of a firm to decide whether to invest in the firm or to continue with the firm or to exit from it. They build their expectations about the estimated growth of the business. Therefore current performance is not the only determinant of market value. Even if the current performance is better in relative terms, poor growth prospects adversely affect the value of the firm. In order to achieve goal congruence, managers' compensation is often linked with the performance of the responsibility centers and also with firm-performance. Therefore, selection of the right measure is critical to the success of a firm. Thus, a new concept of corporate excellence is emerging. This concept states that an organization that maximizes the value of shareholders' wealth is excellent. That is why in recent times, the concept of Economic Value Added (EVA) and Market Value Added (MVA) have gained so much importance. These terms are also related to excellence. *Fortune* magazine has called it "today's hottest financial idea and getting hotter," and management guru Peter Drucker, writing in the *Harvard Business Review*, has described EVA as a vital measure of total factor productivity, one that reflects all the dimensions by which management can increase value. According to Al Ehrbar, "EVA is a measure of corporate performance that differs from most others by including a charge against profit for the cost of all the capital a company employs."[1]

The New York based financial advisory Stern Stewart & Co. postulated a modified concept of economic income in 1990 in the name of Economic Value Added (EVA). EVA is just a variation of residual income. Alfred Marshall was one of the earliest to mention the residual income concept in 1890. He defined Economic Profit as total net gains less the interest on invested capital at the current rate. EVA, the value based benchmark used for judging the financial performance of any business entity may be literally defined as the quantum of economic value generated by a company in excess of its cost of capital.

According to Ashish K. Bhattacharyya and B.V. Phani, "Proponents of EVA argue that EVA is a superior measure as compared to other performance measures on four counts:

- It is nearer to the real cash flows of the business entity.
- It is easy to calculate and understand.
- It has a higher correlation to the market value of the firm.
- Its application to employee compensation leads to the alignment of managerial interests with those of the shareholders, thus minimizing the supposedly dysfunctional behavior of the management."[2]

Mathematically, EVA is the difference between the percent rate of return and the percent cost of capital; or what we may call the return spread times the capital. Thus EVA reflects efficiency as well as growth. The return spread shows efficiency while the amount of capital indicates growth. To increase EVA, a company can improve its efficiency, reduce its cost of capital, or increase its capital. Thus,

**EVA = NOPAT – (Cost of Capital X Capital Employed)**

Where NOPAT is Net Operating Profits After Tax and is calculated as:
*NOPAT= (Profits After Tax + Non- Recurring Expenses + Revenue Expenditure on R&D + Interest Expense + Goodwill written off + Provision for Taxes) - Non-Recurring Income - R&D Amortization - Cash Operating Taxes*

MVA measures the value added by the management over and above the capital invested in the company by the investors. It is said that maximizing Market Value is the best thing that can be done for shareholders. Mathematically, MVA is the difference between the enterprise value and the amount of invested capital. Thus,

**MVA = Market Value of the firm – Economic Capital**

The market value of the firm is the sum of market value of equity, debt, and preference shares. Economic Capital is calculated as:
*Economic Capital = Net Fixed Assets + Investments + Current Assets – (NIBCLs + Miscellaneous Expenditure not written off + Intangible Assets) – (Cumulative Non-Recurring Losses + Capital Expenditure on R&D + Gross Goodwill) – Revaluation Reserve – Cumulative Non-Recurring Gains*
*Where NIBCLs mean Non-Interest Bearing Liabilities*

This is what shareholders ultimately care about, because it answers the question of whether a business is worth more than the original investment or not. Market value alone says nothing at all about wealth creation. It tells the value of a company, of course, but it ignores the vital matter of how much capital the company invested to achieve that value. Wealth creation is determined not by the market value of the company, but by the difference between market value and the capital that investors have committed to the company.

Both EVA and MVA are related to wealth creation and maximization of shareholders' wealth. The shareholder value is the ultimate goal of management. It is based on a combination of past and projected cash flow patterns, the cost of capital, and the expectations of investors. The major deviation in the two concepts is that though both refer to the same concept of shareholder value addition; EVA is more of economic importance while MVA is inclined towards accounting sense.

Implementing them can help companies substantially improve their wealth creation efforts. But, as is true of most worthwhile change initiatives, it takes time, needs an integrated approach and commitment from the top.

## References

1. Ehrbar, Al (1999): *EVA: The Real Key to Creating Wealth;* New York; John Wiley & Sons, Inc.; p. 1.
2. Bhattacharyya, A.K. & Phani, B.V.: *Economic Value Added: In Search of Relevance; Decision; July – December 2000;* Vol. 27 No. 2; pp. 32-33.

# 3

# Corporate Excellence : Some Studies

**History of Similar Studies :** As stated above, discriminant analysis has been used for the prediction of bankruptcy. Also some thinkers have given a number of ratios, which can be used for analyzing the performance of a company. This is also related to measuring corporate excellence of a company. Basically, while measuring corporate excellence, we are just trying to analyze the performance of the company from different angles. These studies have given different measures of performance in their studies. They have used different methods to analyze the performance. These methods include univariate studies, multivariate analysis, etc. Following are some of such studies:

1. Peters and Waterman
2. IDBI study
3. Business World – MARG study
4. Economic Times – HBSAI study
5. Sengupta Committee
6. Beaver
7. Altman.

Now we will discuss these studies in detail:

1. **Peters and Waterman:** They took a sample of 62 companies and they analyzed data for a 20-year period from 1961 to 1980. They selected six measures of long-term superiority. In the words of Peters and Waterman, " the companies were not truly excellent unless their financial performance supported their halo of esteem." Out of the six measures taken by them, three are measures of growth and long-term wealth creation over a twenty-year period and the other three are measures of return on capital and sales. The six are:
   (a) Compound asset growth from 1961 through 1980 (a "least squares" measure that fits a curve to annual growth data).
   (b) Compound equity growth from 1961 through 1980 (a "least squares" measure of annual growth data).

(c) The average ratio of Market value to Book Value. "Market to book" is a standard approximation for what the economists call "wealth creation".
(d) Average return on total capital, 1961 through 1980 (net income divided by total invested capital)
(e) Average return on equity, 1961 through 1980
(f) Average return on sales, 1961 through 1980.[1]

They also gave 8 attributes. The eight attributes that emerged to characterize most nearly the distinction of the excellent, innovative companies are as follows:

- A bias for action- Do it, fix it, try it.
- Close to the customer- To provide unparalleled quality, service, and reliability.
- Autonomy and entrepreneurship- Be creative. Encourage practical risk-taking and support good tries.
- Productivity through people- Respect for the individual and treat them as the root source of the quality and productivity gain.
- Hands-on, value driven-QSC & V (Quality, Service, Cleanliness and Value).
- Stick to the knitting- Stay reasonably close to the businesses you know.
- Simple form, lean staff- The underlying structural forms and systems in the excellent companies are elegantly simple.
- Simultaneous loose-tight properties- Both centralized and decentralized.[2]

2. **IDBI study[3]**: In a first-of-its kind study in the history of Indian industry, an IDBI sponsored study combines quantitative financial research with the opinions of purposively selected monitors of the corporate scene to select India's ten most excellent companies. S.K. Bhattacharyya, former visiting professor of management at Harvard Business School and IFCI professor of management at Indian Institute of Management, Ahmedabad, conducted this study. After much debate and the testing and rejection of a whole host of financial performance yardsticks, Bhattacharyya, with the approval of the advisory committee, selected several yardsticks on the basis of which the financial performance of almost 200 companies was evaluated over the five-year period 1978-79 to 1982-83. These were as follows:
   (a) Growth rate of sales turnover on weighted average basis
   (b) Compound growth rate of assets
   (c) Profit before tax as a return on capital employed

(d) Working capital as a ratio of gross sales
(e) Dividend coverage ratio
(f) Debt equity ratio

In the words of Bhattacharyya, "In my considered opinion, these are the most important dimensions of financial performance. They evaluate an enterprise's performance in terms of growth of sales, management of working capital, asset creation, profitability in relation to sales turnover and soundness of financial policies in relation to funds structuring."

3. **Business World – MARG study[4]:** In India, Business World has pioneered the study of corporate reputations by commissioning the Bombay based Marketing and Research Group Private Ltd. (MARG) to conduct the first ever such poll (in December 1983) of the reputations of some of India's largest corporate entities. The opinion polling exercise was conducted in Bombay, Delhi, Calcutta and Madras among 201 corporate executives drawn from different functional areas and levels of management and having a minimum of five year's experience, to determine India's most respected large companies. Later on, in 1984, this study was extended to determine India's most respected medium-sized companies.

   The most recent BW-MARG poll to determine India's most respected companies has used the following eight attributes
   (a) Quality of Management
   (b) Quality of Product/Services
   (c) Innovativeness
   (d) Financial Soundness
   (e) Quality of Personnel
   (f) Community and Environment Responsibility
   (g) Profitability
   (h) Company to Work For.

4. **Economic Times – HBSAI study[5]:** The idea of instituting a corporate performance award for the first time in India cropped up at one of the discussions which the representatives of the Harvard Business School Association of India (HBSAI) had with The Economic Times during July-August 1983. The Awards Committee selected important quantitative criteria for initial analysis to narrow down the universe of companies. They prepare a primary list of 25 top performers each from among the giant and mini-giant companies in the private corporate sector and a corresponding list of 25 top performers from among the public sector companies. The Committee came to the consensus that the following five criteria are fairly comprehensive performance indicators of any business enterprise:

(a) Gross Surplus Ratio
- Gross Surplus Ratio
- Gross Profit before Depreciation, Interest and Taxes (For awards prior to 1988 it was Gross Profit before Interest and Taxes)
- Total Assets

(b) Sustainable Growth Rate

(c) Net Profit Return on Net Worth

(d) Creation of Value
- Average annual compound growth rate for 5 years of (Number of Equity Share X Stock Price)
- Average annual compound growth rate for 5 years in net worth (excluding new capital issues)

(e) Cash flow as a percentage of total gross assets

Based on these 5 criteria a combined ranking of each of these companies was determined. The first 25 companies from each of the 3 groups were then subjected to a qualitative assessment. Factors that were considered for qualitative assessment were:

1. Contribution to Development
2. Employment Generation
3. Core Sector Projects
4. Backward Area Projects
5. Social/Rural Development expenditure
6. Creation of New Technology – R & D Expenditure
7. Industry Environment and Growth Rate
8. Human Resources Management- Labor and Innovative Management Practices
9. Investment Cycle
10. Conservative vs. Unorthodox Accounting Practices
11. Inflation Accounting; Best Management in an Inflationary Environment
12. Export Performance

5. **Sengupta Committee[6]:** This Committee was formed to assess the performance of the public sector enterprises in the country. It submitted its first report in 1986. It was recommended that for evaluating financial performance of public enterprises, the following criteria should be used:

   (a) Gross margin on assets (for all enterprises)

   (b) Net Profit (for core sector and profit making enterprises)

   (c) Gross Margin on Sales (service enterprises)

In respect of core sector enterprises, the rate of net profit should be at least a stipulated percent and gross margin on capital should be improving over time. In the non-core sector, enterprises should be judged against the industry average for both gross margin on capital employed and the rate of net profit. In evaluating the performance of service enterprises, attention should be focused on direction of change in the gross margin on sales. In loss making enterprises, gross margin should be positive.

In addition, the following are required to be monitored:

1. Ratio of loan liabilities to assets
2. Ratio of wages to value added per worker
3. Cash loss per worker

As far as qualitative assessment of the enterprises was concerned, the Committee gave the following measures:

1. Productivity and Cost Reduction
2. Technical Dynamism
3. Project implementation: It includes:
    - Percentage utilization of plan funds
    - Average slippage in ongoing projects
    - Percentage cost revision for the approved investment programme relative to the previous year
4. Technology Up gradation
5. Relations with Parliament
6. Price Preference
7. Award of contracts
8. Expenditure on township and residential quarters

6. **Beaver[7]:** Beaver was among the first to focus on the ability of ratios to predict failure. A univariate prediction model of corporate failure was developed and tested on observations of 79 failed and 79 non-failed firms over the period 1954-1964. The financial data of the failed corporations were grouped by year, prior to failure, for five years, and were matched with the financial statements of the non-failed firms. Thirty financial ratios were computed over a period of five years prior to failure for each of the 79 failed and 79 non-failed firms. He divided these ratios into six groups as follows:
    - Group I (Cash Flow Ratios)
        1. Cash Flow to Sales
        2. Cash Flow to Total Assets
        3. Cash Flow to Net Worth
        4. Cash Flow to Total Debt

- Group II (Net Income Ratios)
  1. Net Income to Sales
  2. Net Income to Total Assets
  3. Net Income to Net Worth
  4. Net Income to Total Debt
- Group III (Debt to Total Asset Ratios)
  1. Current Liabilities to Total Assets
  2. Long term Liabilities to Total Assets
  3. Current plus Long Term Liabilities to Total Assets
  4. Current plus Long Term plus Preferred Stock to Total Assets
- Group IV (Liquid Asset to Total Asset Ratios)
  1. Cash to Total Assets
  2. Quick Assets to Total Assets
  3. Current Assets to Total Assets
  4. Working Capital to Total Assets
- Group V (Liquid Asset to Current Debt Ratios)
  1. Cash to Current Liabilities
  2. Quick Assets to Current Liabilities
  3. Current Assets to Current Liabilities
- Group VI (Turnover Ratios)
  1. Cash to Sales
  2. Accounts Receivables to Sales
  3. Inventory to Sales
  4. Quick Assets to Sales
  5. Current Assets to Sales
  6. Working Capital to Sales
  7. Net Worth to Sales
  8. Total Assets to Sales
  9. Cash Interval
  10. Defensive Interval
  11. No Credit Intervals

Beaver used three types of analysis in order to establish the predictive power of financial ratios:

1. A comparison of mean values
2. A dichotomous classification test
3. An analysis of likelihood ratio.

Later on, Beaver examined the impact of impact of market prices in the prediction of corporate failure. Using the original sample of data, he found that the stock market prices indeed predicted failure sooner than individual financial ratios.

Beaver's work was one of the most complete studies of the

relationship between financial ratios and business failure. However, it was criticized on the ground of being a univariate approach.

7. **Altman[8]:** Altman developed a model for the prediction of corporate bankruptcy using a sample of 33 bankrupt and 33 non-bankrupt matching firms over the period of 1946-1965. Twenty-two financial ratios were considered in different combinations as predictors of failure. The ratios, which were included, and the weights given were determined by the significance of the contribution they made to the predictive ability of the model. The final set of ratios was determined by F-tests and computer runs analyzing the possible alternatives. The following combination of five ratios did the best overall job in discriminating between the failed firms and the non-failed firms:
   (a) Working Capital/Total Assets (a liquidity measure)
   (b) Retained Earnings/Total Assets (a measure for reinvested earnings)
   (c) EBIT/Total Assets (a profitability measure)
   (d) Market Value of Equity/Book Value of Total Liabilities (a measure for the firms' financial structure or leverage)
   (e) Sales/Total Assets (a measure for the sales generating ability of the firm's assets)

A cut off point for the Z-score was determined in such a way as to minimize the overlap between bankrupt and non-bankrupt groups. The lead given by Altman in applying the Multiple Discriminant Analysis technique to predict corporate failure was followed by several researchers though differ from Altman's in respect of the variables included in the discriminant function.

8. **Springate[9]:** This model was developed in 1978 at Simon Fraser University by Gordon L.V. Springate, following procedures developed by Altman in the U.S. Springate used step-wise multiple discriminate analysis to select four out of 19 popular financial ratios that best distinguished between sound business and those that actually failed. The Springate model takes the following form :

$$Z = 1.03A + 3.07B + 0.66C + 0.4D$$

$Z < 0.862$; then the firm is classified as "failed"

where A = Working Capital/Total Assets
B = Net Profit before Interest and Taxes/Total Assets
C = Net Profit before Taxes/Current Liabilities
D = Sales/Total Assets

This model achieved an accuracy rate of 92.5% using the 40 companies tested by Springate. Botheras (1979)[10] tested the Springate Model on 50 companies with an average asset size of $2.5 million and found an 88.0% accuracy rate.

There are a number of other similar studies, which are given below along with the performance measures used by them:

1. Blum[11]
   (a) Liquidity
      (i) Short-Run Liquidity Flow Position
         (1) The 'quick flow' ratio
         (2) Net quick assets/ Inventory
      (ii) Long-Run Liquidity Flow Position
         (1) Cash flow/ Total liabilities
         (2) Net worth at fair market value/ Total liabilities
         (3) Net worth at book value/ Total liabilities
   (b) Profitability
      (i) Rate of Return to common stockholders who invest for minimum of three years
   (c) Variability and Trend
      (i) Standard deviation of net income over a period
      (ii) Trend 'breaks' for net income
      (iii) Slope for net income
      (iv) Standard deviation of net quick assets to inventory ratio
      (v) Trend breaks of net quick assets to inventory ratio
      (vi) Slope of net quick assets to inventory ratio

2. Libby[12]
   (a) Net income over total assets
   (b) Current assets over total assets
   (c) Cash over total assets
   (d) Current assets over current liabilities
   (e) Sales over current assets

3. Altman, Haldeman & P. Narayanan[13]
   (a) Return on Assets
   (b) Stability of Earnings
   (c) Debt service
   (d) Cumulative Profitability
   (e) Liquidity
   (f) Capitalization
   (g) Size

4. Sapp & Seiler[14]
   (a) Deposit growth rate

(b) Return on Equity
(c) Capital to risk assets ratio
(d) Interest as a percentage of loans

5. Thune and House[15]
(a) Change in sales
(b) EPS
(c) Stock Price
(d) Return on Equity
(e) Return on Capital

6. Van de Ven[16]
(a) Efficiency
(b) Acceptance
(c) Service Quality
(d) Financial Dependence

7. Whitehead and Gup[17]
(a) Deposit growth
(b) Return on Assets
(c) Return on Equity

8. Wood and La Forge[18]
(a) Growth in net income
(b) ROI

9. Ackelsberg and Arlow[19]
(a) Change in sales (Averaged over 3 years)
(b) Change in earnings (Averaged over 3 years)

10. Ansoff[20]: 21 indicators including:
(a) Sales growth rate
(b) Earnings growth rate
(c) Assets growth rate

11. Deakin[21]
(a) Net Income/Total Assets
(b) Cash/Total Assets
(c) Current Assets/Current Liabilities
(d) Sales/Current Assets
(e) Current Assets/Total Assets

12. L.C.Gupta[22]: 56 ratios including:
(a) EBIT/Sales
(b) EBIT/Total Assets
(c) EBIT/Interest
(d) PAT/Net Worth

(e) Depreciation/Net Fixed Assets
(f) Net Worth/Debt
(g) Net Worth/Sales
(h) Current Assets/Current Liabilities
(i) Quick Assets/Current Liabilities
(j) Net Working Capital/Sales
(k) Net Working Capital/Debt
(l) Current Assets/Sales
(m) Net Fixed Assets/Gross Fixed Assets
(n) Quick Assets/Current Assets

13. Bracker[23]
(a) Growth in revenue
(b) Growth in net income
(c) CEO compensation

14. Bracker and Pearson[24]
(a) Growth of sales and profitability
(b) Ratio of costs to revenue

15. Burt[25]: He used averages based on 2 and 3 years' data
(a) Growth in profitability and ROI
(b) Change in ROI

16. Fulmer and Rue[26]
(a) Sales growth
(b) Earnings growth
(c) Return on sales

17. Kallman and Shapiro[27]
(a) Revenue
(b) Profitability
(c) Return on capital
(d) Return on equity

18. Leontiades and Tezel [28]
(a) Return on assets
(b) Return on equity
(c) Price earnings ratio
(d) Growth in sales
(e) Growth in EPS

19. Odom and Boxx[29]: He used growth in attendance, offerings, total additions, and baptisms for measuring performance.

20. Pearce[30]
(a) Return on sales

(b) Return on assets
(c) Sales growth

21. Rhyne[31]
(a) Return to investors (Single year and average of last 10 years)
(b) Return on equity

22. Welch[32]
(a) Price- earnings multiple

23. Klein[33]
(a) Deposit growth
(b) Profitability

24. Kudla[34]
(a) Stock Returns

25. Grinyer and Norburn[35]
(a) Return on Assets

26. Chaganti and Damanpour[36]
(a) Long term debt to capital ratio
(b) Return on Assets
(c) Return on Equity
(d) Price – Earnings Ratio
(e) Total Stock Return

These are some of the studies that tried to find out different performance measures that can be used for the performance evaluation of a company. Testing of excellence is highly related to the measurement of performance because only those companies can be called excellent which outperform other similar companies. On deep analysis of these different studies, certain measures were used in most of the studies. These measures are[37]:

1. Earnings growth
2. Deposit growth
3. EPS growth
4. Sales growth
5. Price- earnings ratio
6. Profitability ratios
7. ROA
8. ROE
9. ROI

Thus, basically the measures used in these studies were indicating towards growth and profitability, as these are very important for an organization to be excellent. If any organization is not profitable, it is not excellent. Also, all profitable companies cannot be called as excellent because another important factor for excellence is sustaining the profitable position and continuous growth. Hence, if it is not growing, we cannot define that organization as an excellent organization.

## References


1. Peters, Thomas J. & Waterman, Robert H. (1998): *In Search of Excellence: Lessons from America's Best Run Companies;* Harper & Row; pp. 22-23.
2. Peters, Thomas J. & Waterman, Robert H. (1998): *In Search of Excellence: Lessons from America's Best Run Companies;* Harper & Row; pp. 15-17.
3. Thakore, Dilip: *India's most excellent companies;* Business World; December 23,1985 – January 5, 1986 ; pp., 40-46.
4. *India's most respected companies 1985;* Business World; February 3-16, 1986; Vol. 5; pp., 38-44.
5. The Economic Times: April 29, 1989; pp., 7 & 9.
6. *Sengupta Committee Report – II: Three indices for assessment of performance;* Business Standard; 9 July, 1986; p. 5.
7. Beaver, W.: *Financial ratios as predictors of failure: Empirical research in accounting;* Journal of Accounting Research; Supplement to Vol. 5; January 1967; pp., 71-111.
8. Altman, E.I.: *Financial ratios, discriminant analysis and the prediction of corporate bankruptcy;* Journal of Finance; September 1968; pp., 589-609.
9. Springate, Gordon L.V.: *Predicting the Possibility of Failure in a Canadian Firm;* Unpublished M.B.A. Research Project; Simon Fraser University; January 1978.
10. Botheras, Donald A: *Use of a Business Failure Prediction Model for Evaluating Potential and Existing Credit Risk;* Unpublished M.B.A. Research Project, Simon Fraser University, March, 1979.
11. Blum, M.: *Failing company discriminant analysis;* Journal of Accounting Research; Spring 1974; pp., 1-25.
12. Libby, R.: *Accounting ratios and the prediction of failure: Some behavioural evidence;* Journal of Accounting Research: Spring 1975; pp., 150-161.
13. Altman, E.I., Haldeman, R. & Narayanan, P.: *Zeta Analysis;* Journal of Banking & Finance; June 1977; pp., 29-54.
14. Sapp, R. W. and R. E. Seiler: *The relationship between long-range planning and financial performance of U.S. commercial banks;* Managerial Planning ; Vol. 29; September/ October 1981; pp., 32-36.
15. Thune, S.S., & House, R.J.: *Where long range planning pays off;* Business Horizons; August 1970; pp., 81-87.
16. Van de Ven, A. H. (1980): *Problem solving, planning, and innovation, Part*

*I. Test of the program planning model;* Human Relations; Vol. 33; pp., 711-740.

17. Whitehead, David D. and B. E. Gup: *Bank and Thrift Profitability: Does Strategic Planning Really Pay?;* Economic Review of the Federal Reserve Bank of Atlanta; Vol. 70; October 1985; pp., 14-25.
18. Wood, D.R., & La Forge, R.L. (1979): *The impact of comprehensive planning on financial performance;* Academy of Management Journal; Vol. 23 No.3; pp., 516-526.
19. Ackelsberg, Robert and P. Arlow (1985): *Small Businesses Do Plan and It Pays Off;* Long Range Planning; Vol. 18 No. 5; pp., 61-67.
20. Quoted from: Boyd, B.K. (1991): *Strategic Planning and Financial Performance: A MetaAnalytic Review;* Journal of Management Studies; Vol. 28 No. 4; pp., 353-374.
21. Deakin, E.B.: *A discriminant analysis of predictors of business failure;* Journal of Accounting Research; March 1972; pp., 167-179
22. Gupta L.C. (1983): *Financial Ratios for Monitoring Corporate Sickness;* Oxford University Press; pp., 133-135.
23. Quoted from: Boyd, B.K. (1991): *Strategic Planning and Financial Performance: A MetaAnalytic Review;* Journal of Management Studies; Vol. 28 No. 4; pp., 353-374.
24. Bracker, Jeffrey S. and J. N. Pearson (1986): *Planning and Performance of Small, Mature Firms;* Strategic Management Journal; Vol. 7; pp., 503-522.
25. Burt, D.N. (1978): *Planning and performance in Australian retailing;* Long Range Planning; Vol. 11 No. 3; pp., 62-66.
26. Fulmer, R.M. & Rue, L.W. (1974): *The Practice and Profitability of Long Range Planning;* Managerial Planning; Vol. 22; pp., 1-7.
27. Kallman, E.J. & Shapiro, H.J. (1978): *The Motor Freight Industry - A Case against Planning;* Long Range Planning; Vol. 11; pp., 81-86.
28. Leontiades, M. & Tezel, A. (1980): *Planning Perceptions and Planning Results;* Strategic Management Journal; Vol. 1; pp., 65-75.
29. Odom, R.Y. & Boxx, W.R. (1988): *Environment, Planning Processes, and organizational performance of churches;* Strategic Management Journal; Vol. 9; pp., 197-205.
30. Quoted from: Boyd, B.K. (1991): *Strategic Planning and Financial Performance: A MetaAnalytic Review;* Journal of Management Studies; Vol. 28 No. 4; pp., 353-374.
31. Rhyne, L.C. (1986): *The Relationship of Strategic Planning to Financial Performance;* Strategic Management Journal; Vol. 7; pp., 423-436.
32. Welch, Jonathan B.: *Strategic Planning Could Improve Your Share Price;* Long Range Planning; Vol. 17; April 1984; pp., 144-147.

33. Klein, H.E. (1981): *The impact of planning on growth and profit;* Journal of Bank Research; Vol. 33 No. 2; pp., 4-9.

34. Kudla, R.J. (1980): *The Effects of Strategic Planning on Common Stock Return;* Academy of Management Journal; Vol. 23 No. 1; pp., 5-20.

35. Grinyer, P.H. & Norburn, D. (1975): *Planning for Existing Markets: Perceptions of Chief Executives and Financial Performance;* The Journal of the Royal Statistical Society; Vol. 138, Series A; pp., 70-97.

36. Chaganti, R. & Damanpour, F.: *Institutional Ownership, Capital Structure, & Firm Performance;* Strategic Management Journal; October 1991; p. 485.

37. Boyd, B.K. (1991): *Strategic Planning and Financial Performance: A Meta-Analytic Review;* Journal of Management Studies; Vol. 28 No. 4; pp., 353-374.

# 4

# Research Methodology and Research Design

**Hypothesis :** The following are the two hypotheses of this research:

1. There are certain ratios that discriminate between the excellent and non-excellent companies. These ratios are as follows:
   (a) Return on Investment
   (b) Debtors Turnover
   (c) Creditors Turnover
   (d) Raw Materials Turnover
   (e) Finished Goods Turnover
   (f) Net Sales/ Total Assets
   (g) Fixed Assets Productivity
   (h) Current Assets Productivity
   (i) Net Sales/ Capital Employed
   (j) Cash to Current Liabilities
   (k) Quick Ratio
   (l) Current Ratio
   (m) Debt Equity Ratio
   (n) PBIT/Interest
   (o) Sales growth
   (p) PBT (NNRT)/Total Assets
   (q) Equity Dividends/PAT
   (r) PAT (NNRT)/Net Sales
   (s) PBIT (NNRT)/Total Assets
   (t) PBDIT (NNRT)/Capital employed
2. Some of these ratios are relatively more important than other ratios in discriminating between excellent and non-excellent companies. The following ratios are likely to be more important than other ratios:
   (a) ROI
   (b) Creditors Turnover
   (c) Raw Materials Turnover
   (d) Net Sales/ Total Assets

(e) Current Assets Productivity
(f) Current Ratio
(g) Debt Equity Ratio
(h) Sales growth
(i) Equity Dividends/PAT
(j) PBT (NNRT)/ Total Assets

**Methodology :** The methodology of this research can be explained under two separate heads:

1. Sample Selection and Data Collection: This section contains description of the nature of information sought for the study and the tapping of sources to collect such information. The period selected for the study and the rationale thereof has also been described in this section.
2. Analysis of Collected Data and Development of the Discriminant model: This section contains the procedure adopted for the selection of variables for the study and the description of statistical techniques applied in the research.

**Sample Selection:** To perform this research, the first step was selection of a sample. For this purpose the list of companies, which appeared in the BT-500 companies, was taken. It was decided to perform the research for 5 years as it was found to be the most suitable period for research. While selecting the sample, it was kept in mind that only those companies are taken in the sample that appear in all the BT-500 lists. It was found that the financial data of many companies for the year 2000-2001 was not available at the time of research. Hence, it was decided to analyze the data for the period 1995-96 to 1999-2000. Looking at the BT-500 lists of these years, it was found that 255 companies are appearing in all the five years' list. To bring homogeneity in the sample, the financial companies were left out from the sample. Thus, 45 out of original set of 255 companies were deleted and the second stage of sample consisted 210 companies. Out of these 210 companies, it was found that for 8 companies, data for the year 1999-2000 was also not available. Hence, we were left with 202 companies.

To make the sample more representative of the Indian industrial scene, it was decided to divide these companies into different industries to which they belonged. While taking out this sample, it was kept in mind that all the industries should get a proper representation, which should be proportionate to the number of listed companies in that industry. For this purpose, the list published by the Bombay Stock Exchange was used. This list is published in the Bombay Stock Exchange Directory, which is divided into 18 volumes and 36 sections. These sections are as follows:

| *Section Number* | *Industry* |
|---|---|
| 18. | Coal and Mining |
| 19. | Cement |
| 20. | Potteries, Tiles, Refractories and Glass |
| 21. | Cotton Spinning Mills |
| 22. | Spinning and Weaving Mills |
| 23. | Jute Textiles |
| 24. | Synthetic Fibres, Silk & Woollen Textiles |
| 25. | Paper, Pulp and Hardboard |
| 26. | Electronics, Electric Equipments and Cables |
| 27. | Steel |
| 28. | Aluminium |
| 29. | Metals, Alloys, Metal Products and Structurals |
| 30. | General Engineering |
| 31. | Chemicals, Dyes, Pharmaceuticals, Refineries and Plastics |
| 32. | Sugar and Breweries |
| 33. | Food Products |
| 34. | Tea Plantations |
| 35. | Coffee, Rubber and Other Plantations |
| 36. | Miscellaneous |

It was found that the BT-500 companies were heavily consisting of the companies from Section 31 i.e. the pharmaceuticals companies. To make the sample more representative of the actual number of companies in a particular industry, companies from this section and other disproportionate sections were removed. It was done in such a way that the final sample of 180 companies was the most proportionate sample from different industries in relation to the number of companies in that industry.

**Data Collection:** After finalizing the sample of companies, the next step is collection of financial data for each of these companies. The financial data of different companies is being published by a number of organizations and all of them analyze the data in a different way. Also, the data is available on a number of websites. After looking at a number of data sets, it was decided to take up the data, which was available online on PROWESS sponsored by CMIE (Center for Monitoring Indian Economy Private Limited). The selection of CMIE data was basically because of its easy availability online on PROWESS and the comprehensiveness of the data. In the CMIE data set, a number of ratios were calculated which included:

1. Comparative Ratio Analysis
2. Structure of Assets/ Liabilities
3. Inventory / Working Capital Cycle
4. Asset Utilization Ratios
5. Liquidity Ratios
6. Profitability Ratios

Thus, a wide range of ratios was available in the CMIE financial data. In the PROWESS, all these data are given in the *Company* Window under the head *Industry Analysis*; sub-head *Financial Analysis*; and topic *Key Ratios*. Regarding nature of the information required, along with the key ratios, information regarding the industry and the size of the company is required. Here, size is related to the net worth of the company. According to the size of the company, the frequency distribution appears as below:

| *Net Worth (in Rs. Crores)* | *No. of Companies* |
|---|---|
| Less than 100 | 31 |
| 100-200 | 47 |
| 200-300 | 23 |
| 300-400 | 28 |
| 400-500 | 12 |
| 500-600 | 6 |
| 600-700 | 6 |
| 700-800 | 4 |
| 800-900 | 4 |
| 900-1000 | 1 |
| More than 1000 | 18 |

It should be noted that all the companies in the last four groups are from Group 1 i.e. excellent firms. Hence, for the purpose of analysis, some groups are clubbed as below:

| *Net Worth (in Rs. Crore)* | *No. of Companies* |
|---|---|
| Less than 100 | 31 |
| 100-200 | 47 |
| 200-300 | 23 |
| 300-500 | 40 |
| More than 500 | 39 |

**Selection of Variables:** Once the data for all the companies is collected, the next major step is to select the variables i.e. financial ratios to be used in further analysis. For this purpose, we have to finalize various measures of corporate excellence.

**About Discriminant Analysis :** Discriminant analysis is a technique, which develops certain rules from sample observations, which enables us to classify a new observation into one of the groups of total population. Here, our attempt will be to develop a rule so that a company can be classified into one of the two groups: excellent and not-so-excellent companies. Thus, discriminant analysis is a useful tool for dividing total population into mutually exclusive groups on the basis of certain clearly defined variables. In discriminant analysis, we analyze different variables on the basis of their discriminating power. Here, discriminating power means the significance of a particular variable in discriminating a large number of companies into two mutually exclusive and clearly defined groups of excellent companies and not-so-excellent companies. The basic assumptions of discriminant analysis are as under:

1. The variables are normally distributed;
2. the groups are discrete and known;
3. each observation in each group is described by a set of characteristics or variables.

The purpose of discriminant function is to derive the linear combination of variables which best discriminate between the groups. It attempts to determine the weights to be given to each of the original variables in order that the resulting composite score will have maximum potentiality for discriminating between the numbers of the two groups.

In this study, financial ratios are used as discriminant variables and the company excellence as the predicted or dependent variable. This analysis takes the simplest form i.e. uni-dimensional, as there are only two groups. The discriminant analysis determines the discriminant coefficients of a set of variables (financial ratios), which do the best job of discriminating between excellent companies and non-excellent companies. When these coefficients are applied to actual ratios, a basis for classification into one of the two mutually exclusive groups exists.

Discriminant analysis is chosen as an appropriate technique since it has the merit of considering an entire profile of ratios common to the relevant companies, as well as the interaction of these properties. Secondly, it has the merit of yielding a model with a relatively small number of selected variables (i.e. ratios), which has the potential of conveying a great deal of information.

It is assumed for the application of Discriminant Analysis that financial ratios used as discriminatory variables are having normal distribution. This assumption is, however, based upon some of the empirical studies, which concluded that financial ratios have normal distribution. These studies were conducted by Bird and McHugh; Horrigan; Deakin etc.

**Limitations of the Model**

1. The rankings of Business Today as given in the list of BT-500 companies are assumed to be ideal. This assumption may not be true.
2. The assumption that the first 250 companies are excellent and the last 250 companies are not-so-excellent may not be true.
3. The study is totally based on quantitative factors and it totally ignores the qualitative factors, which may be equally important for assessing the corporate excellence of the company.

# 5

# Corporate Excellence : Some Measures

**Measures for Corporate Excellence :** The bases of selecting different ratios are a number of studies conducted by different researchers on some related topics like bankruptcy prediction as stated in the last chapter. A number of ratios have been taken up as performance measures in these studies. On analyzing these ratios, it can be easily said that all these ratios indicate one of the following three:

(a) Performance
(b) Investment
(c) Status

Thus, the different measures taken for measuring excellence can also be classified into following three categories:

1. Measures of financial performance
2. Measures of investment
3. Measures of financial status

As stated above, the performance measures can be very easily taken as measures for excellence as the performance is the major indicator of excellence. An excellent company always tries to perform better than its competitors in order to grow and develop in the present highly competitive environment.

1. **Measures of financial performance:** Performance has two very important aspects: *profitability* and *liquidity*. Profitability is the ability of the company to earn maximum profit with minimum investment and the capacity of management to generate surplus in the process of business operations. It is the overall measure of efficiency. Profitability is distinguished from 'Profits'. Profits refer to the absolute quantum of profits whereas the profitability refers to the ability to earn profits. Lord Keynes remarked, 'Profit is the engine that drives the business enterprise'. W.M. Harper remarks, "Profitability is a relative measure – it indicates the most profitable alternative. Profit, on the other hand, is an absolute measure, it

indicates the overall amount of profit earned by a transaction." There are a number of ratios available for measuring profitability of a company. These ratios include EBIT/Sales, Gross Profit ratio, Net profit ratio, EPS, DPS, Dividend Payout ratio, ROCE, ROE, ROA, etc. Thus, in all the profitability ratios, a measure of profit is in the numerator, which is to be divided by a factor, which is indicative of the investment. The term profit in itself is ambiguous. Just by saying the term *profit*, one cannot guess whether the discussion is on accounting profit or economic profit. Even in the category of accounting profit, it is not clear whether it is Gross Profit, Net Profit, Operating Profit, EBDIT, EBIT, PBT, or PAT. Also if we limit our definition of profit to a limited sense, it has many other disadvantages. The most important of these disadvantages is the measuring unit of profit i.e. money. The value of money changes with time and the profits earned in one period and equal amount of profits earned in a different period do not have same value. But profit as a measure does not differentiate between the two. Despite of these disadvantages, profit is very important for proper and smooth running of an organization. Hence, we cannot ignore profit while measuring the excellence. Profit provides for internal resources to an organization and also external financing is much easier for a profitable company than a non-profitable one. Profit also affects the goodwill of the company.

Liquidity means a firms' ability to pay back all its liabilities as and when they become due out of its own resources, i.e., without borrowing from any outside source. A firm cannot be called excellent if it needs external support for paying back its past debts. Thus, a firm should have sufficient funds to pay back all the liabilities in time. As regards liquidity, different ratios available are Current Ratio, Quick Ratio, Acid Test Ratio, etc. All these ratios express a relationship between assets and liabilities as the liabilities have to be paid out of assets. An excellent company has such a proportion of assets and liabilities that its current liabilities can be easily paid out of its current assets. Current assets are the short-term assets and current liabilities are the short-term liabilities. Thus, the relationship between current assets and current liabilities is more important as there is a sense of urgency involved in such transactions. That is why; most of the liquidity ratios establish a relationship between these two components, which can be easily drawn from a company's Balance Sheet.

2. **Measures of investment:** Shareholders are the owners of the firm

and the primary objective of a business is to maximize the value of its shareholders' wealth. Shareholders invest in the firm in the expectation of high returns. For a firm to be truly excellent, it should fulfill the expectations of its shareholders, as they are the providers of funds to the firm and without funds, no company can perform its operations.

Another source of funds is through borrowed funds but that will involve payment of interest at a high rate. This also involves good market standing and reputation, as the funds are available looking at its past performance and current market standing. Hence, for better availability of funds for investment, market standing is important. The shareholders are provided return in two forms: dividend and capital appreciation. All the profits earned by a company are not distributed in the form of dividend and some portion is retained in the form of reserves. These reserves result into the capital appreciation, which is reflected in the market price of shares.

3. **Measures of financial status:** As stated above, funds are available via owned sources (shareholders and retained earnings) as well as borrowed sources (debentures, bonds). Both these sources have their own advantages and disadvantages. Hence it is essential to maintain a proper balance between these two sources. This is explained by debt-equity ratio. Other ratios in this category are debt ratio and equity ratio. Also, growth is an important part of financial status. So, it is important to analyze growth in sales and growth in net worth.

**Ratios Selected for Analysis :** A large number of ratios are available for analysis and it is not possible to include all the ratios available in our analysis. Although it is very difficult to select few of a number of ratios for analysis but to make this analysis possible, I have selected a few important ratios, which are as follows:

1. Return on Investment (X1)
2. Debtors Turnover (X2)
3. Creditors Turnover (X3)
4. Raw Materials Turnover (X4)
5. Finished Goods Turnover (X5)
6. Net Sales/ Total Assets (X6)
7. Fixed Assets Productivity (X7)
8. Current Assets Productivity (X8)
9. Net Sales/ Capital Employed (X9)
10. Cash to Current Liabilities (X10)
11. Quick Ratio (X11)

12. Current Ratio (X12)
13. Debt Equity Ratio (X13)
14. PBIT/Interest (X14)
15. Sales growth (X15)
16. PBT (NNRT)/Total Assets (X16)
17. Equity Dividends/PAT (X17)
18. PAT (NNRT)/Net Sales (X18)
19. PBIT (NNRT)/Total Assets (X19)
20. PBDIT (NNRT)/Capital employed (X20)

The selection of ratios was based on the popularity in the literature i.e. the frequency of appearance of financial ratios in similar literature and also on the basis of various concepts of corporate excellence discussed in the previous chapters. These ratios may be calculated and interpreted in different ways by different analysts. Hence, it is essential to clarify the calculations involved in finding out these ratios for this study. Some important concepts and calculations involved in determination of these ratios are as follows:

1. Sales: Income generated from main business activities like sale of goods and services, fiscal benefits, trading income. It also includes internal transfers but excludes expenses capitalized.
2. Net Sales: Sales excluding indirect taxes and duties such as excise, sales tax, etc.
3. NNRT: Income from non-recurring transactions net of non-recurring expenses. Non-recurring transactions include profit/loss on sales of fixed assets/sale of investments, provisions written back, prior period income/expenses, insurance claims, etc.
4. Interest payments: Interest paid on short term as well as long term loans. Other financial charges such as rollover charges, discounting charges are included here. For aggregates of profits such as PBDIT, PBIT and ratio analysis, lease rent is added to interest payments.
5. PBDIT (NNRT): Profit before depreciation, interest and tax (net of non-recurring transactions).
6. Depreciation: Depreciation provision for the year on owned assets and leased out assets. Depreciation is net of lease equalization and also excludes depreciation on revalued assets.
7. PBIT (NNRT): Profit before interest and tax (net of non-recurring transactions).
8. PBT (NNRT): Profit before tax (net of non-recurring transactions).
9. PAT (NNRT): Profit after tax (net of non-recurring transactions).

10. Current liabilities: Includes sundry creditors, acceptances, interest accrued and due, etc. Short-term borrowings such as cash credit from banks and commercial papers are included in current liabilities but share application money amount is excluded from it.
11. Current assets: Inventories of raw materials, stores, finished and semi-finished goods, cash and bank balances, receivables such as sundry debtors, advances, investments in marketable securities excluding that of in group companies form part of current assets. Inter corporate loans and housing loans to employees are excluded from current assets.
12. Quick Assets: Includes cash and bank balance, sundry debtors (excluding debtors exceeding six months), marketable securities (excluding that of in group companies).
13. Inventories: Stock of raw materials, stores and spares, finished and semi-finished goods.
14. Total Receivables: Sundry debtors, bills receivable, interest receivable, loans and advances, etc. form part of total receivables.
15. Sundry Debtors: Sundry debtors are net of provision. For certain ratios like quick ratio, debtors exceeding six months are excluded from debtors.
16. Total Assets: Total assets are net of revalued assets and the expenditure to the extent not written off.
17. Average: Average is the mean of the current and previous year's value for a particular indicator.
18. Average daily sales: Sales divided by 365 days. Sales are taken net of internal transfers.
19. Average days of debtors: It is arrived at by dividing average debtors by average daily sales. It refers to the credit period (in days) extended to debtors.
20. Debtors turnover ratio: It is calculated by dividing 365 by average days of debtors.
21. Average daily cost of sales: Cost of sales divided by 365 days.
22. Average days of creditors: It is arrived at by dividing average creditors by average daily cost of sales. It refers to the credit period (in days) availed from creditors.
23. Creditors turnover ratio: It is calculated by dividing 365 by average days of creditors.
24. Average days of raw materials and stores: Average raw materials and stores stock divided by average raw materials and stores expenses.

25. Raw materials turnover: 365 divided by average days of raw materials and stores.
26. Average days of finished goods: Average finished goods stock divided by average daily cost of sales.
27. Finished goods turnover: 365 divided by average days of finished goods.
28. Capital employed: A sum of net worth and long term borrowings i.e. excluding short term borrowing such as cash credit from banks and commercial paper. In the case of accumulated losses being higher than long-term borrowings, capital employed related ratios are not calculated.
29. Net worth: Paid up equity and preference capital plus reserves and surplus. Paid up equity and preference capital is net share application money. The reserves are net of revaluation reserves and miscellaneous expenditure to the extent not written off. Accumulated losses, if any, are also deducted from reserves.
30. Total borrowings: Includes short and long term borrowings. Loans from banks, financial institutions, government, deferred sales tax loans, debenture and bonds, fixed deposits, commercial papers, loans from corporates/promoters, foreign currency loans are considered. Though, borrowings such as cash credit from banks or commercial papers form part of total borrowings, for certain ratio calculations, short term debts are treated as current liabilities. Thus, in the calculation of current ratio short-term loans from banks and commercial papers are added to the current liabilities.

Mathematically, these calculations can be represented as follows (as taken from the PROWESS base file):

total_income (sales +other_income +change_in_stocks)
net_sales (sales - indirect_taxes)
fee_based_income (inc_fin_services - (inc_security_trade + inc_dividend + inc_interest + inc_lease_hire + inc_bill_discount + inc_forex_gain + leased_profit_asset_sale))
fund_based_income (inc_fin_services - fee_based_income)
operating_income (sales)
services_operating_inc (sales - sales_mfg - sales_trading - fiscal_benefits - internal_transfer -inc_fin_services)
bank_operating_inc (inc_fin_services + gain_invst_sale)
non_interest_inc (inc_fin_services - inc_interest)
chg_in_wip_stock (change_in_stocks - chg_in_fg_stocks)
mfg_inc_others (sales - sales_mfg - sales_trading - fiscal_benefits - internal_transfer)
ser_inc_others (sales_mfg + fiscal_benefits +inc_fin_services +

internal_transfer)
fin_inc_others (sales - inc_security_trade - inc_dividend - inc_interest - inc_lease_hire - inc_bill_discount - inc_forex_gain)
bank_inc_others (inc_fin_services - inc_security_trade - inc_dividend - inc_interest - inc_lease_hire - inc_bill_discount - inc_forex_gain - inc_comm_brokerage)
exp_raw_mat (tot_raw_mat_expense - exp_stores_spares - purchase_fg_goods-packaging_expenses)
prev_stk_raw_materials (prev(stk_raw_materials))
rawmatpur (tot_raw_mat_expense - exp_stores_spares - purchase_fg_goods + stk_raw_materials - prev_stk_raw_materials)
raw_material_purchase (if (rawmatpur <0.00, 0.0. rawmatpur))
cost_of_production (tot_raw_mat_expense - chg_in_wip_stock + energy + (wages * 0.70) + oth_operating_exp + repairs_plant + depreciation)
selling_cost (advertising + marketing + distribution + bad_debts)
cost_of_sales (cost_of_production + selling_cost + (0 - chg_in_fg_stocks))
admin_n_oth_costs (other_rent + repairs_total - repairs_plant + other_expense + amortization + (wages* 0.30))
total_cost (cost_of_sales + admin_n_oth_costs)
ser_operating_exp (tot_raw_mat_expense + energy+ (wages*0.70)+oth_operating_exp+repairs_plant+depreciation)
fin_operating_exp (tot_raw_mat_expense + (wages*0.70) + oth_operating_exp+depreciation+exp_interest+lease_rent)
bank_operating_exp (tot_raw_mat_expense + (wages*0.70) + oth_operating_exp+depreciation+exp_interest+lease_rent)
mfg_oth_operating_exp (oth_operating_exp+repairs_plant)
ser_oth_operating_exp (oth_operating_exp + tot_raw_mat_expense - purchase_fg_goods -change_in_stocks+energy+depreciation)
fin_oth_operating_exp (tot_raw_mat_expense + energy + oth_operating_exp - change_in_stocks -loss_security_trade - exp_forex_loss - exp_prov_diminution_invst +indirect_taxes-interest_tax)
bank_oth_operating_exp (oth_operating_exp - loss_security_trade - exp_forex_loss -exp_prov_diminution_invst)
mfg_other_exp (other_expense + other_rent)
ser_other_exp (other_expense + other_rent + repairs_total + amortization + indirect_taxes)
fin_other_exp (other_expense + repairs_total + advertising + marketing + distribution + amortization + other_rent)
bank_other_exp (other_expense + repairs_total + advertising + marketing + distribution + amortization + indirect_taxes- interest_tax)
nnrt (extra_ordinary_exp -extra_ordinary_inc)
net_exports (total_exports - total_imports)
retained_profit (net_profit - dividends)
pref_dividends (dividends - equity_dividends)
value_of_output (sales - indirect_taxes + change_in_stocks)
gross_value_added (pbdit_nnrt + wages + lease_rent + other_rent)

net_value_added (gross_value_added - depreciation)
pbdit (net_profit + tax + exp_interest + depreciation + lease_rent)
pbdit_nnrt (net_profit + tax + exp_interest + depreciation + lease_rent - extra_ordinary_inc +extra_ordinary_exp)
pbdit_nnrt_noi (net_profit + tax + exp_interest + depreciation + lease_rent - extra_ordinary_inc +extra_ordinary_exp -other_income)
pbdt (net_profit + tax + depreciation)
pbdt_nnrt (net_profit + tax + depreciation -extra_ordinary_inc +extra_ordinary_exp)
pbdt_nnrt_noi (net_profit + tax + depreciation -extra_ordinary_inc + extra_ordinary_exp - other_income)
pbit (net_profit + tax + exp_interest + lease_rent)
pbit_nnrt (net_profit + tax + exp_interest + lease_rent - extra_ordinary_inc + extra_ordinary_exp)
pbit_nnrt_noi (net_profit + tax + exp_interest + lease_rent - extra_ordinary_inc + extra_ordinary_exp -other_income)
pbt (net_profit + tax )
pbt_nnrt (net_profit + tax -extra_ordinary_inc +extra_ordinary_exp)
pbt_nnrt_noi (net_profit + tax -extra_ordinary_inc +extra_ordinary_exp -other_income)
pat (net_profit)
pat_nnrt (net_profit -extra_ordinary_inc +extra_ordinary_exp)
pat_nnrt_noi (net_profit -extra_ordinary_inc +extra_ordinary_exp -other_income)
cash_profits (net_profit + depreciation + amortization)
cash_profits_nnrt (net_profit + depreciation + amortization - extra_ordinary_inc +extra_ordinary_exp)
cash_profits_nnrt_noi (net_profit + depreciation + amortization - extra_ordinary_inc +extra_ordinary_exp - other_income)
net_worth (equity_capital + pref_capital + reserves - revaluation_reserves - misc_exp_n_w_off)
reserves_n_surplus (reserves - revaluation_reserves - misc_exp_n_w_off)
long_term_borrowings (tot_borrowings - short_term_bank_borr - commercial_paper)
capital_employed (equity_capital + pref_capital + reserves - revaluation_reserves - misc_exp_n_w_off + tot_borrowings - short_term_bank_borr - commercial_paper)
loans_from_corporate_bodies (loan_from_group_cos + loan_from_oth_cos)
total_liab (total_assets - revaluation_reserves - misc_exp_n_w_off - advance_tax)
gfa_net_of_wip_reval (gfa - revaluation_reserves - work_in_progress)
nfa_net_of_wip_reval (nfa - revaluation_reserves - work_in_progress)
loans_to_corporate_bodies (recv_loan_group_cos + recv_loan_oth_cos)

quick_assets (marketable_securities - marketable_security_group + cash_n_bank_bal - application_money + sundry_debtors-debtors_exceed_6mths)
current_assets (marketable_securities - marketable_security_group + inventories + cash_n_bank_bal - application_money + receivables - recv_loan_group_cos -recv_loan_oth_cos -housing_loans)
current_liab_prov (current_liab_n_prov - application_money + short_term_bank_borr + commercial_paper)
working_capital (current_assets - current_liab_prov)
other_receivables (receivables - sundry_debtors - recv_loan_group_cos - recv_loan_oth_cos)
money_at_call (bank_balance - bal_current_account - bal_deposit_account)
money_at_call_total (bank_balance + bal_outside_india - bal_current_account - bal_deposit_account - bal_current_acct_abroad - bal_deposits_abroad)
tot_asset (total_assets - revaluation_reserves - misc_exp_n_w_off - advance_tax)
variable_cost (tot_raw_mat_expense - change_in_stocks + energy + indirect_taxes + (0.7*wages) + repairs_plant + oth_operating_exp + advertising + marketing + distribution)
fixed_cost (repairs_total - repairs_plant + other_expense + depreciation + exp_interest_short + lease_rent + other_rent + exp_forex_loss + bad_debts + amortization + (wages*0.30))
contribution (sales - variable_cost)
operating_profit (contribution - fixed_cost)
break_even_point ((100*fixed_cost)/pv_ratio)
margin_of_safety (if ((sales - break_even_point) < 0.00, 0.00, sales - break_even_point))
operating_leverage (contribution/pbit_nnrt)
financial_leverage (pbit_nnrt/pbt_nnrt)
combined_leverage (contribution/pbt_nnrt)
pv_ratio (if (contribution < 0.00, 0.00, 100*(contribution/sales)))
contribution_to_fc (100*(contribution/fixed_cost))
avg_gfa ((gfa +prev(gfa))/2)
avg_gfa_net_wip_reval (((gfa - revaluation_reserves - work_in_progress) +prev(gfa - revaluation_reserves - work_in_progress))/2)
avg_nfa ((nfa +prev(nfa))/2)
avg_nfa_net_wip_reval ((nfa - revaluation_reserves - work_in_progress +prev(nfa - revaluation_reserves - work_in_progress))/2)
avg_investment ((investments +prev(investments))/2)
avg_inventory ((inventories +prev(inventories))/2)
avg_raw_mat_stock ((stk_raw_materials +prev(stk_raw_materials))/2)
avg_stores_stock ((stk_stores_spares +prev(stk_stores_spares))/2)
avg_wip_stock ((stk_wip +prev(stk_wip))/2)

avg_equity_capital ((equity_capital+prev(equity_capital))/2)
avg_fg_stock ((stk_finished_goods +prev(stk_finished_goods))/2)
avg_cash_bank ((cash_n_bank_bal +prev(cash_n_bank_bal))/2)
avg_debtors ((sundry_debtors +prev(sundry_debtors))/2)
avg_advances ((advances + prev(advances))/2)
avg_net_worth ((net_worth +prev(net_worth))/2)
avg_capital ((equity_capital + pref_capital +prev(equity_capital + pref_capital))/2)
avg_premium ((prem_reserves+prev(prem_reserves))/2)
avg_reserves ((reserves_n_surplus + prev(reserves_n_surplus))/2)
avg_capital_employed (((equity_capital + reserves - revaluation_reserves - misc_exp_n_w_off + tot_borrowings - short_term_bank_borr - commercial_paper)+prev(equity_capital + reserves - revaluation_reserves - misc_exp_n_w_off + tot_borrowings - short_term_bank_borr - commercial_paper))/2)
avg_deposits ((deposits + prev(deposits))/2)
avg_borrowings ((tot_borrowings +prev(tot_borrowings))/2)
avg_creditors ((sundry_creditors +prev(sundry_creditors))/2)
avg_current_liab_prov ((current_liab_prov +prev(current_liab_prov))/2)
avg_current_assets ((current_assets+prev(current_assets))/2)
avg_total_assets ((tot_asset +prev(tot_asset))/2)
avg_daily_sales ((sales-internal_transfer)/365)
avg_daily_rawmat_purchases (raw_material_purchase/365)
avg_daily_stores_expenses (exp_stores_spares/365)
avg_daily_cost_of_production (cost_of_production/365)
avg_daily_cost_of_sales (cost_of_sales/365)
avg_daily_total_cost (total_cost/365)
avg_days_raw_materials ((avg_raw_mat_stock+avg_stores_stock)/(avg_daily_rawmat_purchases+avg_daily_stores_expenses))
avg_days_finished_goods (avg_fg_stock/avg_daily_cost_of_sales)
avg_days_wip_stock (avg_wip_stock/avg_daily_cost_of_production)
avg_days_debtors (avg_debtors/avg_daily_sales)
avg_days_creditors (avg_creditors/avg_daily_cost_of_sales)
avg_working_capital ((working_capital+prev(working_capital))/2)
gross_working_capital_cycle (avg_days_raw_materials+avg_days_finished_goods+avg_days_wip_stock+avg_days_debtors)
net_working_capital_cycle (gross_working_capital_cycle-avg_days_creditors)
source_internal ((reserves + bonus_equity_shares - prem_reserves - revaluation_reserves - intangible_assets + gfa - nfa) - prev(reserves + bonus_equity_shares - prem_reserves - revaluation_reserves - intangible_assets + gfa - nfa))
source_reserves ((reserves + bonus_equity_shares - prem_reserves - revaluation_reserves - intangible_assets) - prev(reserves + bonus_equity_shares - prem_reserves - revaluation_reserves - intangible_assets))
source_revenue_reserves ((reserves - specific_reserves) - prev(reserves - specific_reserves))

source_statutory_reserves (statutory_reserves - prev(statutory_reserves))
source_depreciation ((gfa - nfa) - prev(gfa - nfa))
source_cap_mkt ((equity_capital + pref_capital - bonus_equity_shares + application_money + prem_reserves + debentures + fixed_deposits) - prev(equity_capital + pref_capital -bonus_equity_shares +application_money + prem_reserves + debentures + fixed_deposits))
source_fresh_cap ((equity_capital + pref_capital - bonus_equity_shares) -prev(equity_capital + pref_capital - bonus_equity_shares))
source_share_appl (application_money -prev(application_money))
source_share_prem (prem_reserves -prev(prem_reserves))
source_other_borrowings ((tot_borrowings - loans_from_corporate_bodies - fin_inst_borr-tot_bank_borr - fixed_deposits-debentures) - prev(tot_borrowings - loans_from_corporate_bodies - fin_inst_borr - tot_bank_borr - fixed_deposits - debentures))source_cur_liab_prov (current_liab_n_prov - application_money -prev(current_liab_n_prov - application_money))
source_debenture (debentures -prev(debentures))
source_fxd_deposit (fixed_deposits -prev(fixed_deposits))
source_bank_borr (tot_bank_borr -prev(tot_bank_borr))
source_bank_short (short_term_bank_borr - prev(short_term_bank_borr))
source_fin_inst (fin_inst_borr -prev(fin_inst_borr))
source_corporate_bodies (loans_from_corporate_bodies - prev(loans_from_corporate_bodies))
source_borrowings (source_bank_borr+source_fin_inst+source_corporate_bodies+source_other_borrowings)
source_external (source_cap_mkt+source_borrowings+source_cur_liab_prov)
source_group_cos (loan_from_group_cos - prev(loan_from_group_cos))
source_oth_cos (loan_from_oth_cos -prev(loan_from_oth_cos))
source_deposits (deposits-prev(deposits))
source_term_deposits (term_deposits - prev(term_deposits))
source_saving_deposit (savings_deposits - prev(savings_deposits))
source_demand_deposit (demand_deposits - prev(demand_deposits))
source_misc_deposit (deposits - demand_deposits - savings_deposits - term_deposits - prev(deposits - demand_deposits - savings_deposits - term_deposits))
source_deposit_outside_india (deposits_outside_india - prev(deposits_outside_india))
source_inter_bank (tot_bank_borr -prev(tot_bank_borr))
source_govt_borr (loan_govt_st_credits -prev(loan_govt_st_credits))
source_rbi_borr (rbi_borrowing - prev(rbi_borrowing))
source_foreign_borr (foreign_borrowing -prev(foreign_borrowing))
source_others (tot_borrowings - loans_from_corporate_bodies - fin_inst_borr-tot_bank_borr - fixed_deposits-debentures - prev(tot_borrowings

- loans_from_corporate_bodies - fin_inst_borr - tot_bank_borr - fixed_deposits - debentures))
source_use_total (source_internal + source_external)
source_sundry_creditors (sundry_creditors-prev(sundry_creditors))
use_gfa (gfa - revaluation_reserves -prev(gfa - revaluation_reserves))
use_wip (work_in_progress -prev(work_in_progress))
use_investment (investments -prev(investments))
use_invst_group_cos (invst_group_cos -prev(invst_group_cos))
use_invst_mutual_fund (invst_mutual_funds - prev(invst_mutual_funds))
use_oth_invst (investments -invst_group_cos -invst_mutual_funds - prev(investments -invst_group_cos -invst_mutual_funds))
use_current_asset (inventories + cash_n_bank_bal + receivables - prev(inventories + cash_n_bank_bal + receivables))
use_inventory (inventories -prev(inventories))
use_debtors (sundry_debtors -prev(sundry_debtors))
use_cash_bank (cash_n_bank_bal -prev(cash_n_bank_bal))
use_recv ((receivables - sundry_debtors - loans_to_corporate_bodies) - prev(receivables - sundry_debtors - loans_to_corporate_bodies))
use_loans_corporates (loans_to_corporate_bodies - prev(loans_to_corporate_bodies))
use_loan_group_cos (recv_loan_group_cos - prev(recv_loan_group_cos))
use_loan_oth_cos (recv_loan_oth_cos -prev(recv_loan_oth_cos))
use_advances (advances -prev(advances))
use_lt_advances (advances_term -prev(advances_term))
use_st_advances (advances_short -prev(advances_short))
use_loan_to_assisted_cos (advances_assisted_cos - prev(advances_assisted_cos))
use_loan_to_bank_inst (advances_inst_banks - prev(advances_inst_banks))
use_loan_to_oth_cos (advances - advances_term - advances_short - advances_assisted_cos - advances_inst_banks) - prev(advances - advances_term - advances_short - advances_assisted_cos - advances_inst_banks))
use_housing_loan (housing_loans- prev(housing_loans))
use_adv_foreign_currency (advances_foreign_currency - prev(advances_foreign_currency))
use_loan_priority_sector (advances_priority_sector - prev(advances_priority_sector))
use_loan_public_sector (advances_public_sector - prev(advances_public_sector))
use_invst_govt_securities (invst_govt_security - prev(invst_govt_security))
use_invst_assisted_cos (invst_assisted_cos -prev(invst_assisted_cos))
use_invst_approved_securities (invst_approved_security -

prev(invst_approved_security))
use_invst_outside_india (invst_outside_india -prev(invst_outside_india))
use_invst_associated_banks_etc (invst_group_cos -prev(invst_group_cos))
total_cash_inflow (cf_revenue_inflow + (if(cf_payables > 0.00, cf_payables,0.00))+ (if(cf_receivables > 0.00, cf_receivables,0.00))+ (if(cf_inventories > 0.00, cf_inventories,0.00))+ cf_non_op_inc + cf_fixed_asst_sold + cf_invst_sold + cf_capital_proceeds + cf_loan_proceeds + cf_cash_opening)
total_cash_outflow ((if(cf_payables < 0.00, cf_payables,0.00)) + (if(cf_receivables < 0.00,(cf_receivables* -1),0.00))+ (if(cf_inventories > 0.00, (cf_inventories* -1),0.00)) + (cf_direct_tax + cf_interest + cf_cap_cash_expense+ cf_fixed_asst_pur + cf_invst_purchased + cf_loan_group_cos + cf_loan_repayment + cf_loan_other_cos+ cf_dividend)* - 1 + cf_cash_closing)
operating_cash_flow (cf_revenue_inflow + cf_receivables + cf_inventories + cf_payables + cf_deposits + cf_advances)
npbdit_to_sales (100*pbdit_nnrt/sales)
npbit_to_sales (100*pbit_nnrt/sales)
npat_to_sales (100*pat_nnrt/sales)
ronw_adjusted (100*pat_nnrt/avg_net_worth)
roce_adjusted (100*pbit_nnrt/avg_capital_employed)
current_ratio (current_assets/current_liab_prov)
debt_equity (tot_borrowings/net_worth)
quick_ratio (quick_assets/current_liab_prov)
solvency_ratio (tot_asset/ (tot_borrowings + current_liab_n_prov-advance_tax))
interest_coverage (pbit_nnrt/(exp_interest+lease_rent))
avg_tot_borrowings ((tot_borrowings+prev(tot_borrowings))/2)
govt_fin_inst_share (fin_inst_share+insurance_cos_share)
pe (closing_price/eps)
pb (closing_price/bv_per_share)
yield ((eps_div_rate*faceval)/closing_price)
w_returns (100*(wreturns-1))
daily_traded_shares (no_of_shares)
outstanding_shares (shares)
six_pbdit (six_net_profit+six_exp_interest+six_depreciation+six_tax)

**Selection of Ratios :** Although the task of selecting a few ratios out of a large number of total available ratios but as stated above similar studies have indicated that all these ratios can be categorized into different categories. The ratios selected for this study are stated in the previous pages. These ratios are as follows:

1. Return on Investment (X1)
2. Debtors Turnover (X2)
3. Creditors Turnover (X3)

4. Raw Materials Turnover (X4)
5. Finished Goods Turnover (X5)
6. Net Sales/ Total Assets (X6)
7. Fixed Assets Productivity (X7)
8. Current Assets Productivity (X8)
9. Net Sales/ Capital Employed (X9)
10. Cash to Current Liabilities (X10)
11. Quick Ratio (X11)
12. Current Ratio (X12)
13. Debt Equity Ratio (X13)
14. PBIT/Interest (X14)
15. Sales growth (X15)
16. PBT (NNRT)/Total Assets (X16)
17. Equity Dividends/PAT (X17)
18. PAT (NNRT)/Net Sales (X18)
19. PBIT (NNRT)/Total Assets (X19)
20. PBDIT (NNRT)/Capital employed (X20)

Out of these ratios X1, X16, X18, X19 and X20 measure the profitability of the firm, which is a very important and essential condition for excellence. The ratios X10, X11 and X12 measure the liquidity position of the firm. These two i.e. profitability and liquidity represents the overall financial performance of the firm as these two are the major goals of finance. X2, X3, X4, X5 and X6 represent the turnover ratios. Turnover shows how effectively and efficiently the available resources have been utilized. For a company to be excellent, it is essential that it does not waste the resources available with it. Also the productivity of these resources (assets) is important, which is represented by X7 and X8. For an excellent firm, it is important that sales turnover should increase with additional capital employed. The ratio X9 gives the relationship between sales and capital employed. The ratio X13 shows the balance between the two types of sources of capital i.e. debt and equity. For an excellent firm it is important that it should be able to pay all the interest payments out of its profits. This characteristic is measured by X14. Growth is an essential pre-requisite for excellence. A company, which is stagnant and is not growing may perform good in very short run but it cannot continue to be excellent. This feature i.e. growth is measured by the ratio X15. Shareholders are the owners of the firm and a firm cannot think of being excellent without satisfying the owners (shareholders). They get return in the form of dividend although all the profit is not distributed in the form of dividend. Hence, the proportion of profit distributed in the form of dividend becomes important for measuring excellence. This is measured by the ratio X17.

Now, we will discuss all these ratios in detail:

1. Return on Investment (X1): As stated above, this ratio measures the overall profitability of the firm. It indicates the earning capacity of the investments, which facilitates the management in taking decision relating to capital expenditure and is also of interest to the investors. A firm has to make investments in different projects. A firm invests in expectation of handsome returns. Each rupee of assets has to be matched by a rupee of funds drawn from the financial markets. These funds have to be paid for at the market rate. Payment can come only from the operating surplus derived from the efficient use of assets. It is by relating this surplus to the value of the underlying assets/funds that we find a measure of return on investment. If each rupee of investment by a company produces less than a rupee, that company is eroding the wealth of its shareholders. The funds at the disposal of every firm are limited. For an excellent firm, it is important that the selection of a few investment opportunities should be optimum. An excellent organization is able to derive good returns out if its investments.

2. Debtors Turnover Ratio (X2): This ratio shows how many times debtors turn over during the year. Debtors is the amount owed by customers who have still to pay for goods and services received. It is an indicator of the efficiency of credit management of the firm. For example if the credit terms are 2/10 net 30 then debtors turnover ratio should be around 12 times. If it comes to be less than that, it may mean that the credit management of the firm is not efficient. For any organization to be excellent, it is important to manage debtors effectively and efficiently; otherwise a large number of debtors will eventually become bad debts, which cannot be recovered and the firm will no longer remain profitable and excellent. The key elements of good credit control are:
   - Not selling to anyone who won't pay
   - Monitoring the outstanding level of debt by customer and sticking to credit limits
   - Asking for payments.

3. Creditors Turnover (X3): As it is important to manage debtors well, it is of same importance to manage creditors well as they are also one of the major interest groups. It is like the opposite side of the coin to the debtors turnover ratio. It measures how long a company waits to settle its debts to its suppliers. Creditors are those persons or groups of persons, which provide funds or goods to the

organization on credit. It is important that you pay back the amount in time to them. They have provided you credit on the basis of trust and belief and if you don't return back their money on time, it may lead to disrepute. Also, they may force liquidation of some or all of the assets if their amount is not returned (depending upon the amount due). Also, the organization will not be able to get additional funds easily. Hence, for a firm to be truly excellent, it is important that creditors are paid back their amount in time and they are kept satisfied.

4. Inventory Turnover: The inventory turnover measures how fast the inventory is moving through the firm and generating sales. It is said that inventory is a necessary evil. It is so because a firm cannot think of operating without inventory or stock. It is the inventory that is sold in the market to generate revenue (sales). It is called evil because till the time it is kept in the store it is idle and it is not generating any funds. Hence, it is very important to manage the inventory efficiently. It is very important from the management's point of view because a relatively low figure for the ratio would imply that the company has a lot of stock simply sitting there, and more stock implies less cash and a consequent drain on the company's financial resources. Basically, inventory may be raw materials, work-in-process, and finished goods. The first two types of inventory are used in manufacturing concerns while the third category (finished goods) is used in all the organizations. Some organizations just purchase finished products from the manufacturers and sell it in the market. To keep in view both the types of organizations, i.e. manufacturing organizations and organizations just transferring finished goods from manufacturers to customers, I have taken two of the inventory turnover ratios:
   (a) Raw Materials Turnover Ratio (X4)
   (b) Finished Goods Turnover Ratio (X5)

5. Net Sales/Total Assets (X6): It is also called Assets Turnover Ratio. Same as inventory turnover ratio measures the utilization of inventory, this ratio measures the utilization of assets by an organization. For an organization to be truly excellent, it should utilize the assets available with it to the optimum level. Assets require a huge amount of investment and if they are not fully utilized, the whole investment gets waste. In that case, the profitability of the firm will be affected and the firm will not be able to meet its obligations in time.

6. Productivity: This ratio is related to the above ratio (Assets Turnover Ratio). Productivity is a measure of level of operation of the assets. These assets may be fixed assets or current assets. Fixed assets are long term assets, which are not converted into cash during the normal course of business and current assets are short-term assets, which are in the form of cash or in a form that can be easily converted into cash during the normal course of business. Thus, this ratio may have two components:
   (a) Fixed Assets Productivity (X7): To measure productivity of fixed assets in the organization.
   (b) Current Assets Productivity (X8): To measure productivity of current assets in the organization.

7. Net Sales/Capital Employed (X9): This ratio is used to measure the turnover of the total capital employed. The organization gets capital from a number of sources and it has to return whole amount along with some return. Hence, it is essential that the total capital employed be utilized to the maximum extent. It should be ensured that the capital is turned over in the business maximum number of times to generate maximum sales and thus, maximum revenue. The profit so earned will be used to pay the return to the providers of capital. For a firm to be truly excellent, it should ensure that all dues are paid in time and the providers of capital are kept satisfied.

8. Liquidity Ratios: The first test of a company's financial position is, "Will it have sufficient cash over the immediate future to meet its short-term liabilities as they fall due?" Unless the answer here is positive, the company is in a financial crisis irrespective of its profit performance and such company cannot be said to be excellent. We measure liquidity position of a firm by comparing the values of current assets with its current liabilities. In this study, we have taken three liquidity ratios:
   (a) Cash to Current Liabilities (X10)
   (b) Quick Ratio (X11)
   (c) Current Ratio (X12)

   The first ratio, i.e., cash to current liabilities shows the very short-term liquidity. There may be situations of emergency when cash is required immediately and we cannot wait for other current assets to be converted into cash through operating cycle. For such emergencies, a firm should have sufficient amount of cash that can be used immediately. It is said that the importance of cash as the ultimate form of liquidity should not be underestimated.

The second ratio, i.e., quick ratio shows the short-term liquidity position of the organization. Out of all the current assets, inventory is the asset that takes maximum time to be converted into cash, as it has to go through the total operating cycle. There are a number of situations where payments cannot wait for such a long period. Hence, the firm should have enough current assets except the inventory to meet requirements in such contingencies.

The third ratio, i.e., current ratio indicates the availability of current assets in rupees for every one rupee of current liability. Current ratio provides an idea about the cushion available with the firm to meet its short-term liabilities. It judges the ability of a business to meet its current obligations with a margin of safety, i.e., after making allowance for a possible shrinkage in the value of current assets. This ratio is used to measure current liability coverage, buffer against losses and reserve of liquid funds. In words of R.K.Yorston, E.B.Smyth, S.R.Brown, & W.G.Rodger, "The significance of the current ratio is that it is not only a measure of solvency but is an index of the working capital available to the enterprise." If an enterprise cannot meet its short-term obligations as they become due, it cannot be called as an excellent company.

9. Debt Equity Ratio (X13): This ratio is a great test of the financial strength of the company. It is used to measure the balance in the composition of capital structure. As both debt and equity (owned) sources of capital have some cost involved. It is said that additional debt increases both risk and profit and it is the job of management to maintain a proper balance between these two (debt and equity) in a company's capital structure. For analyzing the composition of capital structure, normally debt-equity ratio is employed as a principal tool for financial analysis. The fundamental object of calculating this ratio is to measure the relative interests of owners and creditors in the company. From the creditors' point of view, it measures the extent to which their interest is covered by owned funds in case of insolvency of the company. Higher the coverage of owned funds, the lower will be the ratio and greater will be the protection to the creditors against the possible losses in the event of liquidation. This ratio is also important for judging the financing policy of the management as to whether they are following over-conservative policy of financing or not.

10. PBIT/Interest (X14): This ratio is also an indicator of the financial strength of the company. It is a measure to ensure that the company

will be able to meet the claims of creditors not only under current economic and business conditions, but also under unfavorable situations that may occur in the future. It indicates a firm's long-term debt-paying capacity. This ratio compares the interest due (payable, not receivable) with the profit generated to meet the payment (PBIT, as interest is paid out of this amount). Thus, it measures how comfortably the company can meet its interest payment. If this measure is adequate, then there is little danger that the firm will not be able to meet its interest obligation. If the firm has a good coverage of interest obligation, it should also be able to refinance the principal when it comes due.

11. Sales Growth (X15): The major portion of a company's income comes from the sales made by the firm. Hence achieving good sales only is not important but it should constantly grow. It is said that growth in sales is an indicator of growth of the firm. If the sales of a company are not growing, it indicates a stagnation stage is creeping into the firm and it will lose heavily. Thus an excellent company should continuously increase its sales. This aspect is measured by this ratio.

12. PBT (NNRT)/Total Assets (X16): This ratio is a measure of the returns on the assets used in the business. Here, the profit is taken net of non-recurring transactions, as these are not part of day-to-day running of a business. For a firm to be really excellent, it is important that the assets should be utilized in a manner so as to give adequate return to the company.

13. Equity Dividends/PAT (X17): All the profits of a business are not distributed to the equity shareholders and some part of the profit is retained with the firm as reserves. This ratio is used to measure the proportion of earnings distributed to shareholders in the form of dividend. The shareholders invest in the firm in the expectation of high returns, which is available in the form of dividends. Thus, this ratio is an indicator of the dividend policy of the firm. For a firm to be really excellent, it is important that it should provide handsome dividend to the shareholders to keep them satisfied and also retain a sufficient amount as reserves to meet the emergency requirements.

14. PAT (NNRT)/Net Sales (X18): This ratio is used to measure the overall profitability of the business enterprise. Although interest and taxes are not a part of day-to-day business, yet they have to be

paid out of the earnings of the business. Hence, in order to assess the overall profitability, this is a good measure. Also PAT is the profit amount that is available for distribution to the shareholders hence this ratio is also an indicator of the firms' concern for its shareholders.

15. PBIT (NNRT)/Total Assets (X19): It is important that all the assets of a company are used not only effectively but also profitably, i.e., we should try to get maximum return out of the utilization of assets. This ratio is an indicator of overall assets management of a company.

16. PBDIT (NNRT)/Capital Employed (X20): This ratio is used to measure the overall return on the amount of capital employed in the business. It is essential for an excellent firm that the capital employed in the business should provide sufficient return, which can be distributed to the different interest groups depending on their claims.

# 6

# Corporate Excellence : Using Discriminant Analysis

**Analysis of data:** All the data collected for 180 companies was analyzed on 3 bases:

1. Year wise Analysis
2. Industry wise Analysis
3. Size wise Analysis

We will discuss the results from all 3 bases one by one in detail.

**Year Wise Analysis**

The data was collected for five years from 1996 till 2000. The results for all the five years are given below:

*FOR 1996*: The best result for the year 1996 was found to be giving 78.1% correct classification. It was found taking X3, X4, X5, X6, X9, X11, X12, X15, X16, X18, X19, and X20. The solution was found to be as follows:

**Table 1: Findings for the year 1996**

**Discriminant**

**Analysis Case Processing Summary**

| *Unweighted Cases* | | *N* | *Percentage* |
|---|---|---|---|
| Valid | | 178 | 98.9 |
| Excluded | Missing or out-of-range group codes | 0 | 0 |
| | At least one missing discriminating variable | 2 | 1.1 |
| | Both missing or out-of-range group codes and at least one missing discriminating variable | 0 | 0 |
| | Total | 2 | 1.1 |
| Total | | 180 | 100.0 |

**Group Statistics**

| Group | | Valid N (listwise) | |
|---|---|---|---|
| | | *Unweighted* | *Weighted* |
| 1. | X 3 | 127 | 127.000 |
| | X 4 | 127 | 127.000 |
| | X 5 | 127 | 127.000 |
| | X 6 | 127 | 127.000 |
| | X 9 | 127 | 127.000 |
| | X 11 | 127 | 127.000 |
| | X 12 | 127 | 127.000 |
| | X 15 | 127 | 127.000 |
| | X 16 | 127 | 127.000 |
| | X 18 | 127 | 127.000 |
| | X 19 | 127 | 127.000 |
| | X 20 | 127 | 127.000 |
| 2. | X 3 | 51 | 51.000 |
| | X 4 | 51 | 51.000 |
| | X 5 | 51 | 51.000 |
| | X 6 | 51 | 51.000 |
| | X 9 | 51 | 51.000 |
| | X 11 | 51 | 51.000 |
| | X 12 | 51 | 51.000 |
| | X 15 | 51 | 51.000 |
| | X 16 | 51 | 51.000 |
| | X 18 | 51 | 51.000 |
| | X 19 | 51 | 51.000 |
| | X 20 | 51 | 51.000 |
| Total | X 3 | 178 | 178.000 |
| | X 4 | 178 | 178.000 |
| | X 5 | 178 | 178.000 |
| | X 6 | 178 | 178.000 |
| | X 9 | 178 | 178.000 |
| | X 11 | 178 | 178.000 |
| | X 12 | 178 | 178.000 |
| | X 15 | 178 | 178.000 |
| | X 16 | 178 | 178.000 |
| | X 18 | 178 | 178.000 |
| | X 19 | 178 | 178.000 |
| | X 20 | 178 | 178.000 |

**Analysis 1**
**Summary of Canonical Discriminant Functions**

Eigenvalues

| *Function* | *Eigenvalue* | *% of Variance* | *Cumulative %* | *Canonical Correlation* |
|---|---|---|---|---|
| 1 | 180[a] | 100.0 | 100.0 | 391 |

Wilks' Lambda

| Test of Funcation (s) | Wilks' Lambda | Chi-square | df | Sig |
|---|---|---|---|---|
| 1 | 847 | 28.190 | 12 | .005 |

Standardized Canonical Discriminant Function Coefficients

| | *Function* |
|---|---|
| | *1* |
| X 3 | .216 |
| X 4 | .219 |
| X 5 | .359 |
| X 6 | -.922 |
| X 9 | 1.034 |
| X 11 | -.977 |
| X 12 | .983 |
| X 15 | -.284 |
| X 16 | -1.610 |
| X 18 | -.551 |
| X 19 | 2.186 |
| X 20 | -.476 |

Structure Matrix

| | *Function* |
|---|---|
| | *1* |
| X 11 | -.358 |
| X 18 | -.296 |
| X 5 | .2.57 |
| X 4 | .206 |
| X 3 | .160 |
| X 16 | -.156 |
| X 15 | -.125 |
| X 12 | .073 |
| X 9 | .065 |
| X 19 | -.045 |
| X 20 | -.030 |
| X 6 | .030 |

Pooled within-groups correlations between discriminating variables and standardized canonical discriminant functions Variables ordered by absolute size of correlation within function.

**Functions at Group Centroids**

| *Group* | *Function* |
|---|---|
| | *1* |
| 1. | -0.268 |
| 2. | 0.666 |

Unstandardized canonical discriminant functions evaluated at group means

**Classification Statistics**

**Classification Processing Summary**

| | | |
|---|---|---|
| Processed | | 180 |
| Excluded | Missing or out-of-range group codes | 0 |
| | At least one missing discriminating variable | 2 |
| Used in Output | | 178 |

**Prior Probabilities for Groups**

| *Group* | *Prior* | *Cases Used in Analysis* | |
|---|---|---|---|
| | | *Unweighted* | *Weighted* |
| 1 | .713 | 127 | 127.000 |
| 2 | .287 | 51 | 51.000 |
| Total | 1.000 | 178 | 178.000 |

**Classification Results**

| | | Group | Predicted Group Membership | | Total |
|---|---|---|---|---|---|
| | | | 1 | 2 | |
| Original | Count | 1 | 124 | 3 | 127 |
| | | 2 | 36 | 15 | 51 |
| | % | 1 | 97.6 | 2.4 | 100.0 |
| | | 2 | 70.6 | 29.4 | 100.0 |

(a) 78.1% of original grouped cases correctly classified.

For 1997 : The best result for the year 1997 was found to be giving 80.3% correct classification. It was found taking X1, X2, X3, X4, X5, X12, X13, X16, and X18. The solution was found to be as follows:

**Table 2 : Findings for the year 1997**

**Discriminant**

**Analysis Case Processing Summary**

| *Unweighted Cases* | | *N* | *Percent* |
|---|---|---|---|
| Valid | | 178 | 98.9 |
| Excluded | Missing or out-of-range group codes | 0 | 0 |
| | At least one missing discriminating variable | 2 | 1.1 |
| | Both missing or out of range group codes and at least one missing discriminating variable | 0 | 0 |
| | Total | 2 | 1.1 |
| Total | | 180 | 100.0 |

**Group Statistics**

| | | *Valid N (listwise)* | |
|---|---|---|---|
| *Group* | | *Unweighted* | *Weighted* |
| 1 | X 1 | 133 | 133.000 |
| | X 2 | 133 | 133.000 |
| | X 3 | 133 | 133.000 |
| | X 4 | 133 | 133.000 |
| | X 5 | 133 | 133.000 |
| | X 12 | 133 | 133.000 |
| | X 13 | 133 | 133.000 |
| | X 16 | 133 | 133.000 |
| | X 18 | 133 | 133.000 |
| 2 | X 1 | 45 | 45.000 |
| | X 2 | 45 | 45.000 |
| | X 3 | 45 | 45.000 |
| | X 4 | 45 | 45.000 |
| | X 5 | 45 | 45.000 |
| | X 12 | 45 | 45.000 |
| | X 13 | 45 | 45.000 |
| | X 16 | 45 | 45.000 |
| | X 18 | 45 | 45.000 |
| Total | X 1 | 178 | 178.000 |
| | X 2 | 178 | 178.000 |
| | X 3 | 178 | 178.000 |
| | X 4 | 178 | 178.000 |
| | X 5 | 178 | 178.000 |
| | X 12 | 178 | 178.000 |
| | X 13 | 178 | 178.000 |
| | X 16 | 178 | 178.000 |
| | X 18 | 178 | 178.000 |

## Analysis 1
## Summary of Canonical Discriminant Functions

### Eigenvalues

| *Function* | *Eigenvalue* | *% of Variance* | *Cumulative %* | *Canonical correlation* |
|---|---|---|---|---|
| 1 | .177[a] | 100.0 | 100.0 | .388 |

(a) First 1 canonical discriminant functions were used in the analysis.

### Wilks' Lambda

| *Test of Function (s)* | *Wilks' Lambda* | *Chi-square* | *df* | *Sig.* |
|---|---|---|---|---|
| 1 | .850 | 27.920 | 9 | .001 |

### Standarized Canonical Discriminant Function Coefficients

| | *Funtion* |
|---|---|
| | *1* |
| X 1 | .659 |
| X 2 | -.267 |
| X 3 | .624 |
| X 4 | .278 |
| X 5 | .680 |
| X 12 | .411 |
| X 13 | -.172 |
| X 16 | -.884 |
| X 18 | -.422 |

### Structure Matrix

| | *Function* |
|---|---|
| | *1* |
| X 5 | .530 |
| X 3 | .383 |
| X 12 | .369 |
| X 16 | -.236 |
| X 18 | -.199 |
| X 1 | -.183 |
| X 2 | -.167 |
| X 4 | .157 |
| X 13 | .067 |

Pooled within-groups correlations between discriminating variables and standardized canonical discriminant functions Variables ordered by absolute size of correlation wihin function.

**Functions at Group Centroids**

| *Group* | *Function* |
|---|---|
| | *1* |
| 1 | -0.243 |
| 2 | 0.719 |

Unstandardized canonical discriminant functions evaluated at group means

**Classification Statistics**

**Classification Processing Summary**

| | | |
|---|---|---|
| Processed | | 180 |
| Excluded | Missing or out-of-range group codes | 0 |
| | At least one missing discriminating variable | 2 |
| Used in Output | | 178 |

**Prior Probabilities for Groups**

| | | *Cases Used in Analysis* | |
|---|---|---|---|
| *Group* | *Prior* | *Unweighted* | *Weighted* |
| 1. | 0.747 | 133 | 133.000 |
| 2. | 0.253 | 45 | 45.000 |
| Total | 1.000 | 178 | 178.000 |

**Classification Results[a]**

| | | | *Predicted Group Membership* | | |
|---|---|---|---|---|---|
| | | *Group* | *1* | *2* | *Total* |
| Original | Count | 1 | 129 | 4 | 133 |
| | | 2 | 31 | 14 | 45 |
| | % | 1 | 97.0 | 3.0 | 100.0 |
| | | 2 | 68.9 | 31.1 | 100.0 |

[a] 80.3% of original grouped cases correctly classified.

For 1998 : The best result for the year 1998 was found to be giving 83.1% correct classification. It was found taking X2, X4, X5, X7, X11, X12, X15, X16, and X19. The solution was found to be as follows:

## Table 3 : Findings for the year 1998

**Discriminant**

### Analysis Case Processing Summary

| *Unweighted of Cases* | | *N* | *Percent* |
|---|---|---|---|
| Valid | | 178 | 98.9 |
| Excluded | Missing or out-of-range group codes | 0 | 0.0 |
| | At least one missing discriminating variable | 2 | 1.1 |
| | Both missing or out-of-range group codes and at least one missing discriminating variable | 0 | 0 |
| | Total | 2 | 1.1 |
| Total | | 180 | 100.0 |

### Group Statistics

| | | *Valid N (listwise)* | |
|---|---|---|---|
| *Group* | | *Unweighted* | *Weighted* |
| 1 | X 2 | 136 | 136.000 |
| | X 4 | 136 | 136.000 |
| | X 5 | 136 | 136.000 |
| | X 7 | 136 | 136.000 |
| | X 11 | 136 | 136.000 |
| | X 12 | 136 | 136.000 |
| | X 15 | 136 | 136.000 |
| | X 16 | 136 | 136.000 |
| | X 19 | 136 | 136.000 |
| 2 | X 2 | 42 | 42.000 |
| | X 4 | 42 | 42.000 |
| | X 5 | 42 | 42.000 |
| | X 7 | 42 | 42.000 |
| | X 11 | 42 | 42.000 |
| | X 12 | 42 | 42.000 |
| | X 15 | 42 | 42.000 |
| | X 16 | 42 | 42.000 |
| | X 19 | 42 | 42.000 |
| Total | X 2 | 178 | 178.000 |
| | X 4 | 178 | 178.000 |
| | X 5 | 178 | 178.000 |
| | X 7 | 178 | 178.000 |
| | X 11 | 178 | 178.000 |
| | X 12 | 178 | 178.000 |
| | X 15 | 178 | 178.000 |
| | X 16 | 178 | 178.000 |
| | X 19 | 178 | 178.000 |

## Analysis 1
## Summary of Canonical Discriminant Functions

Eigenvalues

| *Function* | *Eigenvalue* | *% of Variance* | *Cumulative %* | *Canonical Correlation* |
|---|---|---|---|---|
| 1 | 0.249[a] | 100.0 | 100.0 | .446 |

(a) First 1 canonical discriminent functions were used in the analysis.

Wilks' Lambda

| *Test of Function (s)* | *Wilks' Lambda* | *Chi-square* | *df* | *Sig* |
|---|---|---|---|---|
| 1 | .801 | 38.105 | 9 | .000 |

**Standarized Canonical Discriminant Function Coefficients**

| | *Funtion* |
|---|---|
| | *1* |
| X 2 | 0.176 |
| X 4 | 0.355 |
| X 5 | -0.944 |
| X 7 | 0.042 |
| X 11 | 1.128 |
| X 12 | -0.684 |
| X 15 | -0.365 |
| X 16 | 1.244 |
| X 19 | -0.637 |

**Structure Matrix**

| | *Function* |
|---|---|
| | *1* |
| X 16 | 0.626 |
| X 19 | 0.556 |
| X 7 | 0.492 |
| X 5 | -0.347 |
| X 2 | 0.232 |
| X 12 | -0.169 |
| X 4 | 0.127 |
| X 15 | -0.091 |
| X 11 | -0.006 |

Pooled within-groups correlations between discriminating variables and standardized canonical discriminant functions Variables ordered by absolute size of correlation wihin function.

**Functions at Group Centroids**

| *Group* | *Function* |
|---|---|
| | *1* |
| 1 | 0.276 |
| 2 | -0.893 |

Unstandardized canonical discriminant functions evaluated at group means

**Classification Statistics**

**Classification Processing Summary**

| | | |
|---|---|---|
| Processed | | 180 |
| Excluded | Missing or out-of-range group codes | 0 |
| | At least one missing discriminating variable | 2 |
| Used in Output | | 178 |

**Prior Probabilities for Groups**

| *Group* | *Prior* | *Cases Used in Analysis* | |
|---|---|---|---|
| | | *Unweighted* | *Weighted* |
| 1 | 0.764 | 136 | 136.000 |
| 2 | 0.236 | 42 | 42.000 |
| Total | 1.000 | 178 | 178.000 |

**Classification Results[a]**

| | | | *Predicted Group Membership* | | |
|---|---|---|---|---|---|
| | | *Group* | *1* | *2* | *Total* |
| Original | Count | 1 | 133 | 3 | 136 |
| | | 2 | 27 | 15 | 42 |
| | % | 1 | 97.8 | 2.2 | 100.0 |
| | | 2 | 64.3 | 35.7 | 100.0 |

[a]83.1% of original grouped cases correctly classified

For 1999: The best result for the year 1999 was found to be giving 81% correct classification. It was found taking X4, X7, X9, X11, X15, X16, and X19. The solution was found to be as follows:

**Table 4 : Findings for the year 1999**

**Discriminant**

**Analysis Case Processing Summary**

| *Unweighted Cases* | | *N* | *Percent* |
|---|---|---|---|
| Valid | | 179 | 99.4 |
| Excluded | Missing or out-of-range group codes | 0 | 0.0 |
| | At least one missing discriminating variable | 1 | 0.6 |
| | Both missing or out-of-range group codes and at least one missing discriminating variable | 0 | 0 |
| | Total | 1 | 0.6 |
| Total | | 180 | 100.0 |

**Group Statistics**

| *Group* | | *Valid N (listwise)* | |
|---|---|---|---|
| | | *Unweighted* | *Weighted* |
| 1 | X 4 | 129 | 129.000 |
| | X 7 | 129 | 129.000 |
| | X 9 | 129 | 129.000 |
| | X 11 | 129 | 129.000 |
| | X 15 | 129 | 129.000 |
| | X 16 | 129 | 129.000 |
| | X 19 | 129 | 129.000 |
| 2 | X 4 | 50 | 50.000 |
| | X 7 | 50 | 50.000 |
| | X 9 | 50 | 50.000 |
| | X 11 | 50 | 50.000 |
| | X 15 | 50 | 50.000 |
| | X 16 | 50 | 50.000 |
| | X 19 | 50 | 50.000 |
| Total | X 4 | 179 | 179.000 |
| | X 7 | 179 | 179.000 |
| | X 9 | 179 | 179.000 |
| | X 11 | 179 | 179.000 |
| | X 15 | 179 | 179.000 |
| | X 16 | 179 | 179.000 |
| | X 19 | 179 | 179.000 |

**Analysis 1**

**Summary of Canonical Discriminant Functions**

Eigenvalues

| *Function* | *Eigenvalue* | *% of Variance* | *Cumulative %* | *Canonical Correlation* |
|---|---|---|---|---|
| 1 | 0.299[a] | 100.0 | 100.0 | 0.480 |

(a) First 1 canonical discriminent functions were used in the analysis.

Wilks' Lambda

| *Test of Function (s)* | *Wilks' Lambda* | *Chi-square* | *df* | *Sig* |
|---|---|---|---|---|
| 1 | 0.770 | 45.330 | 7 | 0.000 |

**Standarized Canonical Discriminant Function Coefficients**

| | *Funtion* |
|---|---|
| | *1* |
| X 4 | 0.240 |
| X 7 | 0.246 |
| X 9 | 0.219 |
| X 11 | -0.334 |
| X 15 | 0.304 |
| X 16 | 1.808 |
| X 19 | -1.256 |

**Structure Matrix**

| | *Function* |
|---|---|
| | *1* |
| X 16 | 0.775 |
| X 19 | 0.683 |
| X 7 | 0.677 |
| X 9 | 0.515 |
| X 15 | 0.344 |
| X 4 | 0.140 |
| X 11 | -0.115 |

Pooled within-groups correlations between discriminating variables and standardized canonical discriminant functions Variables ordered by absolute size of correlation within function.

**Functions at Group Centroids**

| *Group* | *Function* |
|---|---|
| | *1* |
| 1 | 0.338 |
| 2 | -0.873 |

Unstandardized canonical discriminant functions evaluated at group means

**Classification Statistics**

**Classification Processing Summary**

| | | |
|---|---|---|
| Processed | | 180 |
| Excluded | Missing or out-of-range group codes | 0 |
| | At least one missing discriminating variable | 1 |
| Used in Output | | 179 |

**Prior Probabilities for Groups**

| Group | Prior | Cases Used in Analysis | |
|---|---|---|---|
| | | Unweighted | Weighted |
| 1 | 0.721 | 129 | 129.000 |
| 2 | 0.279 | 50 | 50.000 |
| Total | 1.000 | 179 | 179.000 |

**Classification Results[a]**

| | | Group | Predicted Group Membership | | Total |
|---|---|---|---|---|---|
| | | | 1 | 2 | |
| Original | Count | 1 | 124 | 5 | 129 |
| | | 2 | 29 | 21 | 50 |
| | % | 1 | 96.1 | 3.9 | 100.0 |
| | | 2 | 58.0 | 42.0 | 100.0 |

[a]81.0% of original grouped cases correctly classified

For 2000: The best result for the year 2000 was found to be giving 83.3% correct classification. It was found taking X1, X3, X4, X6, X7, X8, X9, X10, X13, X15, X16, X17, and X18. The solution was found to be as follows:

**Table 5 : Findings for the year 1998**

**Discriminant**

**Analysis Case Processing Summary**

| Unweighted of Cases | | N | Percent |
|---|---|---|---|
| Valid | | 180 | 100 |
| Excluded | Missing or out-of-range group codes | 0 | .0 |
| | At least one missing discriminating variable | 0 | .0 |
| | Both missing or out-of-range group codes and at least one missing discriminating variable | 0 | .0 |
| | Total | 0 | .0 |
| Total | | 180 | 100.0 |

**Group Statistics**

| Group | | Valid N (listwise) Unweighted | Weighted |
|---|---|---|---|
| 1 | X 1 | 115 | 115.000 |
| | X 3 | 115 | 115.000 |
| | X 4 | 115 | 115.000 |
| | X 6 | 115 | 115.000 |
| | X 7 | 115 | 115.000 |
| | X 8 | 115 | 115.000 |
| | X 9 | 115 | 115.000 |
| | X 10 | 115 | 115.000 |
| | X 13 | 115 | 115.000 |
| | X 15 | 115 | 115.000 |
| | X 16 | 115 | 115.000 |
| | X 17 | 115 | 115.000 |
| | X 18 | 115 | 115.000 |
| 2 | X 1 | 65 | 65.000 |
| | X 3 | 65 | 65.000 |
| | X 4 | 65 | 65.000 |
| | X 6 | 65 | 65.000 |
| | X 7 | 65 | 65.000 |
| | X 8 | 65 | 65.000 |
| | X 9 | 65 | 65.000 |
| | X 10 | 65 | 65.000 |
| | X 13 | 65 | 65.000 |
| | X 15 | 65 | 65.000 |
| | X 16 | 65 | 65.000 |
| | X 17 | 65 | 65.000 |
| | X 18 | 65 | 65.000 |
| Total | X 1 | 180 | 180.000 |
| | X 3 | 180 | 180.000 |
| | X 4 | 180 | 180.000 |
| | X 6 | 180 | 180.000 |
| | X 7 | 180 | 180.000 |
| | X 8 | 180 | 180.000 |
| | X 9 | 180 | 180.000 |
| | X 10 | 180 | 180.000 |
| | X 13 | 180 | 180.000 |
| | X 15 | 180 | 180.000 |
| | X 16 | 180 | 180.000 |
| | X 17 | 180 | 180.000 |
| | X 18 | 180 | 180.000 |

**Analysis 1**

**Summary of Canonical Discriminant Functions**

Eigenvalues

| *Function* | *Eigenvalue* | *% of Variance* | *Cumulative %* | *Canonical Correlation* |
|---|---|---|---|---|
| 1 | 0.469[a] | 100.0 | 100.0 | 0.565 |

(a) First 1 canonical discriminent functions were used in the analysis.

Wilks' Lambda

| *Test of Funcation (s)* | *Wilks' Lambda* | *Chi-square* | *df* | *Sig* |
|---|---|---|---|---|
| 1 | 0.681 | 65.971 | 13 | 0.000 |

**Standarized Canonical Discriminant Function Coefficients**

| | *Funtion* |
|---|---|
| | *1* |
| X 1 | -0.953 |
| X 3 | -0.275 |
| X 4 | -0.160 |
| X 6 | -0.730 |
| X 7 | 0.199 |
| X 8 | 0.489 |
| X 9 | 0.892 |
| X 10 | 0.099 |
| X 13 | -0.177 |
| X 15 | -0.134 |
| X 16 | 1.239 |
| X 17 | 0.399 |
| X 18 | -0.121 |

**Structure Matrix**

| | *Funtion* |
|---|---|
| | *1* |
| X 16 | 0.693 |
| X 1 | 0.623 |
| X 7 | 0.599 |
| X 8 | 0.575 |
| X 17 | 0.467 |
| X 6 | 0.390 |
| X 13 | -0.371 |
| X 9 | 0.365 |
| X 4 | -0.213 |
| X 10 | 0.187 |
| X 18 | 0.148 |
| X 15 | 0.059 |
| X 3 | -0.052 |

Pooled within-groups correlations between discriminating variables and standardized canonical discriminant functions Variables ordered by absolute size of correlation wihin function.

### Functions at Group Centroids

| Group | Function |
|---|---|
| | *1* |
| 1 | 0.512 |
| 2 | -0.906 |

Unstandardized canonical discriminant functions evaluated at group means

## Classification Statistics

### Classification Processing Summary

| | | |
|---|---|---|
| Processed | | 180 |
| Excluded | Missing or out-of-range group codes | 0 |
| | At least one missing discriminating variable | 0 |
| Used in Output | | 180 |

### Prior Probabilities for Groups

| | | Cases Used in Analysis | |
|---|---|---|---|
| *Group* | *Prior* | *Unweighted* | *Weighted* |
| 1 | 0.639 | 115 | 115.000 |
| 2 | 0.361 | 65 | 65.000 |
| Total | 1.000 | 180 | 180.000 |

### Classification Results[a]

| | | | Predicted Group Membership | | |
|---|---|---|---|---|---|
| | | *Group* | *1* | *2* | *Total* |
| Original | Count | 1 | 110 | 5 | 115 |
| | | 2 | 25 | 40 | 65 |
| | % | 1 | 95.7 | 4.3 | 100.0 |
| | | 2 | 38.5 | 61.5 | 100.0 |

[a]83.3% of original grouped cases correctly classified

**Results :** Looking at the above solutions, we find that for different years different sets of ratios are giving the best result. Now the problem is to select the set of ratios, which discriminates best between the excellent and not-so-excellent companies. For this purpose some measures are available like *wilks' lambda, canonical correlation, eigenvalue and significance test of lambda.* Let's explain each of them one by one.

**Wilks' lambda:** Wilks' lambda is a multivariate test of significance, sometimes called U-statistic. Wilks' Lambda is the proportion of the total variance in the discriminant scores not explained by differences among the groups. Lambda ranges between 0 and 1, with values close to 1 indicating the group means are not different.

**Eigenvalue:** The eigenvalue is the ratio of between groups sum of squares to within groups sum of squares. The largest eigenvalue corresponds to the eigenvector in the direction of the maximum spread of the groups means. The square root of each eigenvalue provides an indication of length of corresponding eigenvector.

**Canonical Correlation:** The canonical correlation for a discriminant function is the square root of the ratio between groups sum of squares to total sum of squares. Squared, it is the proportion of the total variability explained by differences between groups. Canonical correlation measures the association between the discriminant scores and the groups. Values close to 1 indicate a strong correlation between the discriminant scores and the groups.

**Significance test:** A chi-square transformation of Wilks' lambda is used along with the degrees of freedom to determine the significance. If significance value is small (less than 0.10) this indicates that group means differ. If the significance value is large, this indicates that group means do not differ.

These measures for all the sets of ratios is given below:

**Table 6: Analysis of yearwise results**

| *Year* | *Wilk's Lambda* | *Eigen Value* | *Canonical Correlation* | *Significance Test* |
|---|---|---|---|---|
| 1996 | 0.847 | 0.180 | 0.391 | 0.005 |
| 1997 | 0.850 | 0.177 | 0.388 | 0.001 |
| 1998 | 0.801 | 0.249 | 0.446 | 0.000 |
| 1999 | 0.770 | 0.299 | 0.480 | 0.000 |
| 2000 | 0.681 | 0.469 | 0.565 | 0.000 |

From the above discussion and looking at the above table it is clear that the result for the year 2000 is the best of all the five results discussed earlier. So we will analyze the solution for the year 2000 in detail.
Another point to be noticed while analyzing these solutions was that the correct classification for Group 1, i.e., excellent companies for all the five years was more than 95 %. Looking at the solutions, following were correct classifications for different groups:

**Table 7: Correct Classifications Groupwise for Different Years**

| *Year* | *Group 1* | *Group 2* |
|---|---|---|
| 1996 | 97.6 % | 29.4 % |
| 1997 | 97 % | 31.1 % |
| 1998 | 97.8 % | 35.7 % |
| 1999 | 96.1 % | 42 % |
| 2000 | 95.7 % | 61.5 % |

Looking at the above table, it is clear that the selected ratios have more discriminating power as far as excellent companies are concerned. Another interpretation for this result can be that since the sample of the companies was taken from the BT-500 companies, which represent the top 500 companies in the country; there was always a possibility that the bottom 250 companies (classified in Group 2 in the present study) are not really non-excellent.

As discussed above, the solution for the year 2000 is the best of the five years, we can say that the set of ratios that discriminates the two groups best is as follows:

1. X1 (Return on Investment)
2. X3 (Creditors Turnover)
3. X4 (Raw Materials Turnover)
4. X6 (Net Sales/Total Assets)
5. X7 (Fixed Assets Productivity)
6. X8 (Current Assets Productivity)
7. X9 (Net Sales/Capital Employed)
8. X10 (Cash to Current Liabilities)
9. X13 (Debt Equity Ratio)
10. X15 (Sales Growth)
11. X16 (PBT (NNRT)/Total Assets)
12. X17 (Equity Dividends/PAT)
13. X18 (PAT (NNRT)/Net Sales)

The other results related to year 2000 are as follows:

**Table 8: Regression Analysis for the year 2000**

**Regression**

**Variables Entered / Removed[b]**

| *Model* | *Variables Entered* | *Variables Removed* | *Method* |
|---|---|---|---|
| 1 | X 18, X 4, X 13, X 3, X 10, X 17, X 9, X 15, X 7, X 8, X 16, X 6, X 1[a] | | Enter |

[a]All reuested variables entered.

[b]Dependent Variable : Discriminant Scores from Function 1 for Analysis 1

**Model Summary**

| Model | R | R Square | Adjusted R Square | Std. Error of the Estimate |
|---|---|---|---|---|
| 1 | 1.000[a] | 1.000 | 1.000 | .0000000 |

(a) Predictors : (Constant), X 18, X 4, X 13, X 3, X 10, X 17, X9, X 15, X 7, X 8, X 16, X 6, X 1

**Coefficients[a]**

| *Model* | | *Unstandardized Coefficients* | | *Standardi Zed Coefficien ts* | | |
|---|---|---|---|---|---|---|
| | | *B* | *Std. Error* | *Beta* | *t* | *Sig.* |
| 1 | (Constant) | -.665 | 0.000 | | - | - |
| | X 1 | -6.27E-02 | 0.000 | -0.854 | - | - |
| | X 3 | -4.68E-02 | 0.000 | -0.227 | - | - |
| | X 4 | -5.06E-03 | 0.000 | -0.133 | - | - |
| | X 6 | -1.407 | 0.000 | -0.624 | - | - |
| | X 7 | .517 | 0.000 | 0.177 | - | - |
| | X 8 | 1.994 | 0.000 | 0.433 | - | - |
| | X 9 | .808 | 0.000 | 0.759 | - | - |
| | X 10 | .190 | 0.000 | 0.082 | - | - |
| | X 13 | -6.00E-02 | 0.000 | -0.151 | - | - |
| | X 15 | -5.73E-03 | 0.000 | -0.111 | - | - |
| | X 16 | .118 | 0.000 | 1.131 | - | - |
| | X 17 | 1.267E-02 | 0.000 | 0.346 | - | - |
| | X 18 | -2.79E-05 | 0.000 | -0.101 | - | - |

a. Dependent Variable : Discriminant Scores from Function 1 for Analysis 1

The discriminant function, which discriminates the two groups best, is found out as:

**S = -.06271X1 -.0468X3 -.00506X4 –1.407X6 +.517X7 +1.994X8 +.808X9 +.19X10 -.06X13 -.00573X15 +.118X16 +.01267X17 -.0000279X18 -.665**

Another important finding to study is the relationship between the discriminant scores and all the variables. This analysis is helpful in finding out the outliers. Outliers are the extreme observations, which unduly affect the analysis results. An outlier in a group will have a greater effect on the extent of variation of a particular variable within that group. Since it is not possible to determine the total effect of outliers, the analysis would become meaningful by removing them. The outliers can be easily detected using a curve fit between the discriminant scores and the variables.

**Table 9: Curve Fit for the year 2000**

## Curve Fit

MODEL: MOD_1.
Independent: DIS1_1

| Dependent | Mth | Rsq | d.f. | F | Sigf | b0 | b1 |
|---|---|---|---|---|---|---|---|
| X 1 | LIN | .482 | 178 | 165.49 | .000 | 18.8110 | 9.4632 |
| X 3 | LIN | .004 | 178 | .70 | .404 | 7.3248 | -.3036 |
| X 4 | LIN | .065 | 178 | 12.37 | .001 | 12.7036 | -6.7134 |
| X 6 | LIN | .208 | 178 | 46.79 | .000 | 1.0097 | .2022 |
| X 7 | LIN | .452 | 178 | 146.56 | .000 | .4767 | .2306 |
| X 8 | LIN | .421 | 178 | 129.38 | .000 | .4196 | .1410 |
| X 9 | LIN | .184 | 178 | 40.21 | .000 | 1.6601 | .4029 |
| X 10 | LIN | .051 | 178 | 9.53 | .002 | .3036 | .0976 |
| X 13 | LIN | .190 | 178 | 41.71 | .000 | 1.2324 | -1.0969 |
| X 15 | LIN | .005 | 178 | .90 | .343 | 12.2729 | 1.3760 |
| X 16 | LIN | .576 | 178 | 241.78 | .000 | 7.5534 | 7.2952 |
| X 17 | LIN | .290 | 178 | 72.81 | .000 | 34.3766 | 14.7108 |
| X 18 | LIN | .032 | 178 | 5.83 | .017 | -231.08 | 642.516 |

**X 1**

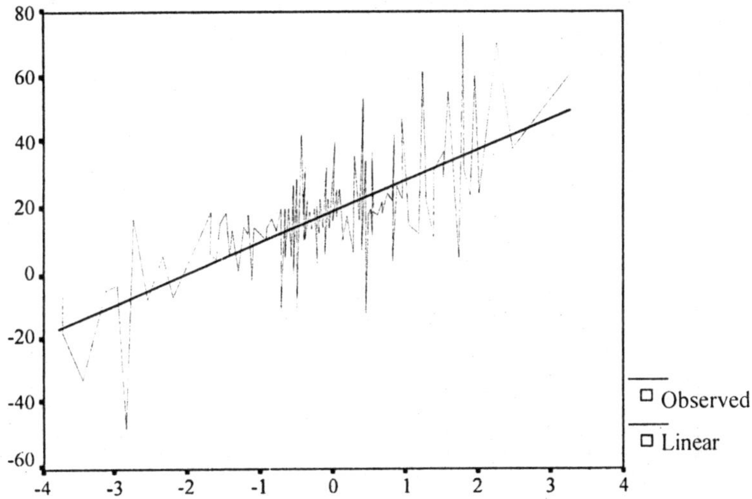


Discriminant Scores from Function 1 for Analysis 1

**X 3**

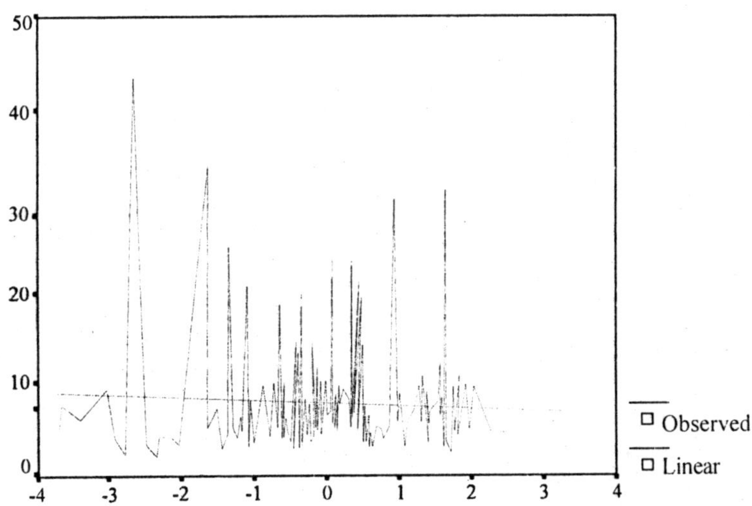


Discriminant Scores from Function 1 for Analysis 1

**X 4**

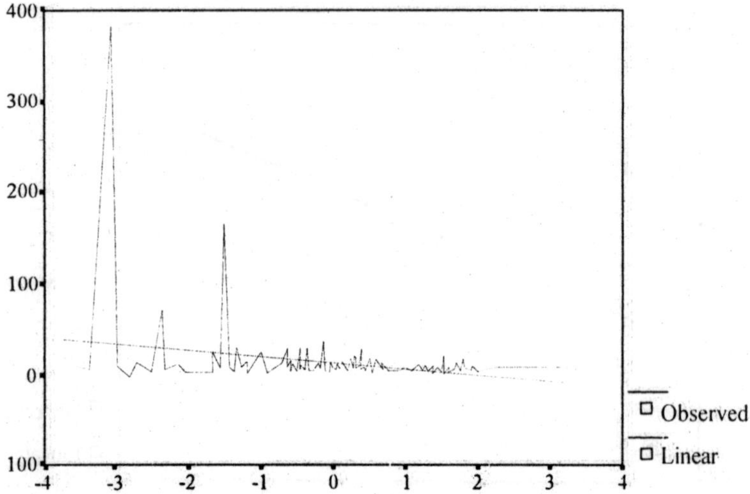


Discriminant Scores from Function 1 for Analysis 1

**X 6**

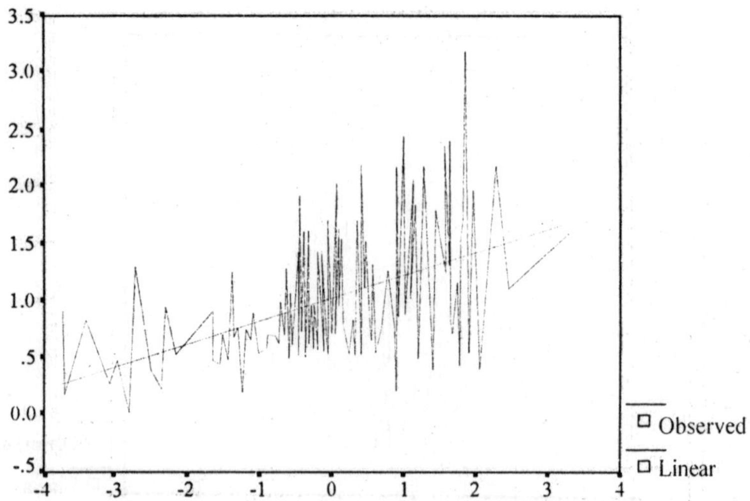


Discriminant Scores from Function 1 for Analysis 1

**X 7**

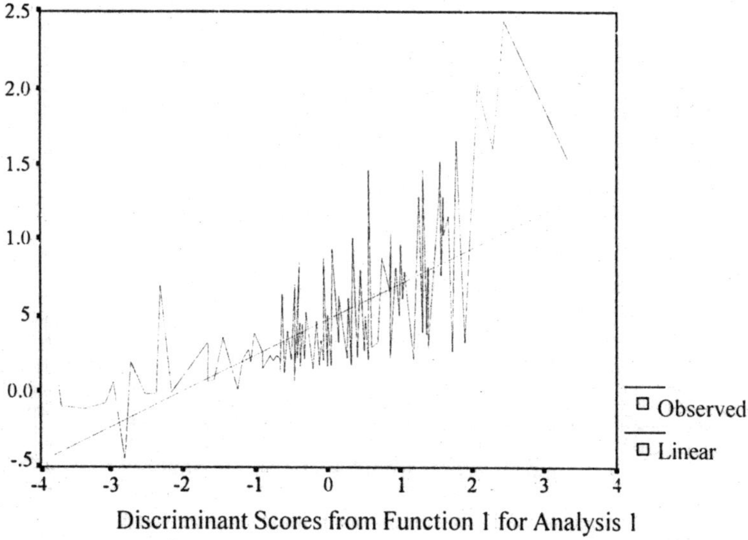
2.5
2.0
1.5
1.0
5
0.0
-.5
-4
-3
-2
-1
0
1
2
3
4
Observed
Linear
Discriminant Scores from Function 1 for Analysis 1

**X 8**

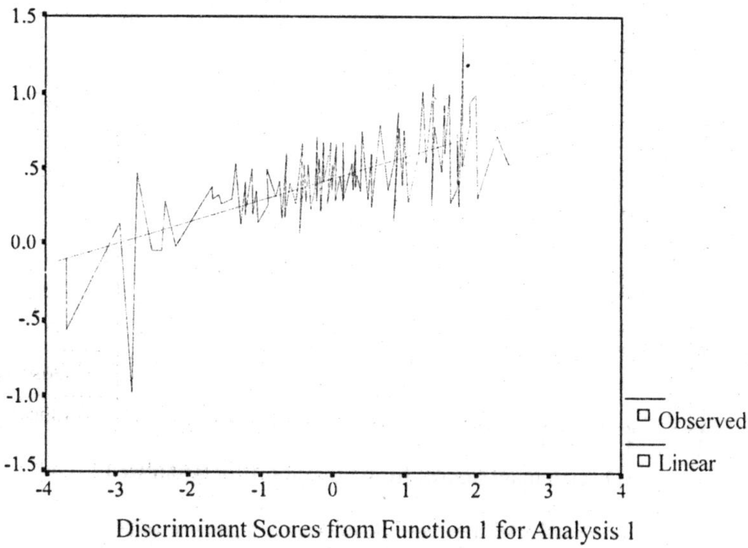
1.5
1.0
.5
0.0
-.5
-1.0
-1.5
-4
-3
-2
-1
0
1
2
3
4
Observed
Linear
Discriminant Scores from Function 1 for Analysis 1

**X 9**

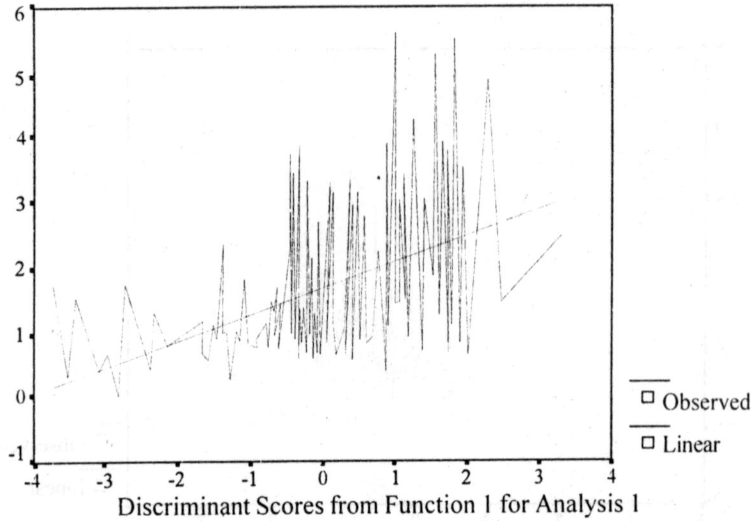
6
5
4
3
2
1
0
-1
-4
-3
-2
-1
0
1
2
3
4
Observed
Linear
Discriminant Scores from Function 1 for Analysis 1

**X 10**

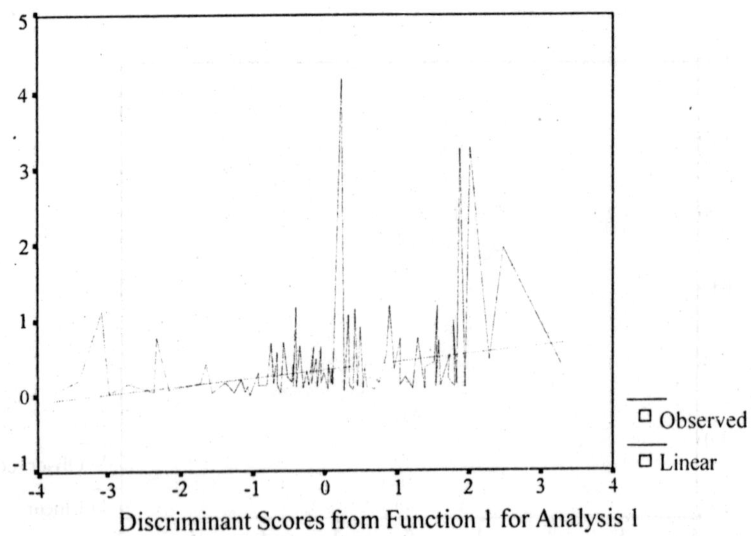
5
4
3
2
1
0
-1
-4
-3
-2
-1
0
1
2
3
4
Observed
Linear
Discriminant Scores from Function 1 for Analysis 1

**X 13**

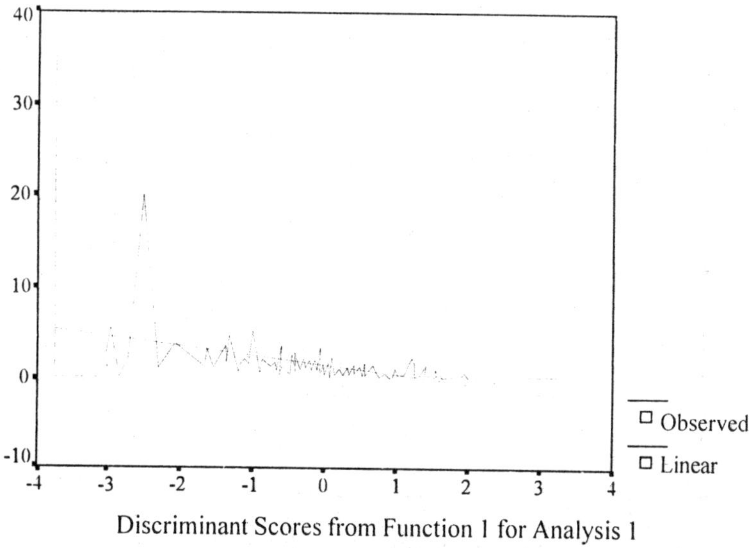
40
30
20
10
0
-10
-4
-3
-2
-1
0
1
2
3
4
Observed
Linear
Discriminant Scores from Function 1 for Analysis 1

**X 15**

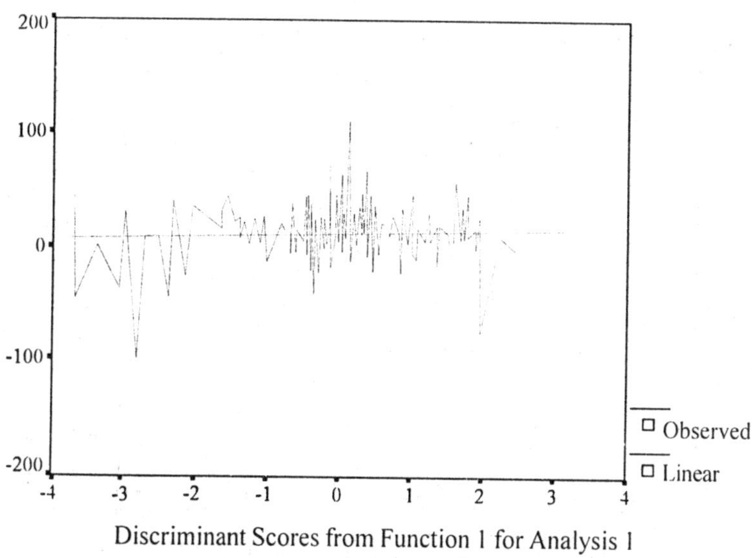
200
100
0
-100
-200
-4
-3
-2
-1
0
1
2
3
4
Observed
Linear
Discriminant Scores from Function 1 for Analysis 1

**X 16**

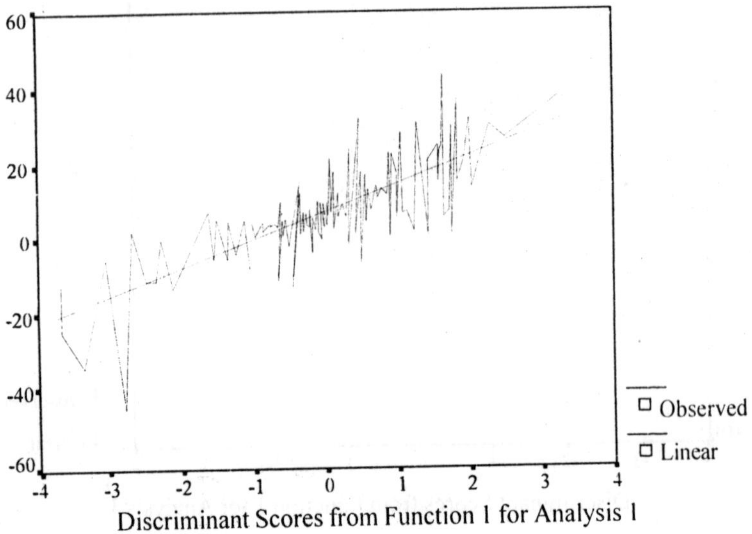
60
40
20
0
-20
-40
-60
-4
-3
-2
-1
0
1
2
3
4
Observed
Linear
Discriminant Scores from Function 1 for Analysis 1

**X 17**

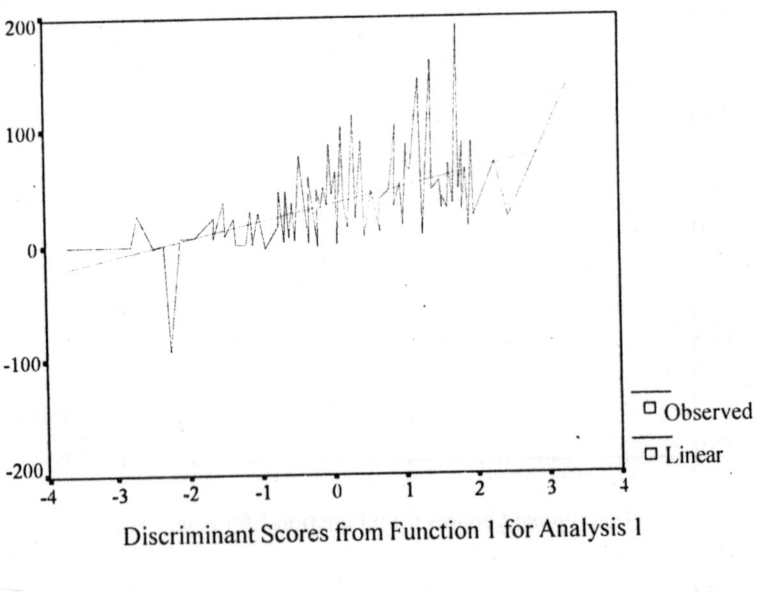
200
100
0
-100
-200
-4
-3
-2
-1
0
1
2
3
4
Observed
Linear
Discriminant Scores from Function 1 for Analysis 1

**X 18**

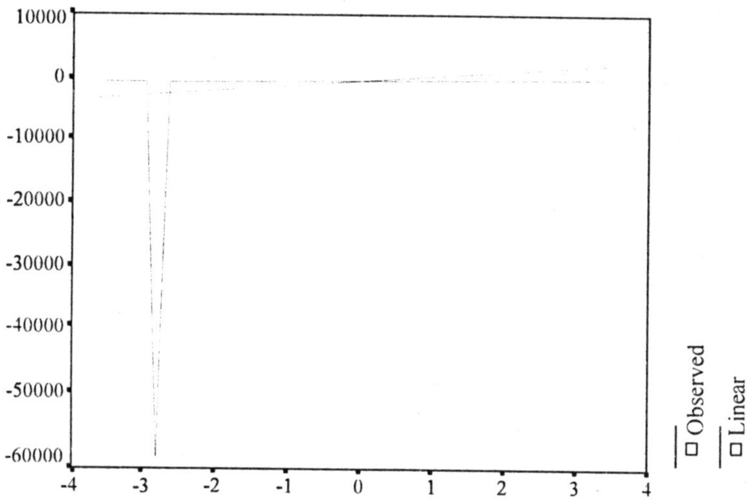


Discriminant Scores from Function 1 for Analysis 1

From the above analysis, it is clear that some outliers are present in X3, X4, X7, X13, and X18. We should remove these outliers for more effective analysis.

After removing the outliers from the data, the solution looks as follows:

**Table 10: Findings after Removing Outliers for the year 2000**

**Discriminant**

**Analysis Case Processing Summary**

| *Unweighted Cases* | | *N* | *Percentage* |
|---|---|---|---|
| Valid | | 174 | 100.0 |
| Excluded | Missing or out-of-range group codes | 0 | 0.0 |
| | At least one missing discriminating variable | 0 | 0.0 |
| | Both missing or out of range group codes and at least one missing discriminating variable | 0 | 0.0 |
| | Total | 0 | 0.0 |
| Total | | 174 | 100.0 |

**Group Statistics**

| Group | | Valid N (listwise) | |
|---|---|---|---|
| | | Unweighted | Weighted |
| 1 | X 1 | 113 | 113.000 |
| | X 3 | 113 | 113.000 |
| | X 4 | 113 | 113.000 |
| | X 6 | 113 | 113.000 |
| | X 7 | 113 | 113.000 |
| | X 8 | 113 | 113.000 |
| | X 9 | 113 | 113.000 |
| | X 10 | 113 | 113.000 |
| | X 13 | 113 | 113.000 |
| | X 15 | 113 | 113.000 |
| | X 16 | 113 | 113.000 |
| | X 17 | 113 | 113.000 |
| | X 18 | 113 | 113.000 |
| 2 | X 1 | 61 | 61.000 |
| | X 3 | 61 | 61.000 |
| | X 4 | 61 | 61.000 |
| | X 6 | 61 | 61.000 |
| | X 7 | 61 | 61.000 |
| | X 8 | 61 | 61.000 |
| | X 9 | 61 | 61.000 |
| | X 10 | 61 | 61.000 |
| | X 13 | 61 | 61.000 |
| | X 15 | 61 | 61.000 |
| | X 16 | 61 | 61.000 |
| | X 17 | 61 | 61.000 |
| | X 18 | 61 | 61.000 |
| Total | X 1 | 174 | 174.000 |
| | X 3 | 174 | 174.000 |
| | X 4 | 174 | 174.000 |
| | X 6 | 174 | 174.000 |
| | X 7 | 174 | 174.000 |
| | X 8 | 174 | 174.000 |
| | X 9 | 174 | 174.000 |
| | X 10 | 174 | 174.000 |
| | X 13 | 174 | 174.000 |
| | X 15 | 174 | 174.000 |
| | X 16 | 174 | 174.000 |
| | X 17 | 174 | 174.000 |
| | X 18 | 174 | 174.000 |

## Analysis 1
## Summary of Canonical Discriminant Functions

### Eigenvalues

| *Function* | *Eigenvalue* | *% of Variance* | *Cumulative %* | *Canonical Correlation* |
|---|---|---|---|---|
| 1 | 0.420[a] | 100.0 | 100.0 | 0.544 |

(a) First 1 canonical discriminant functions were used in the analysis

### Wilks' Lambda

| *Test of Funcation (s)* | *Wilks' Lambda* | *Chi-square* | *df* | *Sig* |
|---|---|---|---|---|
| 1 | 0.704 | 58.044 | 13 | 0.000 |

### Standardized Canonical Discriminant Function Coefficients

| | *Function* |
|---|---|
| | *1* |
| X 1 | -0.936 |
| X 3 | -0.237 |
| X 4 | -0.098 |
| X 6 | -0.798 |
| X 7 | 0.251 |
| X 8 | 0.472 |
| X 9 | 0.910 |
| X 10 | -0.036 |
| X 13 | -0.221 |
| X 15 | -0.161 |
| X 16 | 1.186 |
| X 17 | 0.395 |
| X 18 | 01.014 |

**Structure Matrix**

| | *Function* |
|---|---|
| | *1* |
| X 16 | 0.684 |
| X 1 | 0.606 |
| X 7 | 0.602 |
| X 8 | 0.658 |
| X 18 | 0.504 |
| X 13 | -0.474 |
| X 17 | 0.474 |
| X 6 | 0.397 |
| X 9 | 0.376 |
| X 4 | -0.207 |
| X 10 | 0.177 |
| X 3 | 0.010 |
| X 15 | -0.007 |

Pooled within-groups correlations between discriminating variables and standardized canonical discriminant functions Variables ordered by abssolute size of correlation within function.

**Functions at Group Centroids**

| *Group* | *Function* |
|---|---|
| | *1* |
| 1 | 0.473 |
| 2 | -0.877 |

Unstandardized canonical discriminant functions evaluated at group means

**Classification Statistics**

**Classification Processing Summary**

| | | |
|---|---|---|
| Processed | | 174 |
| Excluded | Missing or out-of-range group codes | 0 |
| | At least one missing discriminating variable | 0 |
| Used in Output | | 174 |

**Prior Probabilities for Groups**

| | | *Cases Used in Analysis* | |
|---|---|---|---|
| *Group* | *Prior* | *Unweighted* | *Weighted* |
| 1 | 0.649 | 113 | 113.000 |
| 2 | 0.351 | 61 | 61.000 |
| Total | 1.000 | 174 | 174.000 |

**Classification Results[a]**

| | | Group | *Predicted Group Membership* 1 | 2 | *Total* |
|---|---|---|---|---|---|
| Original | Count | 1 | 108 | 5 | 113 |
| | | 2 | 25 | 36 | 61 |
| | % | 1 | 95.6 | 4.4 | 100.0 |
| | | 2 | 41.0 | 59.0 | 100.0 |

[a]82.8% of original grouped cases correctly classified

The new discriminant function without the outliers can be found out as :

**Table 11 : Regression Analvsis after Removing Outlines for the year 2000**

**Regression**

**Variables Entered / Removed[b]**

| *Model* | *Variables Entered* | *Variables Removed* | *Method* |
|---|---|---|---|
| 1 | X 18, X 9, X 4, X 17, X 3, X 15, X 13, X 10, X 7, X 8, X 1, X 6, X 16[a] | | Enter |

[a]All requested variables entered.
[b]Dependent Variable : Discriminant Scores from Function 1 for Analysis 1

**Model Summary**

| *Model* | *R* | *R Square* | *Adjusted R Square* | *Std. Error of the Estimate* |
|---|---|---|---|---|
| 1 | 1.000[a] | 1.000 | 1.000 | 0.0000000 |

[a]Predictors : (Constant), X 18, X 9, X 4, X 17, X 3, X 15, X 13, X 10, X 7, X 8, X 1, X 6, X 16

**Coefficients[a]**

| Model | | Unstandardized Coefficients | | Standardized Coefficients | | |
|---|---|---|---|---|---|---|
| | | B | Std. Error | Beta | t | Sig. |
| 1 | (Constant) | -0.527 | 0.000 | | - | - |
| | X 1 | -6.40E-02 | 0.000 | 0.844 | - | - |
| | X 3 | -4.59E-02 | 0.000 | -0.199 | - | - |
| | X 4 | -6.89E-03 | 0.000 | -0.083 | - | - |
| | X 6 | -1.536 | 0.000 | -0.691 | - | - |
| | X 7 | 0.700 | 0.000 | 0.226 | - | - |
| | X 8 | 2.088 | 0.000 | 0.422 | - | - |
| | X 9 | 0.819 | 0.000 | 0.786 | - | - |
| | X 10 | -8.73E-02 | 0.000 | -0.030 | - | - |
| | X 13 | -0.129 | 0.000 | -0.194 | - | - |
| | X 15 | -7.4E-03 | 0.000 | -0.135 | - | - |
| | X 16 | 0.118 | 0.000 | 1.088 | - | - |
| | X 17 | 1.240E-02 | 0.000 | 0.346 | - | - |
| | X 18 | 8.416E-04 | 0.000 | 0.12 | - | - |

[a]Dependent Variable : Discriminant Scores from Function 1 for Analysis 1

Thus, the new discriminant function will come as:

**S= -.064X1-.0459X3-.00689X4-.536X6+.7X7+2.088X8+.819X9-.0873X10-.129X13-.0074X15+.118X16+.0124X17+.0008416X18-.527**

Now, to test whether outliers are totally removed or not, we will again plot the curve between the discriminant scores and different variables.

**Table 12: Curve Fit after removing outliers for the year 2000**

**Curve Fit**

MODEL: MOD_1.

Independent: DIS1_1

| *Dependent* | *Mth* | *Rsq* | *d.f.* | *F* | *Sigf* | *b0* | *b1* |
|---|---|---|---|---|---|---|---|
| X 1 | LIN | .461 | 172 | 146.95 | .000 | 18.8719 | 9.5209 |
| X 3 | LIN | .000 | 172 | .02 | .877 | 7.1543 | .0544 |
| X 4 | LIN | .049 | 172 | 8.87 | .003 | 10.8845 | -2.8442 |
| X 6 | LIN | .215 | 172 | 47.18 | .000 | 1.0087 | .2222 |
| X 7 | LIN | .433 | 172 | 131.52 | .000 | .4664 | .2262 |
| X 8 | LIN | .414 | 172 | 121.44 | .000 | .4244 | .1384 |
| X 9 | LIN | .196 | 172 | 42.02 | .000 | 1.6583 | .4523 |
| X 10 | LIN | .073 | 172 | 13.62 | .000 | .2646 | .1002 |
| X 13 | LIN | .222 | 172 | 48.95 | .000 | 1.1019 | -.7523 |
| X 15 | LIN | .000 | 172 | .003 | .957 | 13.0237 | .0804 |
| X 16 | LIN | .570 | 172 | 227.62 | .000 | 7.5233 | 7.3824 |
| X 17 | LIN | .302 | 172 | 74.30 | .000 | 34.2904 | 16.3303 |
| X 18 | LIN | .338 | 172 | 87.63 | .000 | 3.4211 | 8.8970 |

**X 1**

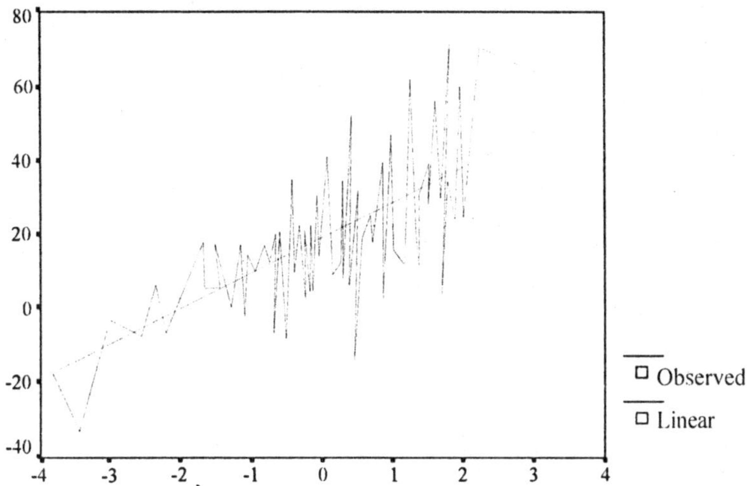


Discriminant Scores from Function 1 for Analysis 1

**X 3**

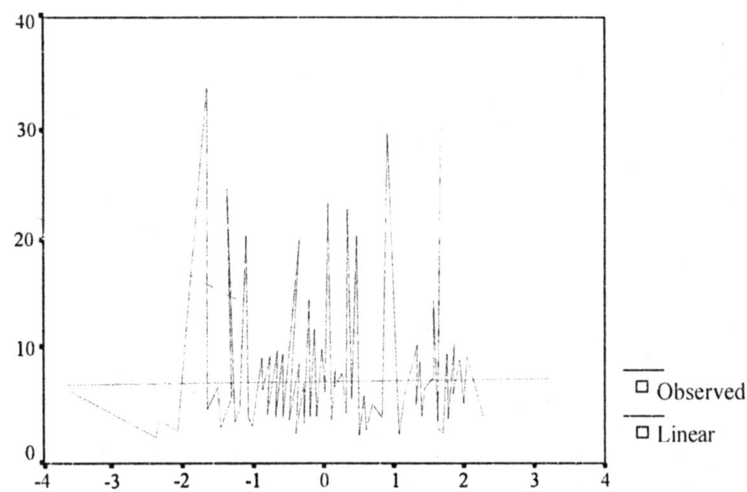


Discriminant Scores from Function 1 for Analysis 1

**X 4**

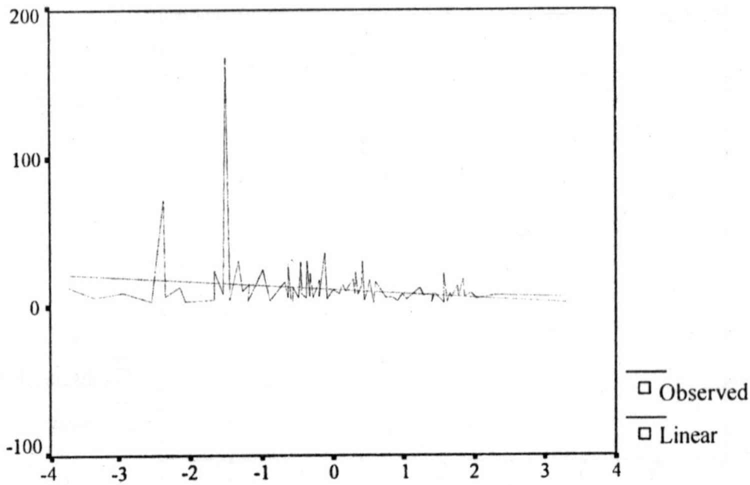


Discriminant Scores from Function 1 for Analysis 1

**X 6**

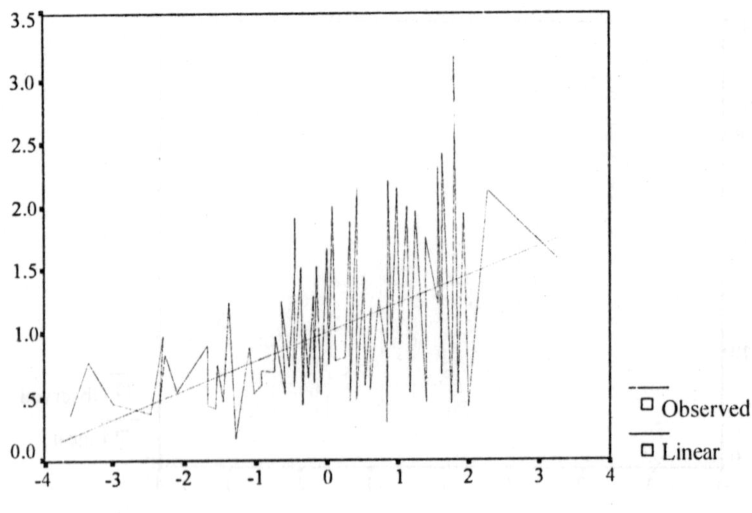


Discriminant Scores from Function 1 for Analysis 1

**X 7**

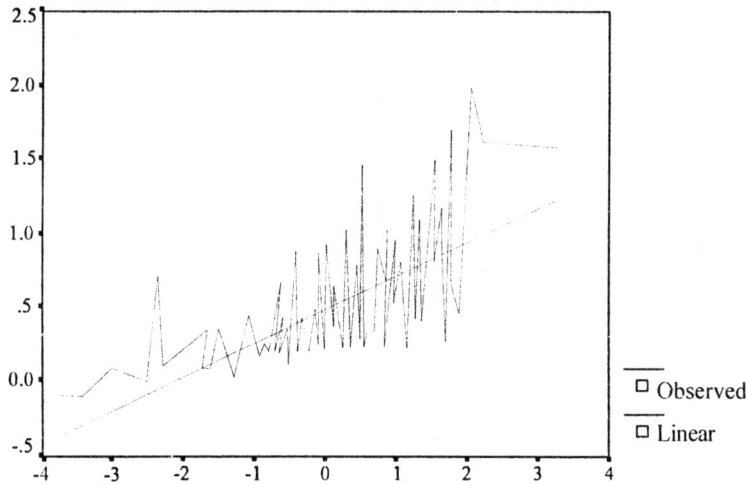


Discriminant Scores from Function 1 for Analysis 1

**X 8**

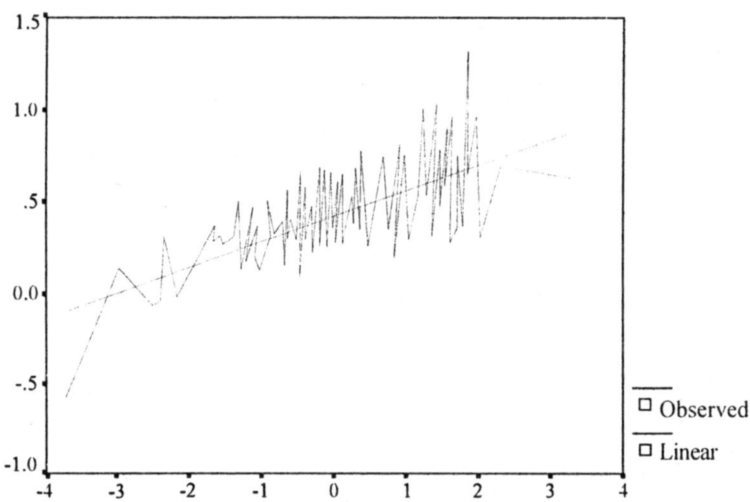


Discriminant Scores from Function 1 for Analysis 1

**X 9**

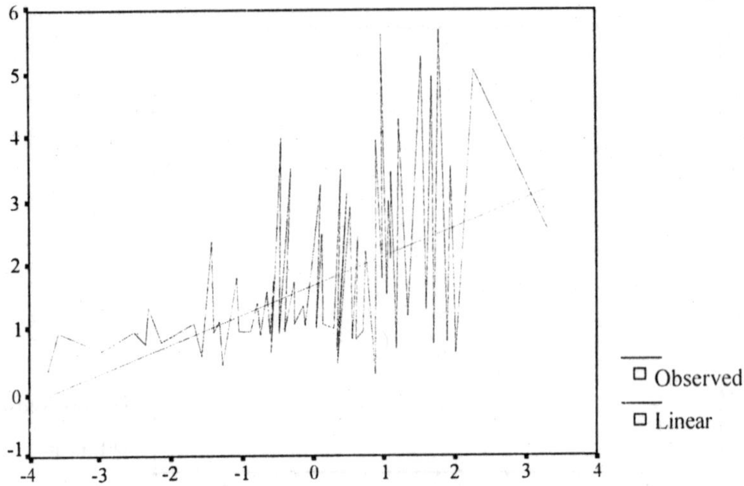


Discriminant Scores from Function 1 for Analysis 1

**X 10**

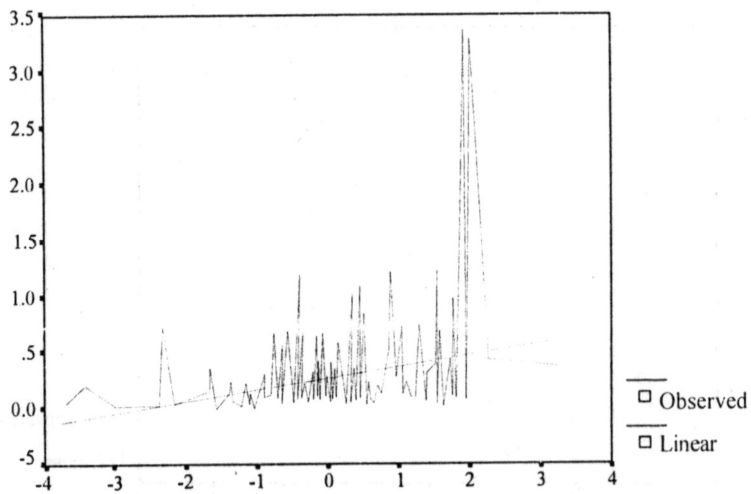


Discriminant Scores from Function 1 for Analysis 1

**X 13**

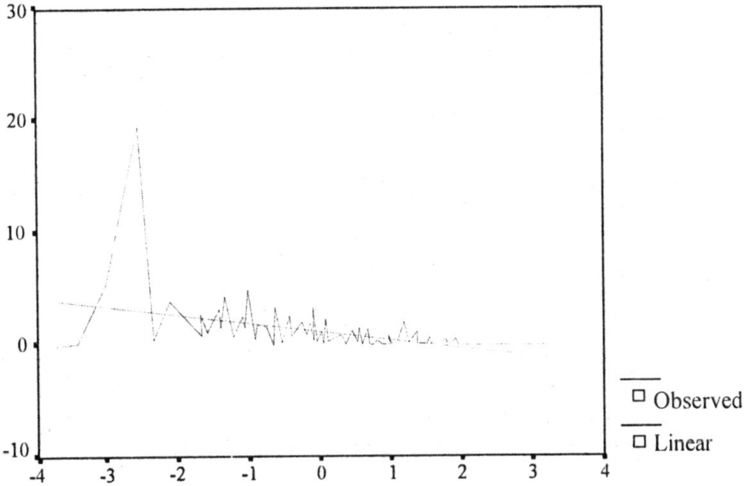


Discriminant Scores from Function 1 for Analysis 1

**X 15**

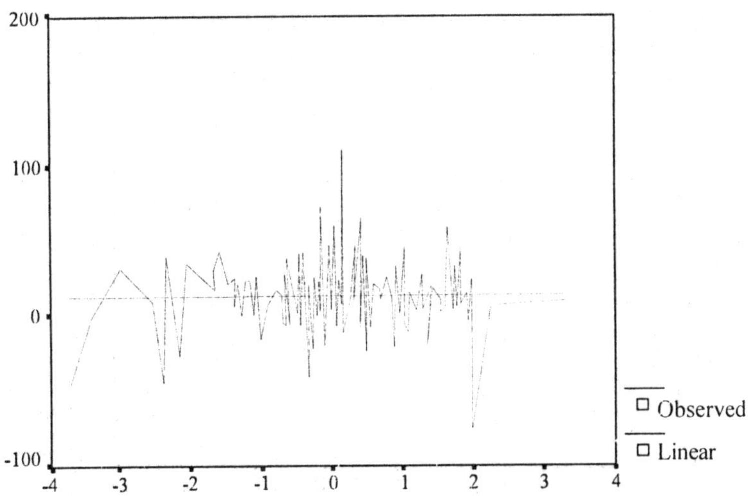


Discriminant Scores from Function 1 for Analysis 1

**X 16**

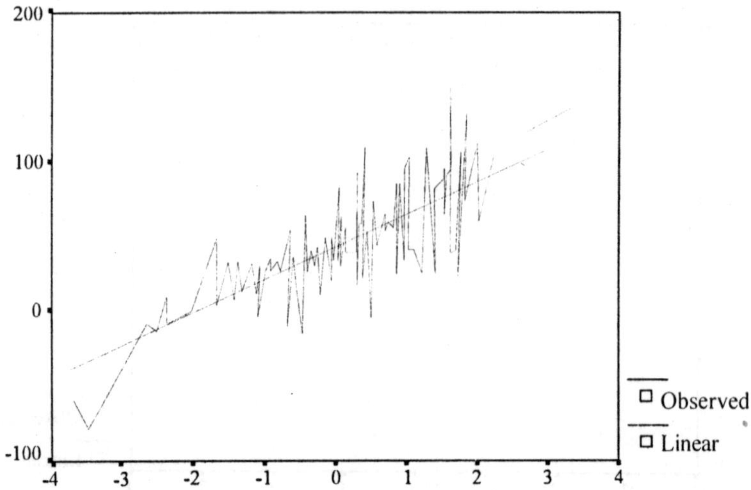


Discriminant Scores from Function 1 for Analysis 1

**X 17**

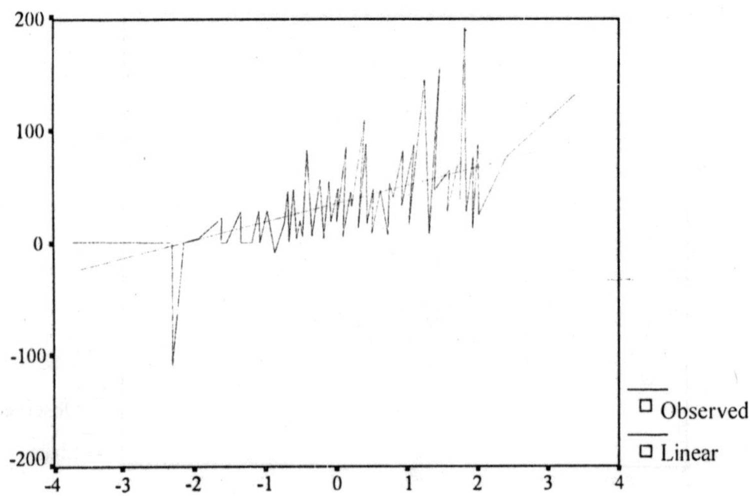


Discriminant Scores from Function 1 for Analysis 1

**X 18**

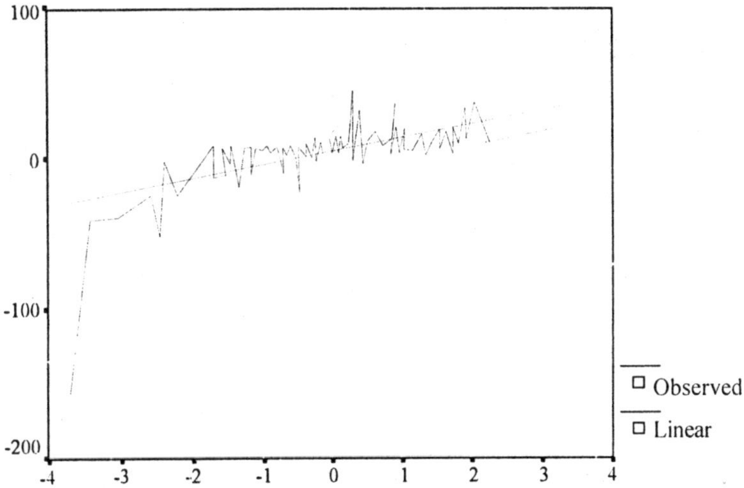


Discriminant Scores from Function 1 for Analysis 1

Another important point to be noticed here is that if we remove X4 and X18 from our analysis, the solution improves as follows :

**Table 13: Improved Finding for the year 2000**

**Discriminant**

**Analysis Case Processing Summary**

| *Unweighted Cases* | | *N* | *Percentage* |
|---|---|---|---|
| Valid | | 174 | 100.0 |
| Excluded | Missing or out-of-range group codes | 0 | 0.0 |
| | At least one missing discriminating variable | 0 | 0.0 |
| | Both-of-range group codes and at least one missing discriminating variable | 0 | 0.0 |
| | Total | 0 | 0.0 |
| Total | | 174 | 100.0 |

**Group Statistics**

| Group | | Valid N (listwise) | |
|---|---|---|---|
| | | *Unweighted* | *Weighted* |
| 1 | X 1 | 113 | 113.000 |
| | X 3 | 113 | 113.000 |
| | X 4 | 113 | 113.000 |
| | X 6 | 113 | 113.000 |
| | X 7 | 113 | 113.000 |
| | X 8 | 113 | 113.000 |
| | X 9 | 113 | 113.000 |
| | X 10 | 113 | 113.000 |
| | X 13 | 113 | 113.000 |
| | X 15 | 113 | 113.000 |
| | X 16 | 113 | 113.000 |
| | X 17 | 113 | 113.000 |
| 2 | X 1 | 61 | 61.000 |
| | X 3 | 61 | 61.000 |
| | X 4 | 61 | 61.000 |
| | X 6 | 61 | 61.000 |
| | X 7 | 61 | 61.000 |
| | X 8 | 61 | 61.000 |
| | X 9 | 61 | 61.000 |
| | X 10 | 61 | 61.000 |
| | X 13 | 61 | 61.000 |
| | X 15 | 61 | 61.000 |
| | X 16 | 61 | 61.000 |
| | X 17 | 61 | 61.000 |
| Total | X 1 | 174 | 174.000 |
| | X 3 | 174 | 174.000 |
| | X 4 | 174 | 174.000 |
| | X 6 | 174 | 174.000 |
| | X 7 | 174 | 174.000 |
| | X 8 | 174 | 174.000 |
| | X 9 | 174 | 174.000 |
| | X 10 | 174 | 174.000 |
| | X 13 | 174 | 174.000 |
| | X 15 | 174 | 174.000 |
| | X 16 | 174 | 174.000 |
| | X 17 | 174 | 174.000 |

**Analysis 1**
**Summary of Canonical Discriminant Functions**

**Eigenvalues**

| *Function* | *Eigenvalue* | *% of Variance* | *Cumulative %* | *Canonical Correlation* |
|---|---|---|---|---|
| 1 | 0.416[a] | 100.0 | 100.0 | 0.542 |

(a)First 1 canonical discriminant functions were used in the analysis

**Wilks' Lambda**

| *Test of Funcation (s)* | *Wilks' Lambda* | *Chi-square* | *df* | *Sig* |
|---|---|---|---|---|
| 1 | 0.706 | 57.932 | 11 | 0.000 |

**Standardized Canonical Discriminant Function Coefficients**

| | *Function* |
|---|---|
| | *1* |
| X 1 | -0.974 |
| X 3 | -0.232 |
| X 6 | -0.824 |
| X 7 | 0.275 |
| X 8 | 0.485 |
| X 9 | 0.938 |
| X 10 | -0.033 |
| X 13 | -0.228 |
| X 15 | -0.163 |
| X 16 | 1.213 |
| X 17 | 0.398 |

**Structure Matrix**

| | *Function* |
|---|---|
| | *1* |
| X 16 | 0.687 |
| X 1 | 0.608 |
| X 7 | 0.604 |
| X 8 | 0.571 |

| | |
|---|---|
| X 13 | -0.477 |
| X 17 | 0.476 |
| X 6 | 0.399 |
| X 9 | 0.377 |
| X 10 | 0.177 |
| X 3 | 0.010 |
| X 15 | -0.007 |

Pooled within-groups correlations between discriminating variables and standardized canonical discriminant functions Variables ordered by abssolute size of correlation within function.

### Functions at Group Centroids

| *Group* | *Function* |
|---|---|
| | *1* |
| 1 | 0.471 |
| 2 | -0.873 |

Unstandardized canonical discriminant functions evaluated at group means.

## Classification Statistics

### Classification Processing Summary

| | | |
|---|---|---|
| Processed | | 174 |
| Excluded | Missing or out-of-range group codes | 0 |
| | At least one missing discriminating variable | 0 |
| Used in Output | | 174 |

### Prior Probabilities for Groups

| | | *Cases Used in Analysis* | |
|---|---|---|---|
| *Group* | *Prior* | *Unweighted* | *Weighted* |
| 1 | 0.649 | 113 | 113.000 |
| 2 | 0.351 | 61 | 61.000 |
| Total | 1.000 | 174 | 174.000 |

**Classification Results**[a]

| | | Group | *Predicted Group Membership* 1 | 2 | *Total* |
|---|---|---|---|---|---|
| Original | Count | 1 | 108 | 5 | 113 |
| | | 2 | 22 | 39 | 61 |
| | % | 1 | 95.6 | 4.4 | 100.0 |
| | | 2 | 36.1 | 63.9 | 100.0 |

[a] 84.5% of original grouped cases correctly classified.

## Regression

**Variables Entered / Removed**

| *Model* | *Variables Entered* | *Variables Removed* | *Method* |
|---|---|---|---|
| 1 | X 17, X 15, X 9, X 10, X 3, X 13, X 8, X 7, X 16, X 6, X 1[a], | | Enter |

[a] All requested variables entered.
[b] Dependent Variable : Discriminant Scores from Function 1 for Analysis 1.

**Model Summary**

| *Model* | *R* | *R Square* | *Adjusted R Square* | *Std. Error of the Estimate* |
|---|---|---|---|---|
| 1 | 1.000[a] | 1.000 | 1.000 | .0000000 |

(a) Predictors : (Constant), X 17, X 15, X 9, X 10, X 3, X 13, X 8, X 7, X 16, X 6, X 1

**Coefficients[a]**

| Model | | *Unstandardized Coefficients* | | *Standardized Coefficients* | | |
|---|---|---|---|---|---|---|
| | | *B* | *Std. Error* | *Beta* | *t* | *Sig.* |
| 1 | (Constant) | -0.625 | 0.000 | | - | - |
| | X 1 | -6.67E-02 | 0.000 | -0.880 | - | - |
| | X 3 | -4.48E-02 | 0.000 | -0.195 | - | - |
| | X 6 | -1.586 | 0.000 | -0.715 | - | - |
| | X 7 | 0.766 | 0.000 | 0.248 | - | - |
| | X 8 | 2.145 | 0.000 | 0.434 | - | - |
| | X 9 | 0.845 | 0.000 | 0.812 | - | - |
| | X 10 | -8.09E-02 | 0.000 | -0.028 | - | - |
| | X 13 | -0.133 | 0.000 | -0.200 | - | - |
| | X 15 | -7.51E-03 | 0.000 | -0.137 | - | - |
| | X 16 | 0.121 | 0.000 | 1.115 | - | - |
| | X 17 | 1.251E-02 | 0.000 | 0.350 | - | - |

[a] Dependent Variable : Discriminant Scores from Function 1 for Analysis 1.

Hence, now the discriminant function will look like :

**S = -0.625-0.0667X1-0.0448X3-1.586X6+0.766X7+2.145X8+0.845X9-0.0809X10-0.133X13-0.00751X15+0.121X16+0.01251X17**

This discriminant function correctly classifies 84.5% of the total cases correctly.

Now, we will find out some other measures of these variables like mean, standard deviation, etc.

**Table 14 : Descriptives for the year 2000**

**Descriptives**

**Descriptive Statistics**

| | N | Range | Minimum | Maximum | Mean | Std. Deviation | Variance |
|---|---|---|---|---|---|---|---|
| X 1 | 174 | 104.95 | -32.97 | 71.98 | 19.4084 | 15.6593 | 245.212 |
| X 3 | 174 | 32.14 | 1.70 | 33.84 | 7.1574 | 5.1590 | 26.616 |
| X 4 | 174 | 167.59 | .00 | 167.59 | 10.7242 | 14.3382 | 205.583 |
| X 6 | 174 | 3.04 | .15 | 3.19 | 1.0212 | .5347 | .286 |
| X 7 | 174 | 2.17 | -.11 | 2.06 | .4791 | .3837 | .147 |
| X 8 | 174 | 1.90 | -.57 | 1.33 | .4322 | .2401 | 5.765E-02 |
| X 9 | 174 | 5.52 | .18 | 5.70 | 1.6838 | 1.1396 | 1.299 |
| X 10 | 174 | 3.34 | -.02 | 3.32 | .2703 | .4128 | .170 |
| X 13 | 174 | 19.76 | .00 | 19.76 | 1.0595 | 1.7843 | 3.184 |

| | | | | | | | |
|---|---|---|---|---|---|---|---|
| X 15 | 174 | 187.35 | -75.19 | 112.16 | 13.0283 | 21.6470 | 468.594 |
| X 16 | 174 | 77.09 | -33.53 | 43.56 | 7.9393 | 10.9201 | 119.248 |
| X 17 | 174 | 315.36 | -125.00 | 190.36 | 35.2106 | 33.1930 | 1101.772 |
| Valid N (listwise) | 174 | | | | | | |

For finding out the cut-off point between the two groups, we will now list down the discriminant scores for all the companies.

**Table 15 : Discriminant Scores for the year 2000**

| *Rank* | *Discriminant Scores* |
|---|---|
| Group 1 | |
| 1 | 2.31742 |
| 2 | 1.34390 |
| 5 | 1.79401 |
| 6 | -0.15532 |
| 10 | -0.06579 |
| 12 | -0.22147 |
| 13 | 0.98809 |
| 14 | 1.13251 |
| 15 | 0.26087 |
| 16 | 0.41278 |
| 17 | 0.50651 |
| 18 | 1.90440 |
| 20 | 3.40438 |
| 21 | 1.75988 |
| 22 | 0.94283 |
| 23 | 0.41182 |
| 27 | 0.19681 |
| 28 | 1.85899 |
| 29 | -0.08024 |
| 31 | 0.20095 |
| 33 | 1.74762 |
| 34 | -0.25242 |
| 40 | -0.39529 |
| 42 | 1.78585 |
| 43 | 1.52557 |
| 44 | 1.96289 |
| 45 | 1.66284 |
| 46 | 0.68533 |
| 47 | -0.51574 |

| Rank | Discriminant Scores |
|---|---|
| 50 | 0.25481 |
| 52 | 1.32393 |
| 53 | 1.22028 |
| 60 | 0.48913 |
| 61 | 0.82314 |
| 62 | 1.17650 |
| 63 | 0.01342 |
| 65 | 1.61669 |
| 67 | 0.35640 |
| 69 | 1.02045 |
| 71 | 2.12063 |
| 72 | -0.59269 |
| 73 | -0.36446 |
| 74 | 0.37834 |
| 75 | 1.67385 |
| 77 | -0.39141 |
| 81 | 1.34175 |
| 82 | -0.31460 |
| 83 | 1.46624 |
| 85 | 1.10133 |
| 88 | -0.43320 |
| 89 | 1.64805 |
| 90 | 1.79882 |
| 92 | -0.33069 |
| 93 | 0.43023 |
| 94 | 0.08136 |
| 96 | -0.15956 |
| 97 | -0.40299 |
| 98 | 0.93996 |
| 100 | 1.60696 |
| 101 | 0.15418 |
| 103 | 1.66377 |
| 105 | -0.24370 |
| 107 | 0.33634 |
| 109 | -0.31756 |
| 110 | 0.62002 |
| 113 | 1.43905 |
| 124 | 1.98099 |
| 128 | -0.40871 |
| 129 | -0.41773 |
| 131 | 0.76161 |
| 134 | -0.26832 |

| *Rank* | *Discriminant Scores* |
|---|---|
| 142 | -0.52017 |
| 143 | -0.39706 |
| 144 | 1.77722 |
| 146 | -0.27903 |
| 155 | -0.54004 |
| 156 | 1.16659 |
| 157 | -0.62127 |
| 164 | 0.29500 |
| 167 | -0.12408 |
| 168 | 1.09237 |
| 169 | 0.16283 |
| 174 | 0.70445 |
| 177 | -1.68741 |
| 182 | 0.84389 |
| 184 | -0.22675 |
| 186 | 0.80317 |
| 189 | -0.51864 |
| 199 | 0.04398 |
| 200 | -0.00017 |
| 201 | 0.75184 |
| 204 | 0.38847 |
| 205 | -0.10061 |
| 207 | 0.75796 |
| 208 | 0.51849 |
| 212 | -1.18183 |
| 215 | -0.16804 |
| 217 | 1.41930 |
| 220 | 0.51105 |
| 222 | -0.49506 |
| 228 | -0.35157 |
| 229 | 0.03603 |
| 230 | -0.72088 |
| 232 | 0.35283 |
| 234 | -0.84837 |
| 235 | -0.27350 |
| 236 | 0.63650 |
| 237 | -0.32400 |
| 239 | -0.60931 |
| 240 | -0.07929 |
| 241 | -0.45448 |
| 242 | -0.72325 |
| 243 | -0.08012 |

| *Rank* | *Discriminant Scores* |
|---|---|
| **Group 2** | |
| 258 | -0.06247 |
| 259 | 0.13159 |
| 262 | -1.35563 |
| 263 | -0.74823 |
| 265 | -0.69641 |
| 266 | -1.22240 |
| 267 | -0.02333 |
| 269 | -0.83541 |
| 270 | -0.87937 |
| 271 | -0.07156 |
| 273 | -0.99955 |
| 276 | -0.26688 |
| 277 | 1.73380 |
| 281 | -0.77214 |
| 282 | -0.95672 |
| 283 | -0.84303 |
| 284 | -0.67894 |
| 285 | -0.44988 |
| 287 | -0.71213 |
| 288 | -1.73400 |
| 290 | -0.38290 |
| 295 | -1.56808 |
| 305 | -0.67122 |
| 307 | -1.02805 |
| 308 | 0.71725 |
| 310 | -2.48478 |
| 311 | -0.48435 |
| 313 | -0.07497 |
| 326 | -0.69131 |
| 328 | 0.31630 |
| 330 | -1.72605 |
| 336 | 0.79965 |
| 338 | -0.77272 |
| 346 | -0.27262 |
| 349 | -0.11390 |

| *Rank* | *Discriminant Scores* |
|---|---|
| 364 | -0.05989 |
| 373 | 0.54593 |
| 374 | -1.62644 |
| 377 | -1.88758 |
| 382 | -0.69997 |
| 383 | -0.96648 |
| 384 | -1.43703 |
| 391 | -1.49263 |
| 419 | -1.19070 |
| 421 | 0.36577 |
| 426 | -3.54170 |
| 429 | -0.11765 |
| 438 | -2.35980 |
| 439 | -1.19239 |
| 443 | -2.41584 |
| 445 | -0.57377 |
| 454 | 1.44562 |
| 455 | -1.29131 |
| 457 | -3.99751 |
| 460 | -0.71854 |
| 466 | -3.67114 |
| 479 | -0.68238 |
| 480 | -3.42597 |
| 481 | -2.49025 |
| 494 | -1.29846 |
| 500 | -1.30037 |

Looking at the above table, it is very clear that all companies having a discriminant score above 1.73380 are classified into group 1, while those having scores below –1.68741 are clearly in group 2. So, we can now safely say that the companies having discriminant scores above 1.73380 are excellent while the companies having discriminant scores below –1.68741 are not-so-excellent companies. The value that gives minimum misclassification for the above-mentioned cases is –0.63, so we can say that *if the discriminant score of a company is more than –0.63 it is in Group 1, otherwise it is in Group 2.*

### Industry Wise Analysis

As stated in the last chapter, the industry wise classification is based on the different sections given in the Stock Exchange Official Directory. The number of companies (in our sample) in each section is given below:

**Table 16: Industrywise Classification of Companies in Sample**

| *Section* | *Name of the Industry* | *Number of Companies* |
|---|---|---|
| 18 | Coal and Mining | 1 |
| 19 | Cement | 8 |
| 20 | Potteries, Tiles, Refraction and Glass | 3 |
| 21 | Cotton Spinning Mills | 4 |
| 22 | Spinning and Weaving Mills | 3 |
| 23 | Jute Textiles | 0 |
| 24 | Synthetic Fibres, Silk and Woollen Textiles | 8 |
| 25 | Paper, Pulp and Hardboard | 2 |
| 26 | Electronics, Electric Equipments and Cables | 20 |
| 27 | Steel | 1 |
| *Section* | *Name of the Industry* | *Number of Companies* |
| 28 | Aluminium | 2 |
| 29 | Metals, Alloys, Metal Products and Structurals | 15 |
| 30 | General Engineering | 27 |
| 31 | Chemicals, Dyes, Pharaceuticals, Refineries and Plastics | 51 |
| 32 | Sugar and Breweries | 5 |
| 33 | Food Products | 4 |
| 34 | Tea Plantations | 1 |
| 35 | Coffee, Rubber and Other Plantations | 0 |
| 36 | Miscellaneous | 25 |

From the above table it is clear that most of the sections do not have enough companies in our sample to be classified into two groups. Only Sections19, 24, 26, 29, 30, 31, and 36 have sufficient number of companies, so we will use discriminant analysis for all these sections to classify the companies into two groups, i.e., excellent and non-excellent.

**Section 19 (Cement Industry) :** The sample selected included 8 companies from this section out of which 3 were excellent and remaining 5 were not-so-excellent companies.
The best results for this section were as follows:

**Table 17: Findings for the Cement Companies**

**Discriminant**

**Analysis Case Processing Summary**

| *Unweighted Cases* | | *N* | *Percent* |
|---|---|---|---|
| Valid | | 8 | 100.0 |
| Excluded | Missing or out-of-range group codes | 0 | 0.0 |
| | At least one missing discriminating variable | 0 | 0.0 |
| | Both missing or out-of-range group cases and at least one missing discriminating variable | 0 | 0.0 |
| | Total | 0 | 0.0 |
| Total | | 8 | 100.0 |

**Group Statistics**

| | | *Valid N (listwise)* | |
|---|---|---|---|
| *Group* | | *Unweighted* | *Weighted* |
| 1 | X 4 | 3 | 3.000 |
| | X 7 | 3 | 3.000 |
| | X 8 | 3 | 3.000 |
| | X 19 | 3 | 3.000 |
| 2 | X 4 | 5 | 5.000 |
| | X 7 | 5 | 5.000 |
| | X 8 | 5 | 5.000 |
| | X 19 | 5 | 5.000 |
| Total | X 4 | 8 | 8.000 |
| | X 7 | 8 | 8.000 |
| | X 8 | 8 | 8.000 |
| | X 19 | 8 | 8.000 |

## Analysis 1
## Summary of Canonical Discriminant Functions

### Eigenvalues

| *Function* | *Eigenvalue* | *% of Variance* | *Cumulative %* | *Canonical Correlation* |
|---|---|---|---|---|
| 1 | 84.675[a] | 100.0 | 100.0 | 0.994 |

(a) First 1 canonical discriminant functions were used in the analysis

### Wilks' Lambda

| *Test of Funcation (s)* | *Wilks' Lambda* | *Chi-square* | *df* | *Sig* |
|---|---|---|---|---|
| 1 | 0.012 | 17.802 | 4 | 0.001 |

### Standardized Canonical Discriminant Function Coefficients

| | *Function* |
|---|---|
| | *1* |
| X 4 | 3.187 |
| X 7 | 8.885 |
| X 8 | 11.415 |
| X 19 | -19.102 |

### Structure Matrix

| | *Function* |
|---|---|
| | *1* |
| X 8 | .126 |
| X 4 | .123 |
| X 19 | .075 |
| X 7 | .068 |

Pooled within-groups correlations between discriminating variables and standardized canonical discriminant functions Variables ordered by abssolute size of correlation within function.

**Functions at Group Centroids**

| *Group* | *Function* |
|---|---|
| | *1* |
| 1 | 10.288 |
| 2 | -6.173 |

Unstandardized canonical discriminant functions evaluated at group means

## Classification Statistics

**Classification Processing Summary**

| | | |
|---|---|---|
| Processed | | 8 |
| Excluded | Missing or out-of-range group codes | 0 |
| | At least one missing discriminating variable | 0 |
| Used in Output | | 8 |

**Prior Probabilities for Groups**

| *Group* | *Prior* | *Cases Used in Analysis* | |
|---|---|---|---|
| | | *Unweighted* | *Weighted* |
| 1 | 0.375 | 3 | 3.000 |
| 2 | 0.625 | 5 | 5.000 |
| Total | 1.000 | 8 | 8.000 |

**Classification Results[a]**

| | | | *Predicted Group Membership* | | |
|---|---|---|---|---|---|
| | | *Group* | *1* | *2* | *Total* |
| Original | Count | 1 | 3 | 0 | 3 |
| | | 2 | 0 | 5 | 5 |
| | % | 1 | 100 | 0.0 | 100.0 |
| | | 2 | 0.0 | 100.0 | 100.0 |

[a] 100.0% of original grouped cases correctly classified.

Thus it is classify all the cases correctly.

To find out the discriminant function

**Table 18 : Regression Analysis for the Cement Companies**

**Regression**

**Variables Entered / Removed**

| *Model* | *Variables Entered* | *Variables Removed* | *Method* |
|---|---|---|---|
| 1 | X 19, X 4, X 8, X 7[a], | | Enter |

(a) All requested variables entered.
(b) Dependent Variable : Discriminant Scores from Function 1 for Analysis 1.

**Model Summary**

| *Model* | *R* | *R Square* | *Adjusted R Square* | *Std. Error of the Estimate* |
|---|---|---|---|---|
| 1 | 1.000[a] | 1.000 | 1.000 | .0000000 |

a. Predictors : (Constant), X 19, X 4, X 8, X 7

**Coefficients[a]**

| Model | | Unstandardized Coefficients | | Standardi Zed Coefficien ts | | |
|---|---|---|---|---|---|---|
| | | B | Std. Error | Beta | t | Sig. |
| 1 | (Constant) | -23.342 | 0.000 | | - | - |
| | X 4 | 0.775 | 0.000 | 0.520 | - | - |
| | X 7 | 88.743 | 0.000 | 1.130 | - | - |
| | X 8 | 44.156 | 0.000 | 1.886 | - | - |
| | X 19 | -1.928 | 0.000 | -2.505 | - | - |

[a] Dependent Vasiable : Discriminant Scroes from function 1 for Analysis 1

Thus the discriminant function for cement industry comes to be-

$$S_{Cement} = .775X4+88.743X7+44.156X8-1.928X19-23.342$$

Here to find out the cut-off score:

**$D_1$=10.288 and $D_2$=-6.173**; hence the cut-off score should be $(D_1+D_2)/2$, i.e., ***2.0575***

**Section 24 (Synthetic Fibres, Silk and Woollen Textiles):** The sample selected included 8 companies from this section out of which 5 were excellent and remaining 3 were not-so-excellent companies.
The best results for this section were as follows:

**Table 19: Findings for the Fibres and Textile Companies**

**Discriminant**

**Analysis Case Processing Summary**

| *Unweighted Cases* | | *N* | *Percentage* |
|---|---|---|---|
| Valid | | 8 | 100.0 |
| Excluded | Missing or out-of-range group codes | 0 | 0.0 |
| | At least one missing discriminating variable | 0 | 0.0 |
| | Both missing or out-of-range group codes and at least one missing discriminating variable | 0 | 0.0 |
| | Total | 0 | 0.0 |
| Total | | 8 | 100.0 |

**Group Statistics**

| *Group* | | *Valid N (listwise)* | |
|---|---|---|---|
| | | *Unweighted* | *Weighted* |
| 1 | X 7 | 3 | 3.000 |
| 2 | X 7 | 5 | 5.000 |
| Total | X 7 | 8 | 8.000 |

**Analysis 1**
**Summary of Canonical Discriminant Functions**

**Eigenvalues**

| *Function* | *Eigenvalue* | *% of Variance* | *Cumulative %* | *Canonical Correlation* |
|---|---|---|---|---|
| 1 | 2.047[a] | 100.0 | 100.0 | 0.820 |

[a]First 1 canonical discriminant functions were used in the analysis.

**Wilks' Lambda**

| *Test of Function (s)* | *Wilks' Lambda* | *Chi-square* | *df* | *Sig* |
|---|---|---|---|---|
| 1 | 0.328 | 6.128 | 1 | 0.013 |

**Standardized Canonical Discriminant Function Coefficients**

| | *Function* |
|---|---|
| | *1* |
| X 7 | 1.000 |

**Structure Matrix**

| | *Function* |
|---|---|
| | *1* |
| X 7 | 1.000 |

Pooled within-groups correlations between discriminating variables and standardized canonical discriminant functions Variables ordered by abssolute size of correlation within function.

**Functions at Group Centroids**

| *Group* | *Function* |
|---|---|
| | *1* |
| 1 | 0.960 |
| 2 | -1.600 |

Unstandardized canonical discriminant functions evaluated at group means

**Classification Statistics**

**Classification Processing Summary**

| | | |
|---|---|---|
| Processed | | 8 |
| Excluded | Missing or out-of-range group codes | 0 |
| | At least one missing discriminating variable | 0 |
| Used in Output | | 8 |

**Prior Probabilities for Groups**

| Group | Prior | Cases Used in Analysis | |
|---|---|---|---|
| | | *Unweighted* | *Weighted* |
| 1 | 0.625 | 5 | 5.000 |
| 2 | 0.375 | 3 | 3.000 |
| Total | 1.000 | 8 | 8.000 |

**Classification Results**[a]

| | | Group | Predicted Group Membership | | Total |
|---|---|---|---|---|---|
| | | | *1* | *2* | |
| Original | Count | 1 | 5 | 0 | 5 |
| | | 2 | 0 | 3 | 3 |
| | % | 1 | 100 | 0.0 | 100.0 |
| | | 2 | 0.0 | 100.0 | 100.0 |

[a]100.0% of original grouped cases correctly classified.

In this section, just one variable, i.e., X7 is classifying all the cases correctly. It can be easily observed looking at the values of X7 for different companies in this section, which are as follows:

| Rank | X7 | Group |
|---|---|---|
| 6 | 0.21 | 1 |
| 34 | 0.17 | 1 |
| 128 | 0.21 | 1 |
| 174 | 0.34 | 1 |
| 235 | 0.28 | 1 |
| 285 | 0.11 | 2 |
| 295 | 0.11 | 2 |
| 480 | 0.07 | 2 |

Thus, we see that all companies in Group 1 have values of X7 greater than or equal to 0.17 while the companies in Group 2 have values less than or equal to 0.11. Hence, we can say that for this section, X7 best classifies the companies into two groups. Graphically, it can be represented as follows :

**Table 20 : Graphical Representation of Finding for the Fibres and Textile Companies**

**X 7**

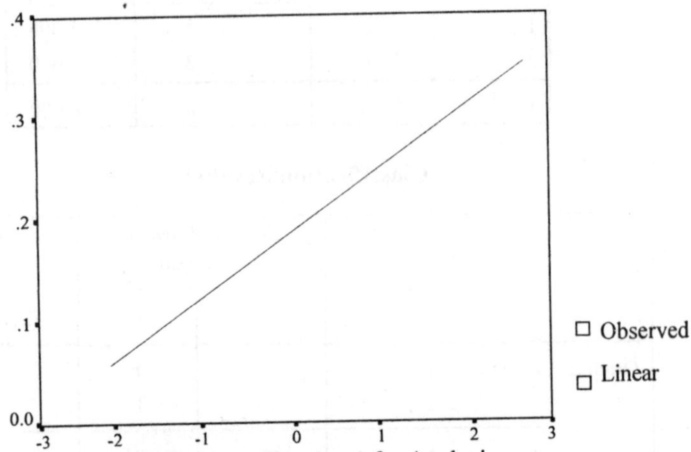


Discriminant scores from function 1 for Analysis.

Thus, we see that the relationship between X7 and discriminant scores is linear hence; we can easily say that for the companies of this section X7 is the best discriminatory variable.

**Section 26 (Electronics, Electric Equipments and Cables):** The sample selected included 20 companies from this section out of which 14 were excellent and remaining 6 were not-so-excellent companies.

The best results for this section were as follows :

**Table 21: Findings for the Electronics, Electric Equipments and Cables Companies**

**Discriminant**

**Analysis Case Processing Summary**

| *Unweighted Cases* | | *N* | *Percent* |
|---|---|---|---|
| Valid | | 20 | 100.0 |
| Excluded | Missing or out-of-range group codes | 0 | 0.0 |
| | At least one missing discriminating variable | 0 | 0.0 |
| | Both-of-range group codes and at least one missing discriminating variable | 0 | 0.0 |
| | Total | 0 | 0.0 |
| Total | | 20 | 100.0 |

**Group Statistics**

| Group | | Valid N (listwise) | |
|---|---|---|---|
| | | *Unweighted* | *Weighted* |
| 1 | X 2 | 14 | 14.000 |
| | X 5 | 14 | 14.000 |
| | X 7 | 14 | 14.000 |
| | X 8 | 14 | 14.000 |
| | X 11 | 14 | 14.000 |
| | X 12 | 14 | 14.000 |
| | X 13 | 14 | 14.000 |
| | X 14 | 14 | 14.000 |
| | X 16 | 14 | 14.000 |
| 2 | X 2 | 6 | 6.000 |
| | X 5 | 6 | 6.000 |
| | X 7 | 6 | 6.000 |
| | X 8 | 6 | 6.000 |
| | X 11 | 6 | 6.000 |
| | X 12 | 6 | 6.000 |
| | X 13 | 6 | 6.000 |
| | X 14 | 6 | 6.000 |
| | X 16 | 6 | 6.000 |
| Total | X 2 | 20 | 20.000 |
| | X 5 | 20 | 20.000 |
| | X 7 | 20 | 20.000 |
| | X 8 | 20 | 20.000 |
| | X 11 | 20 | 20.000 |
| | X 12 | 20 | 20.000 |
| | X 13 | 20 | 20.000 |
| | X 14 | 20 | 20.000 |
| | X 16 | 20 | 20.000 |

**Analysis 1**
**Summary of Canonical Discriminant Functions**

**Eigenvalues**

| *Function* | *Eigenvalue* | *% of Variance* | *Cumulative %* | *Canonical Correlation* |
|---|---|---|---|---|
| 1 | 2.480[a] | 100.0 | 100.0 | .844 |

[a]First 1 canonical discriminant functions were used in the analysis

**Wilks' Lambda**

| *Test of Funcation (s)* | *Wilks' Lambda* | *Chi-square* | *df* | *Sig* |
|---|---|---|---|---|
| 1 | 0.287 | 16.835 | 9 | 0.051 |

**Standardized Canonical Discriminant Function Coefficients**

| | *Function* |
|---|---|
| | *1* |
| X 2 | 0.177 |
| X 5 | 1.835 |
| X 7 | -2.027 |
| X 8 | 1.415 |
| X 11 | -2.828 |
| X 12 | 2.822 |
| X 13 | -0.955 |
| X 14 | 2.687 |
| X 16 | -2.019 |

**Structure Matrix**

| | *Function* |
|---|---|
| | *1* |
| X 5 | 0.368 |
| X 7 | -0.246 |
| X 2 | 0.163 |
| X 13 | -0.089 |
| X 14 | -0.083 |
| X 8 | 0.043 |
| X 11 | 0.026 |
| X 16 | 0.025 |
| X 12 | -0.001 |

Pooled within-groups correlations between discriminating variables and standardized canonical discriminant functions Variables ordered by abssolute size of correlation within function.

**Functions at Group Centroids**

| *Group* | *Function* |
|---|---|
| | *1* |
| 1 | -0.978 |
| 2 | 2.282 |

Unstandardized canonical discriminant functions evaluated at group means.

**Classification Statistics**

**Classification Processing Summary**

| | | |
|---|---|---|
| Processed | | 20 |
| Excluded | Missing or out-of-range group codes | 0 |
| | At least one missing discriminating variable | 0 |
| Used in Output | | 20 |

**Prior Probabilities for Groups**

| *Group* | *Prior* | *Cases Used in Analysis* | |
|---|---|---|---|
| | | *Unweighted* | *Weighted* |
| 1 | 0.700 | 14 | 14.000 |
| 2 | 0.300 | 6 | 6.000 |
| Total | 1.000 | 20 | 20.000 |

**Classification Results**

| | | | *Predicted Group Membership* | | |
|---|---|---|---|---|---|
| | | *Group* | *1* | *2* | *Total* |
| Original | Count | 1 | 14 | 0 | 14 |
| | | 2 | 0 | 6 | 6 |
| | % | 1 | 100 | 0.0 | 100.0 |
| | | 2 | 0.0 | 100.0 | 100.0 |

(a) 100.0% of original grouped cases correctly classified.

Thus, the set of ratios containing X2, X5, X7, X8, X11, X12, X13, X14 and X16 is classifying all the companies of this section correctly.

To find out the discriminant function

**Table 22 : Regression Analysis for the Electronics, Electric Equipments and Cables Companies**

**Regression**

**Variables Entered / Removed**

| *Model* | *Variables Entered* | *Variables Removed* | *Method* |
|---|---|---|---|
| 1 | X 16, X 2, X 5, X 14, X 12, X 8, X 7, X 11[a] | | Enter |

[a]All requested variables entered.
[b]Dependent Variable : Discriminant Scores from Function 1 for Analysis 1.

**Model Summary**

| *Model* | *R* | *R Square* | *Adjusted R Square* | *Std. Error of the Estimate* |
|---|---|---|---|---|
| 1 | 1.000[a] | 1.000 | 1.000 | 0.0000000 |

[a]Predictors : (Constant), X 16, X 2, X 5, X 14, X 13, X 12, X 8, X 7, X 11

**Coefficients[a]**

| Model | | Unstandardized Coefficients | | Standardized Coefficients | t | Sig. |
|---|---|---|---|---|---|---|
| | | B | Std. Error | Beta | | |
| 1 | (Constant) | -1.674 | .000 | | - | - |
| | X 2 | 5.531E-02 | .000 | .098 | - | - |
| | X 5 | 1.542E-02 | .000 | 1.137 | - | - |
| | X 7 | -4.761 | .000 | -1.165 | - | - |
| | X 8 | 11.375 | .000 | .760 | - | - |
| | X 11 | -2.602 | .000 | -1.517 | - | - |
| | X 12 | 1.695 | .000 | 1.513 | - | - |
| | X 13 | -1.482 | .000 | -.517 | - | - |
| | X 14 | .103 | .000 | 1.453 | - | - |
| | X 16 | -.242 | .000 | -1.803 | - | - |

[a]Dependent Variable : Discriminant scores from Functions 1 for Analysis 1.

Thus, the function that classifies all the companies of this section correctly into the two groups can be expressed as follows:

$S_{Electric}$ **= .05531X2+ .01542X5- 4.761X7+ 11.375X8-2.602X11+ 1.695X12- 1.482X13+ .104X14- .242X16- 1.674**

Here to find out the cut-off score:

**$D_1$=-.978 and $D_2$=2.282**; hence the cut-off score should be $(D_1+D_2)/2$, i.e., ***0.653.***

**Section 29 (Metals, Alloys, Metal Products & Structurals):** The sample selected included 15 companies from this section out of which 2 were excellent and remaining 13 were not-so-excellent companies.

The best results for this section were found to be as follows:

**Table 23: Findings for Metals, Alloys, Metal Products and Structurals Companies**

**Discriminant**

**Analysis Case Processing Summary**

| *Unweighted Cases* | | *N* | *Percent* |
|---|---|---|---|
| Valid | | 15 | 100.0 |
| Excluded | Missing or out-of-range group codes | 0 | 0.0 |
| | At least one missing discriminating variable | 0 | 0.0 |
| | Both-of-range group codes and at least one missing discriminating variable | 0 | 0.0 |
| | Total | 0 | 0.0 |
| Total | | 15 | 100.0 |

**Group Statistics**

| Group | | Valid N (listwise) Unweighted | Weighted |
|---|---|---|---|
| 1 | X 16 | 2 | 2.000 |
| | X 18 | 2 | 2.000 |
| 2 | X 16 | 13 | 13.000 |
| | X 18 | 13 | 13.000 |
| Total | X 16 | 15 | 15.000 |
| | X 18 | 15 | 15.000 |

**Analysis 1**
**Summary of Canonical Discriminant Functions**

**Eigenvalues**

| Function | Eigenvalue | % of Variance | Cumulative % | Canonical Correlation |
|---|---|---|---|---|
| 1 | 0.907[a] | 100.0 | 100.0 | 0.690 |

(a) First 1 canonical discriminant functions were used in the analysis

**Wilks' Lambda**

| Test of Funcation (s) | Wilks' Lambda | Chi-square | df | Sig |
|---|---|---|---|---|
| 1 | 0.524 | 7.745 | 2 | 0.021 |

**Standardized Canonical Discriminant Function Coefficients**

| | Function 1 |
|---|---|
| X 16 | 3.003 |
| X 18 | -2.610 |

**Structure Matrix**

| | *Function* |
|---|---|
| | *1* |
| X 16 | 0.534 |
| X 18 | 0.232 |

Pooled within-groups correlations between discriminating variables and standardized canonical discriminant functions Variables ordered by abssolute size of correlation within function.

**Functions at Group Centroids**

| *Group* | *Function* |
|---|---|
| | *1* |
| 1 | 2.260 |
| 2 | -0.348 |

Unstandardized canonical discriminant functions evaluated at group means.

## Classification Statistics

**Classification Processing Summary**

| | | |
|---|---|---|
| Processed | | 15 |
| Excluded | Missing or out-of-range group codes | 0 |
| | At least one missing discriminating variable | 0 |
| Used in Output | | 15 |

**Prior Probabilities for Groups**

| | | *Cases Used in Analysis* | |
|---|---|---|---|
| *Group* | *Prior* | *Unweighted* | *Weighted* |
| 1 | 0.133 | 2 | 2.000 |
| 2 | 0..867 | 13 | 13.000 |
| Total | 1.000 | 15 | 15.000 |

**Classification Results[a]**

| | | Group | Predicted Group Membership 1 | 2 | Total |
|---|---|---|---|---|---|
| Original | Count | 1 | 2 | 0 | 2 |
| | | 2 | 0 | 13 | 13 |
| | % | 1 | 100 | 0.0 | 100.0 |
| | | 2 | 0.0 | 100.0 | 100.0 |

[a] 100.0% of original grouped cases correctly classified.

Thus, taking X 16 and X 18 together classifies all the companies of this section correctly.

To find out the discriminant function.

**Table 24 : Regression Analysis for the Metals, Alloys, Metal Products and Structurals Companier**

**Regression**

**Variables Entered / Removed[b]**

| *Model* | *Variables Entered* | *Variables Removed* | *Method* |
|---|---|---|---|
| 1 | X 18, X 16[a] | | Enter |

[a] All requested variables entered.
[b] Dependent Variable : Discriminant Scores from Function 1 for Analysis 1.

**Model Summary**

| *Model* | *R* | *R Square* | *Adjusted R Square* | *Std. Error of the Estimate* |
|---|---|---|---|---|
| 1 | 1.000[a] | 1.000 | 1.000 | 0.0000000 |

(a) Predictors : (Constant), X 18, X 16

**Coefficients**[a]

| Model | | Unstandardized Coefficients | | Standardized Coefficients | t | Sig. |
|---|---|---|---|---|---|---|
| | | B | Std. Error | Beta | | |
| 1 | (Constant) | -1.396 | .000 | | - | - |
| | X 16 | .753 | .000 | 2.440 | - | - |
| | X 18 | -.169 | .000 | -1.936 | - | - |

[a]Dependent Variable : Discriminant Scores from Function 1 for Analysis 1

Hence, the discriminant function that classifies all the companies of this section correctly into the two groups can be expressed as follows:

$$S_{Metals} = .753X16 - .169X18 - 1.396$$

Now to find out the cut-off score:

**$D_1$=2.260 and $D_2$= -.348**; hence the cut-off score should be $(D_1+D_2)/2$, i.e., ***0.956***

**Section 30 (General Engineering):** The sample selected included 27 companies from this section out of which 19 were excellent companies and the remaining 8 were not-so-excellent companies.

The best results for this section were found to be as follows :

**Table 25: Findings for General Engineering Companies**

**Discriminant**

**Analysis Case Processing Summary**

| *Unweighted Cases* | | *N* | *Percentage* |
|---|---|---|---|
| Valid | | 27 | 100.0 |
| Excluded | Missing or out-of-range group codes | 0 | 0.0 |
| | At least one missing discriminating variable | 0 | 0.0 |
| | Both-of-range group codes and at least one missing discriminating variable | 0 | 0.0 |
| | Total | 0 | 0.0 |
| Total | | 27 | 100.0 |

**Group Statistics**

| Group | | Valid N (listwise) Unweighted | Weighted |
|---|---|---|---|
| 1 | X 7 | 19 | 19.000 |
| | X 8 | 19 | 19.000 |
| | X 10 | 19 | 19.000 |
| | X 11 | 19 | 19.000 |
| | X 12 | 19 | 19.000 |
| | X 15 | 19 | 19.000 |
| | X 16 | 19 | 19.000 |
| | X 17 | 19 | 19.000 |
| | X 19 | 19 | 18.000 |
| 2 | X 7 | 8 | 8.000 |
| | X 8 | 8 | 8.000 |
| | X 10 | 8 | 8.000 |
| | X 11 | 8 | 8.000 |
| | X 12 | 8 | 8.000 |
| | X 15 | 8 | 8.000 |
| | X 16 | 8 | 8.000 |
| | X 17 | 8 | 8.000 |
| | X 19 | 8 | 8.000 |
| Total | X 7 | 27 | 27.000 |
| | X 8 | 27 | 27.000 |
| | X 10 | 27 | 27.000 |
| | X 11 | 27 | 27.000 |
| | X 12 | 27 | 27.000 |
| | X 15 | 27 | 27.000 |
| | X 16 | 27 | 27.000 |
| | X 17 | 27 | 27.000 |
| | X 19 | 27 | 27.000 |

**Analysis 1**
**Summary of Canonical Discriminant Functions**

**Eigenvalues**

| *Function* | *Eigenvalue* | *% of Variance* | *Cumulative %* | *Canonical Correlation* |
|---|---|---|---|---|
| 1 | 1.640[a] | 100.0 | 100.0 | 0.788 |

[a]First 1 canonical discriminant functions were used in the analysis.

**Wilks' Lambda**

| *Test of Funcation (s)* | *Wilks' Lambda* | *Chi-square* | *df* | *Sig* |
|---|---|---|---|---|
| 1 | 0.379 | 19.903 | 9 | 0.019 |

**Standardized Canonical Discriminant Function Coefficients**

| | *Function* |
|---|---|
| | *1* |
| X 7 | 0.599 |
| X 8 | 2.194 |
| X 10 | 0.856 |
| X 11 | -2.613 |
| X 12 | 2.281 |
| X 15 | -0.542 |
| X 16 | 2.628 |
| X 17 | 0.845 |
| X 19 | -4.609 |

**Structure Matrix**

| | *Function* |
|---|---|
| | *1* |
| X 7 | 0.280 |
| X 8 | 0.253 |
| X 10 | 0.227 |
| X 11 | 0.217 |
| X 12 | 0.201 |
| X 15 | 0.195 |
| X 16 | 0.158 |
| X 17 | 0.044 |
| X 19 | 0.027 |

Pooled within-groups correlations between discriminating variables and standardized canonical discriminant functions Variables ordered by absolute size of correlation within function.

**Functions at Group Centroids**

| Group | Function |
|---|---|
| | *1* |
| 1 | 0.800 |
| 2 | -1.899 |

Unstandardized canonical discriminant functions evaluated at group means

**Classification Statistics**

**Classification Processing Summary**

| | | |
|---|---|---|
| Processed | | 27 |
| Excluded | Missing or out-of-range group codes | 0 |
| | At least one missing discriminating variable | 0 |
| Used in Output | | 27 |

**Prior Probabilities for Groups**

| | | Cases Used in Analysis | |
|---|---|---|---|
| *Group* | *Prior* | *Unweighted* | *Weighted* |
| 1 | .704 | 19 | 19.000 |
| 2 | .296 | 8 | 8.000 |
| Total | 1.000 | 27 | 27.000 |

**Classification Results[a]**

| | | | Predicted Group Membership | | |
|---|---|---|---|---|---|
| | | *Group* | *1* | *2* | *Total* |
| Original | Count | 1 | 19 | 0 | 19 |
| | | 2 | 0 | 8 | 8 |
| | % | 1 | 100 | .0 | 100.0 |
| | | 2 | 12.5 | 87.5 | 100.0 |

[a]96.3% of original grouped cases correctly classified.

Hence for this group taking a combination of X7, X8, X10, X11, X12, X15, X16, X17, and X19 classifies maximum number of companies, i.e., 96.3% of this section correctly.

To find out the discriminant function:

**Table 26: Regression Analysis for General Engineering Companies**

**Regression**

**Variables Entered / Removed[b]**

| *Model* | *Variables Entered* | *Variables Removed* | *Method* |
|---|---|---|---|
| 1 | X 19, X 17, X 10, X 12, X 15, X 7, X 11, X 8, X16[a] | | Enter |

[a]All requested variables entered.
[b]Dependent Variable : Discriminant Scores from Function 1 for Analysis 1

**Model Summary**

| *Model* | *R* | *R Square* | *Adjusted R Square* | *Std. Error of the Estimate* |
|---|---|---|---|---|
| 1 | 1.000[a] | 1.000 | 1.000 | 0.0000000 |

[a]Predictors : (Constant), X 19, X 17, X 10, X 12, X 15, X 7, X 11, X 8, X 16

**Coefficients[a]**

| Model | | Unstandardized Coefficients | | Standardized Coefficients | t | Sig. |
|---|---|---|---|---|---|---|
| | | B | Std. Error | Beta | | |
| 1 | (Constant) | -3.485 | 0.000 | | - | - |
| | X 7 | 1.809 | 0.000 | 0.387 | - | - |
| | X 8 | 6.017 | 0.000 | 1.434 | - | - |
| | X 10 | 4.229 | 0.000 | 0.543 | - | - |
| | X 11 | -6.932 | 0.000 | -1.611 | - | - |
| | X 12 | 3.566 | 0.000 | 1.432 | - | - |
| | X 15 | -1.70E-02 | 0.000 | -0.334 | - | - |
| | X 16 | 0.172 | 0.000 | 1.679 | - | - |
| | X 17 | 3.133E-02 | 0.000 | 0.542 | - | - |
| | X 19 | -0.329 | 0.000 | -2.929 | - | - |

[a]Dependent Variable : Discriminant Scores from function 1 for Analysis1

Thus, the discriminant function classifying the companies of this section correctly is as follows:

$$S_{Engineering} = 1.809X7+6.017X8+4.229X10-6.932X11+3.566X12-.017X15+.172X16+.03133X17-.329X19-3.485$$

Now to find out the cut-off score:

$D_1$**=0.800 and** $D_2$**= -1.899**; hence the cut-off score should be $(D_1+D_2)/2$, i.e., ***-0.549***

**Section 31 (Chemicals, Dyes, Pharmaceuticals, Refineries and Plastics):** The sample selected included 51 companies from this section out of which 42 were excellent companies and the remaining 9 were not-so-excellent companies.

The best results for this section were found to be as follows :

**Table 27: Findings for Chemicals, Dyes, Pharmaceuticals, Refineries and Plastics Companies**

**Discriminant**

**Analysis Case Processing Summary**

| *Unweighted Cases* | | *N* | *Percentage* |
|---|---|---|---|
| Valid | | 51 | 100.0 |
| Excluded | Missing or out-of-range group codes | 0 | 0.0 |
| | At least one missing discriminating variable | 0 | 0.0 |
| | Both missing or out-of-range group codes and at least one missing discriminating variable | 0 | 0.0 |
| | Total | 0 | 0.0 |
| Total | | 51 | 100.0 |

**Group Statistics**

| Group | | Valid N (listwise) | |
|---|---|---|---|
| | | Unweighted | Weighted |
| 1 | X 16 | 42 | 42.000 |
| | X 1 | 42 | 42.000 |
| | X 2 | 42 | 42.000 |
| 2 | X 16 | 9 | 9.000 |
| | X 1 | 9 | 9.000 |
| | X 2 | 9 | 9.000 |
| Total | X 16 | 51 | 51.000 |
| | X 1 | 51 | 51.000 |
| | X 2 | 51 | 51.000 |

**Analysis 1**
**Summary of Canonical Discriminant Functions**

**Eigenvalues**

| *Function* | *Eigenvalue* | *% of Variance* | *Cumulative %* | *Canonical Correlation* |
|---|---|---|---|---|
| 1 | 0.323[a] | 100.0 | 100.0 | 0.494 |

(a) First 1 canonical discriminant functions were used in the analysis

**Wilks' Lambda**

| *Test of Funcation (s)* | *Wilks' Lambda* | *Chi-square* | *df* | *Sig* |
|---|---|---|---|---|
| 1 | 0.756 | 13.302 | 3 | 0.004 |

**Standardized Canonical Discriminant Function Coefficients**

| | *Function* |
|---|---|
| | *1* |
| X 16 | 1.350 |
| X 1 | -0.329 |
| X 2 | -0.548 |

**Structure Matrix**

| | *Function* |
|---|---|
| | *1* |
| X 16 | 0.840 |
| X 1 | 0.669 |
| X 2 | -0.156 |

Pooled within-groups correlations between discriminating variables and standardized canonical discriminant functions Variables ordered by abssolute size of correlation within function.

**Functions at Group Centroids**

| *Group* | *Function* |
|---|---|
| | *1* |
| 1 | 0.258 |
| 2 | -1.204 |

Unstandardized canonical discriminant functions evaluated at group means.

## Classification Statistics

**Classification Processing Summary**

| | | |
|---|---|---|
| Processed | | 51 |
| Excluded | Missing or out-of-range group codes | 0 |
| | At least one missing discriminating variable | 0 |
| Used in Output | | 51 |

**Prior Probabilities for Groups**

| | | *Cases Used in Analysis* | |
|---|---|---|---|
| *Group* | *Prior* | *Unweighted* | *Weighted* |
| 1 | .824 | 42 | 42.000 |
| 2 | .176 | 9 | 9.000 |
| Total | 1.000 | 51 | 51.000 |

**Classification Results**[a]

| | | Group | Predicted Group Membership 1 | 2 | Total |
|---|---|---|---|---|---|
| Original | Count | 1 | 42 | 0 | 42 |
| | | 2 | 6 | 3 | 9 |
| | % | 1 | 100 | .0 | 100.0 |
| | | 2 | 66.7 | 33.3 | 100.0 |

[a]88.2% of original grouped cases correctly classified.

Hence for this group taking a combination of X1, X2, and X16 classifies maximum number of companies, i.e., 88.2% of this section correctly.

To find out the discriminant function:

**Table 28: Regression Analysis for Chemicals, Dyes, Pharmaceuticals, Refineries and Plastics Companies**

## Regression

**Variables Entered / Removed**[b]

| *Model* | *Variables Entered* | *Variables Removed* | *Method* |
|---|---|---|---|
| 1 | X 16, X 1, X 2[a] | | Enter |

[a]All requested variables entered.
[b]Dependent Variable : Discriminant Scores from Function 1 for Analysis 1.

**Model Summary**

| *Model* | *R* | *R Square* | *Adjusted R Square* | *Std. Error of the Estimate* |
|---|---|---|---|---|
| 1 | 1.000[a] | 1.000 | 1.000 | 0.0000000 |

[a]Predictors : (Constant), X 16, X 2, X 1.

**Coefficients[a]**

| Model | | Unstandardized Coefficients | | Standardized Coefficients | t | Sig. |
|---|---|---|---|---|---|---|
| | | B | Std. Error | Beta | | |
| 1 | (Constant) | -0.518 | 0.000 | | - | - |
| | X 1 | -2.15E-02 | 0.000 | -0.306 | - | - |
| | X 2 | -5.20E-02 | 0.000 | -0.478 | - | - |
| | X 16 | 0.136 | 0.000 | 1.301 | - | - |

Thus, the discriminant function classifying the companies of this section correctly is as follows:

$$S_{Pharmaceuticals} = -.0215X1-.052X2+.136X16-.518$$

Now to find out the cut-off score:

**$D_1$=0.258 and $D_2$= -1.204**; hence the cut-off score should be $(D_1+D_2)/2$, i.e., ***-0.527***

**Section 36 (Miscellaneous):** The sample selected included 25 companies from this section out of which 16 were excellent companies and the remaining 9 were not-so-excellent companies.

The best results for this section were found to be as follows:

**Table 29: Findings for Companies in Miscellaneous Section**

**Discriminant**

**Analysis Case Processing Summary**

| *Unweighted Cases* | | *N* | *Percent* |
|---|---|---|---|
| Valid | | 25 | 100.0 |
| Excluded | Missing or out-of-range group codes | 0 | 0.0 |
| | At least one missing discriminating variable | 0 | 0.0 |
| | Both missing or out-of-range group codes and at least one missing discriminating variable | 0 | 0.0 |
| | Total | 0 | 0.0 |
| Total | | 25 | 100.0 |

**Group Statistics**

| Group | | Valid N (listwise) | |
|---|---|---|---|
| | | *Unweighted* | *Weighted* |
| 1 | X 3 | 16 | 16.000 |
| | X 4 | 16 | 16.000 |
| | X 5 | 16 | 16.000 |
| | X 6 | 16 | 16.000 |
| | X 7 | 16 | 16.000 |
| | X 8 | 16 | 16.000 |
| | X 9 | 16 | 16.000 |
| | X 10 | 16 | 16.000 |
| | X 11 | 16 | 16.000 |
| | X 12 | 16 | 16.000 |
| | X 13 | 16 | 16.000 |
| | X 14 | 16 | 16.000 |
| | X 15 | 16 | 16.000 |
| | X 16 | 16 | 16.000 |
| | X 17 | 16 | 16.000 |
| | X 18 | 16 | 16.000 |
| | X 19 | 16 | 16.000 |
| | X 20 | 16 | 16.000 |
| 2 | X 3 | 9 | 9.000 |
| | X 4 | 9 | 9.000 |
| | X 5 | 9 | 9.000 |
| | X 6 | 9 | 9.000 |
| | X 7 | 9 | 9.000 |
| | X 8 | 9 | 9.000 |
| | X 9 | 9 | 9.000 |
| | X 10 | 9 | 9.000 |
| | X 11 | 9 | 9.000 |
| | X 12 | 9 | 9.000 |
| | X 13 | 9 | 9.000 |
| | X 14 | 9 | 9.000 |
| | X 15 | 9 | 9.000 |
| | X 16 | 9 | 9.000 |
| | X 17 | 9 | 9.000 |
| | X 18 | 9 | 9.000 |
| | X 19 | 9 | 9.000 |
| | X 20 | 9 | 9.000 |
| Total | X 3 | 25 | 25.000 |
| | X 4 | 25 | 25.000 |

| | | |
|---|---|---|
| X 5 | 25 | 25.000 |
| X 6 | 25 | 25.000 |
| X 7 | 25 | 25.000 |
| X 8 | 25 | 25.000 |
| X 9 | 25 | 25.000 |
| X 10 | 25 | 25.000 |
| X 11 | 25 | 25.000 |
| X 12 | 25 | 25.000 |
| X 13 | 25 | 25.000 |
| X 14 | 25 | 25.000 |
| X 15 | 25 | 25.000 |
| X 16 | 25 | 25.000 |
| X 17 | 25 | 25.000 |
| X 18 | 25 | 25.000 |
| X 19 | 25 | 25.000 |
| X 20 | 25 | 25.000 |

## Analysis 1
## Summary of Canonical Discriminant Functions

### Eigenvalues

| *Function* | *Eigenvalue* | *% of Variance* | *Cumulative %* | *Canonical Correlation* |
|---|---|---|---|---|
| 1 | 2.339[a] | 100.0 | 100.0 | 0.837 |

[a]First 1 canonical discriminant functions were used in the analysis

### Wilks' Lambda

| *Test of Funcation (s)* | *Wilks' Lambda* | *Chi-square* | *df* | *Sig* |
|---|---|---|---|---|
| 1 | 0.300 | 16.878 | 18 | 0.532 |

### Standardized Canonical Discriminant Function Coefficients

| | *Function* |
|---|---|
| | *1* |
| X 3 | -0.789 |
| X 4 | 1.542 |
| X 5 | -2.592 |

| | |
|---|---|
| X 6 | -7.414 |
| X 7 | -3.372 |
| X 8 | 1.469 |
| X 9 | 8.323 |
| X 10 | 0.388 |
| X 11 | -0.475 |
| X 12 | 3.394 |
| X 13 | 1.438 |
| X 14 | 0.223 |
| X 15 | -1.433 |
| X 16 | 6.106 |
| X 17 | -0.380 |
| X 18 | -2.332 |
| X 19 | 3.645 |
| X 20 | -6.397 |

**Structure Matrix**

| | *Function* |
|---|---|
| | *1* |
| X 16 | -0.461 |
| X 20 | -0.450 |
| X 19 | -0.400 |
| X 17 | -0.395 |
| X 8 | -0.381 |
| X 18 | -0.336 |
| X 6 | -0.283 |
| X 3 | -0.262 |
| X 13 | 0.247 |
| X 7 | -0.220 |
| X 4 | -0.163 |
| X 9 | -0.158 |
| X 14 | -0.146 |
| X 11 | -0.112 |
| X 5 | -0.096 |
| X 15 | -0.058 |
| X 10 | -0.048 |
| X 12 | -0.045 |

Pooled within-groups correlations between discriminating variables and standardized canonical discriminant functions Variables ordered by absolute size of correlation within function.

**Functions at Group Centroids**

| *Group* | *Function* |
|---|---|
| | *1* |
| 1 | -1.100 |
| 2 | -1.956 |

Unstandardized canonical discriminant functions evaluated at group means.

## Classification Statistics

**Classification Processing Summary**

| | | |
|---|---|---|
| Processed | | 25 |
| Excluded | Missing or out-of-range group codes | 0 |
| | At least one missing discriminating variable | 0 |
| Used in Output | | 25 |

**Prior Probabilities for Groups**

| *Group* | *Prior* | *Cases Used in Analysis* | |
|---|---|---|---|
| | | *Unweighted* | *Weighted* |
| 1 | 0.640 | 16 | 16.000 |
| 2 | 0.360 | 9 | 9.000 |
| Total | 1.000 | 25 | 25.000 |

**Classification Results[a]**

| | | | *Predicted Group Membership* | | |
|---|---|---|---|---|---|
| | | *Group* | *1* | *2* | *Total* |
| Original | Count | 1 | 16 | 0 | 16 |
| | | 2 | 0 | 9 | 9 |
| | % | 1 | 100.00 | 0.0 | 100.0 |
| | | 2 | 0 | 100.00 | 100.0 |

[a] 100.0% of original grouped cases correctly classified.

Hence for this group taking a combination of all the ratios except X 1 and X 2 classifies all the companies of this section correctly.
To find out the discriminant function :

**Table 30 : Regression Analysis for Companies in Miscellaneous Section**

## Regression

**Variables Entered / Removed[b]**

| *Model* | *Variables Entered* | *Variables Removed* | *Method* |
|---|---|---|---|
| 1 | X 20, X 5, X 15, X 4, X 14, X 3, X 11, X 13, X 9, X 10, X 17, X 12, X 8, X 7, X 18, X 19, X 6, X 16[a] | | Enter |

[a] All requested variables entered.
[b] Dependent Variable : Discriminant Scores from Function 1 for Analysis 1

**Model Summary**

| *Model* | *R* | *R Square* | *Adjusted R Square* | *Std. Error of the Estimate* |
|---|---|---|---|---|
| 1 | 1.000[a] | 1.000 | 1.000 | .0000000 |

[a] Predictors : (Constant), X 20, X 5, X 15, X 4, X 14, X 3, X 11, X 13, X 9, X 10, X 17, X 12, X 8, X 7, X 18, X 19, X 6, X 16.

**Coefficients[a]**

| Model | | Unstandardized Coefficients | | Standardized Coefficients | t | Sig. |
|---|---|---|---|---|---|---|
| | | B | Std. Error | Beta | | |
| 1 | (Constant) | -2.221 | 0.000 | | - | - |
| | X 3 | -0.204 | 0.000 | -465 | - | - |
| | X 4 | -0.322 | 0.000 | 0.870 | - | - |
| | X 5 | -0.145 | 0.000 | -1.434 | - | - |
| | X 6 | -17.124 | 0.000 | -4.421 | - | - |
| | X 7 | -8.489 | 0.000 | -1.947 | - | - |
| | X 8 | 8.776 | 0.000 | 0.931 | - | - |
| | X 9 | 8.681 | 0.000 | 4.686 | - | - |
| | X 10 | 1.492 | 0.000 | 0.213 | - | - |
| | X 11 | -2.217 | 0.000 | -264 | - | - |
| | X 12 | 7.438 | 0.000 | 1.862 | - | - |
| | X 13 | 1.849 | 0.000 | 0.841 | - | - |
| | X 14 | 2.578E-03 | 0.000 | 0.125 | - | - |
| | X 15 | -9.25E-02 | 0.000 | -0.787 | - | - |
| | X 16 | 0.712 | 0.000 | 4.088 | - | - |
| | X 17 | -1.34E-02 | 0.000 | -0.243 | - | - |
| | X 18 | -0.339 | 0.000 | -1.435 | - | - |
| | X 19 | 0.456 | 0.000 | 2.338 | - | - |
| | X 20 | -0.519 | 0.000 | -4.251 | - | - |

[a] Dependent Variable : Discriminant Scores from Function 1 for Analysis 1.

Hence the discriminant function that classifies all the companies of this section correctly is as follows:

$$S_{Miscellaneous} = .204X3 + .322X4 - .145X5 - 17.124X6 - 8.489X7 + 8.776X8 + 8.691X9 + 1.492X10 - 2.217X11 + 7.438X12 + 1.849X13 + .002578X14 - .0925X15 + .712X16 - .0134X17 - .339X18 + .456X19 - .519X20 - 2.221$$

To find out the cut-off score:

**$D_1$=-1.1 and $D_2$=1.956**; hence the cut off score will be 0.428.

Now to summarize the industry wise classification; we can look into the following table:

**Table 31: Summary for Industrywise Classification**

| *Section* | *Number* | *Correct Classification* | *Eigen Value* | *Canonical Correlation* | *Wilk's Lambda* | *Significance Test* |
|---|---|---|---|---|---|---|
| 19 | 8 | 100 % | 84.675 | 0.994 | 0.012 | 0.001 |
| 24 | 8 | 100 % | 2.047 | 0.820 | 0.328 | 0.013 |
| 26 | 20 | 100 % | 2.480 | 0.844 | 0.287 | 0.051 |
| 29 | 15 | 100 % | 0.907 | 0.690 | 0.524 | 0.021 |
| 30 | 27 | 96.3 % | 1.640 | 0.788 | 0.379 | 0.019 |
| 31 | 51 | 88.2 % | 0.323 | 0.494 | 0.756 | 0.004 |
| 36 | 25 | 100 % | 2.339 | 0.837 | 0.300 | 0.532 |

**Size wise Analysis**

As stated earlier, size is related to the net worth of the company. The previous studies discussed in Chapter 2 have taken size of investment or size of total assets as the size of the company. But since the investment in assets can be increased by heavy borrowings or through issue of securities, which form liabilities and required to be paid back as and when due; I think that the difference between the amount of total assets and total liabilities, i.e., net worth is a better indicator of the size of the company. Also, if we look at the General Accounting Equation (Assets = Liabilities + Capital), the net worth is indicator of the capital available to the firm.

All the companies of the sample have been divided into 5 slabs depending upon their net worth as follows:

**Table 32: Sizewise Classification of Companies**

| *Net Worth (in Rs. Crores)* | *Number of Companies* | *Group 1* | *Group 2* |
|---|---|---|---|
| <100 | 29 | 10 | 19 |
| 100-200 | 45 | 32 | 13 |
| 200-300 | 23 | 10 | 13 |
| 300-500 | 38 | 26 | 12 |
| >500 | 39 | 35 | 4 |

Here, it should be kept in mind that the outliers have been already removed. Hence, the total of number of companies is coming to be 174 and not 180.

**Companies having Net Worth less than Rs. 100 Crores:** The number of such companies in our sample was 29 with 10 of them in Group 1, i.e., excellent companies and remaining 19 not-so-excellent companies.

The best results for such companies are as follows:

**Table 33: Findings for Companies having Net Worth less than Rs. 100 Crores**

**Discriminant**

**Analysis Case Processing Summary**

| *Unweighted Cases* | | *N* | *Percentage* |
|---|---|---|---|
| Valid | | 29 | 100.0 |
| Excluded | Missing or out-of-range group codes | 0 | 0.0 |
| | At least one missing discriminating variable | 0 | 0.0 |
| | Both missing or out-of-range group codes and at least one missing discriminating variable | 0 | 0.0 |
| | Total | 0 | 0.0 |
| Total | | 29 | 100.0 |

**Group Statistics**

| *Group* | | *Valid N (listwise)* | |
|---|---|---|---|
| | | *Unweighted* | *Weighted* |
| 1 | X 2 | 10 | 10.000 |
| | X 3 | 10 | 10.000 |
| | X 6 | 10 | 10.000 |
| | X 7 | 10 | 10.000 |
| | X 9 | 10 | 10.000 |
| | X 10 | 10 | 10.000 |
| | X 11 | 10 | 10.000 |
| | X 12 | 10 | 10.000 |
| | X 14 | 10 | 10.000 |
| | X 17 | 10 | 10.000 |
| | X 19 | 10 | 10.000 |
| | X 20 | 10 | 10.000 |

| | | | |
|---|---|---|---|
| 2 | X 2 | 19 | 19.000 |
| | X 3 | 19 | 19.000 |
| | X 6 | 19 | 19.000 |
| | X 7 | 19 | 19.000 |
| | X 9 | 19 | 19.000 |
| | X 10 | 19 | 19.000 |
| | X 11 | 19 | 19.000 |
| | X 12 | 19 | 19.000 |
| | X 14 | 19 | 19.000 |
| | X 17 | 19 | 19.000 |
| | X 19 | 19 | 19.000 |
| | X 20 | 19 | 19.000 |
| Total | X 2 | 29 | 29.000 |
| | X 3 | 29 | 29.000 |
| | X 6 | 29 | 29.000 |
| | X 7 | 29 | 29.000 |
| | X 9 | 29 | 29.000 |
| | X 10 | 29 | 29.000 |
| | X 11 | 29 | 29.000 |
| | X 12 | 29 | 29.000 |
| | X 14 | 29 | 29.000 |
| | X 17 | 29 | 29.000 |
| | X 19 | 29 | 29.000 |
| | X 20 | 29 | 29.000 |

**Analysis 1**

**Summary of Canonical Discriminant Functions**

**Eigenvalues**

| *Function* | *Eigenvalue* | *% of Variance* | *Cumulative %* | *Canonical Correlation* |
|---|---|---|---|---|
| 1 | 2.997[a] | 100.0 | 100.0 | 0.866 |

(a) First 1 canonical discriminant functions were used in the analysis.

**Wilks' Lambda**

| *Test of Funcation (s)* | *Wilks' Lambda* | *Chi-square* | *df* | *Sig* |
|---|---|---|---|---|
| 1 | 0.250 | 29.097 | 12 | 0.004 |

**Standardized Canonical Discriminant Function Coefficients**

| | *Function* |
|---|---|
| | *1* |
| X 2 | -0.889 |
| X 3 | -0.129 |
| X 6 | 0.715 |
| X 7 | 1.646 |
| X 9 | -0.250 |
| X 10 | 1.786 |
| X 11 | -1.721 |
| X 12 | 0.346 |
| X 14 | -1.280 |
| X 17 | 0.692 |
| X 19 | -0.443 |
| X 20 | 0.261 |

**Structure Matrix**

| | *Function* |
|---|---|
| | *1* |
| X 7 | 0.553 |
| X 9 | 0.321 |
| X 17 | 0.291 |
| X 20 | 0.287 |
| X 19 | 0.257 |
| X 14 | 0.230 |
| X 6 | 0.167 |
| X 10 | 0.142 |
| X 12 | 0.104 |
| X 11 | 0.102 |
| X 2 | -0.075 |
| X 3 | -0.010 |

Pooled within-groups correlations between discriminating variables and standardized canonical discriminant functions Variables ordered by abssolute size of correlation within function.

**Functions at Group Centroids**

| *Group* | *Function* |
|---|---|
| | *1* |
| 1 | 2.303 |
| 2 | -1.212 |

Unstandardized canonical discriminant functions evaluated at group means

**Classification Statistics**

**Classification Processing Summary**

| | | |
|---|---|---|
| Processed | | 29 |
| Excluded | Missing or out-of-range group codes | 0 |
| | At least one missing discriminating variable | 0 |
| Used in Output | | 29 |

**Prior Probabilities for Groups**

| | | *Cases Used in Analysis* | |
|---|---|---|---|
| *Group* | *Prior* | *Unweighted* | *Weighted* |
| 1 | 0.345 | 10 | 10.000 |
| 2 | 0.655 | 19 | 19.000 |
| Total | 1.000 | 29 | 29.000 |

**Classification Results**[a]

| | | | *Predicted Group Membership* | | |
|---|---|---|---|---|---|
| | | *Group* | *1* | *2* | *Total* |
| Original | Count | 1 | 9 | 1 | 10 |
| | | 2 | 0 | 19 | 19 |
| | % | 1 | 90.0 | 10.0 | 100.0 |
| | | 2 | 0 | 100.00 | 100.0 |

[a] 96.6% of original grouped cases correctly classified.

It is classifying all but one cases correctly. Now, to find out the discriminant functions and cut-off scores :

**Table 34 : Regression Analysis for Companies having Net Worth less than Rs. 100 Crores**

**Regression**

**Variables Entered / Removed**[b]

| *Model* | *Variables Entered* | *Variables Removed* | *Method* |
|---|---|---|---|
| 1 | X 20, X 10, X 2, X 3, X 17, X 16, X 12, X 14, X 9, X 7, X 11, X19[a] | | Enter |

[a] All requested variables entered.
[b] Dependent Variable : Discriminant Scores from Function 1 for Analysis 1

**Model Summary**

| *Model* | *R* | *R Square* | *Adjusted R Square* | *Std. Error of the Estimate* |
|---|---|---|---|---|
| 1 | 1.000[a] | 1.000 | 1.000 | 7.2402E-08 |

a. Predictors : (Constant), X 20, X 10, X 2, X 3, X 17, X 6, X 12, X 14, X 9, X 7, X 11, X 19

**Coefficients[a]**

| Model | | Unstandardized Coefficients | | Standardized Coefficients | | |
|---|---|---|---|---|---|---|
| | | B | Std. Error | Beta | .t | Sig. |
| 1 | (Constant) | -1.764 | 0.000 | | -2.5E+07 | .000 |
| | X 2 | -8.34E-02 | 0.000 | -0.448 | -5.1E+07 | .000 |
| | X 3 | -3.56E-02 | 0.000 | -0.064 | -6454796 | .000 |
| | X 6 | 1.291 | 0.000 | 0.373 | 1.4E+07 | .000 |
| | X 7 | 4.224 | 0.000 | 1.140 | 5.6E+07 | .000 |
| | X 9 | -0.244 | 0.000 | -0.143 | -4655822 | .000 |
| | X 10 | 2.992 | 0.000 | 0.920 | 3.9E+07 | .000 |
| | X 11 | -2.353 | 0.000 | -0.874 | -2.9E+07 | .000 |
| | X 12 | 0.419 | 0.000 | 0.176 | 7920346 | .000 |
| | X 14 | -5.79E-02 | 0.000 | -0.689 | -4.6E+07 | .000 |
| | X 17 | 2.078E-02 | 0.000 | 0.388 | 3.7E+07 | .000 |
| | X 19 | -3.87E-02 | 0.000 | -0.243 | -5164872 | .000 |
| | X 20 | 1.199E-02 | 0.000 | 0.146 | 3699502 | .000 |

(a) Dependent Variable : Discriminant Scores from Function 1 for Analysis 1.

Hence, the discriminant function that best discriminates between the two groups of companies having net worth less than Rs. 100 Crores is as follows:

**$S_1$= -.0834X2-.0356X3+1.291X6+4.224X7-.244X9+2.992X10-2.353X11+.419X12-.0579X14+.02078X17-.0387X19+.01199X20-1.764**

To find out the cut-off score:
**$D_1$=2.303 and $D_2$= -1.212**; hence the cut-off score should be ***0.545***

**Companies having Net Worth between Rs. 100 Crores and Rs. 200 Crores:** The number of such companies in our sample was 45 with 32 of them in Group 1, i.e., excellent companies and remaining 13 not-so-excellent companies.

The best results for such companies are as follows:

**Table 35: Findings for Companies having Net Worth between Rs. 100 Crores and Rs. 200 Crores**

**Discriminant**

**Analysis Case Processing Summary**

| *Unweighted Cases* | | *N* | *Percent* |
|---|---|---|---|
| Valid | | 45 | 100.0 |
| Excluded | Missing or out-of-range group codes | 0 | 0.0 |
| | At least one missing discriminating variable | 0 | 0.0 |
| | Both missing or out-of-range group codes and at least one missing discriminating variable | 0 | 0.0 |
| | Total | 0 | 0.0 |
| Total | | 45 | 100.0 |

**Group Statistics**

| *Group* | | *Valid N (listwise)* | |
|---|---|---|---|
| | | *Unweighted* | *Weighted* |
| 1 | X6 | 32 | 32.000 |
| | X 8 | 32 | 32.000 |
| | X 9 | 32 | 32.000 |
| | X 11 | 32 | 32.000 |
| | X 12 | 32 | 32.000 |
| | X 17 | 32 | 32.000 |
| | X 19 | 32 | 32.000 |
| | X 20 | 32 | 32.000 |
| | X 3 | 32 | 32.000 |
| | X 5 | 32 | 32.000 |

| | | | |
|---|---|---|---|
| 2 | X 6 | 13 | 13.000 |
| | X 8 | 13 | 13.000 |
| | X 9 | 13 | 13.000 |
| | X 11 | 13 | 13.000 |
| | X 12 | 13 | 13.000 |
| | X 17 | 13 | 13.000 |
| | X 19 | 13 | 13.000 |
| | X 20 | 13 | 13.000 |
| | X 3 | 13 | 13.000 |
| | X 5 | 13 | 13.000 |
| Total | X 6 | 45 | 45.000 |
| | X 8 | 45 | 45.000 |
| | X 9 | 45 | 45.000 |
| | X 11 | 45 | 45.000 |
| | X 12 | 45 | 45.000 |
| | X 17 | 45 | 45.000 |
| | X 19 | 45 | 45.000 |
| | X 20 | 45 | 45.000 |
| | X 3 | 45 | 45.000 |
| | X 5 | 45 | 45.000 |

## Analysis 1
## Summary of Canonical Discriminant Functions

### Eigenvalues

| *Function* | *Eigenvalue* | *% of Variance* | *Cumulative %* | *Canonical Correlation* |
|---|---|---|---|---|
| 1 | .605[a] | 100.0 | 100.0 | 0.614 |

[a]First 1 canonical discriminant functions were used in the analysis

### Wilks' Lambda

| *Test of Function (s)* | *Wilks' Lambda* | *Chi-square* | *df* | *Sig* |
|---|---|---|---|---|
| 1 | 0.623 | 17.969 | 10 | 0.055 |

**Standardized Canonical Discriminant Function Coefficients**

| | *Function* |
|---|---|
| | *1* |
| X 6 | 1.614 |
| X 8 | -0.588 |
| X 9 | -1.696 |
| X 11 | -0.509 |
| X 12 | 0.590 |
| X 17 | 0.455 |
| X 19 | -1.460 |
| X 20 | 2.432 |
| X 3 | 0.129 |
| X 5 | -.375 |

**Structure Matrix**

| | *Function* |
|---|---|
| | *1* |
| X 20 | 0.703 |
| X 19 | 0.543 |
| X 6 | 0.506 |
| X 9 | 0.395 |
| X 8 | 0.345 |
| X 5 | -0.291 |
| X 3 | 0.206 |
| X 11 | 0.130 |
| X 12 | 0.117 |
| X 17 | 0.003 |

Pooled within-groups correlations between discriminating variables and standardized canonical discriminant functions Variables ordered by absolute size of correlation within function.

**Functions at Group Centroids**

| *Group* | *Function* |
|---|---|
| | *1* |
| 1 | 0.484 |
| 2 | -1.193 |

Unstandardized canonical discriminant functions evaluated at group means.

## Classification Statistics

### Classification Processing Summary

| | | |
|---|---|---|
| Processed | | 45 |
| Excluded | Missing or out-of-range group codes | 0 |
| | At least one missing discriminating variable | 0 |
| Used in Output | | 45 |

### Prior Probabilities for Groups

| | | *Cases Used in Analysis* | |
|---|---|---|---|
| *Group* | *Prior* | *Unweighted* | *Weighted* |
| 1 | .711 | 32 | 32.000 |
| 2 | .289 | 13 | 13.000 |
| Total | 1.000 | 45 | 45.000 |

### Classification Results[a]

| | | | *Predicted Group Membership* | | |
|---|---|---|---|---|---|
| | | *Group* | *1* | *2* | *Total* |
| Original | Count | 1 | 29 | 3 | 32 |
| | | 2 | 2 | 11 | 13 |
| | % | 1 | 90.6 | 9.4 | 100.0 |
| | | 2 | 15.4 | 84.6 | 100.0 |

[a] 88.9% of original grouped cases correctly classified.

Thus, it is classifying 88.9% of the companies of this slab correctly. Now, to find out the discriminant function and cut-off score :

**Table 36 : Regression Analysis for Companies having Net Worth between Rs. 100 Crores Rs. 200 Crores**

**Regression**

**Variables Entered / Removed[b]**

| *Model* | *Variables Entered* | *Variables Removed* | *Method* |
|---|---|---|---|
| 1 | X 20, X 12, X 5, X 17, X 9, X 3, X 8, X 11, X 6, X 19[a] | | Enter |

[a] All requested variables entered.
[b] Dependent Variable : Discriminant Scores from Function 1 for Analysis 1

**Model Summary**

| *Model* | *R* | *R Square* | *Adjusted R Square* | *Std. Error of the Estimate* |
|---|---|---|---|---|
| 1 | 1.000[a] | 1.000 | 1.000 | 8.4909E-08 |

(a) Predictors : (Constant), X 20, X 12, X 5, X 17, X 9, X 3, X 8, X 11, X 6, X 19.

**Coefficients[a]**

| Model | | Unstandardized Coefficients | | Standardized Coefficients | | |
|---|---|---|---|---|---|---|
| | | B | Std. Error | Beta | t | Sig. |
| 1 | (Constant) | -3.208 | 0.000 | | -5.3E+07 | 0.000 |
| | X 3 | 2.636E-02 | 0.000 | 0.103 | 5969280 | 0.000 |
| | X 5 | -1.23E-02 | 0.000 | -0.304 | -2.5E+07 | 0.000 |
| | X 6 | 3.219 | 0.000 | 1.369 | 3.4E+07 | 0.000 |
| | X 8 | -2.609 | 0.000 | -0.480 | -2.9E+07 | 0.000 |
| | X 9 | -1.407 | 0.000 | -1.401 | -3.1E+07 | 0.000 |
| | X 11 | -1.328 | 0.000 | -0.404 | -2.3E+07 | 0.000 |
| | X 12 | 0.722 | 0.000 | 0.468 | 2.2E+07 | 0.000 |
| | X 17 | 1.138E-02 | 0.000 | 0.359 | 3.3E+07 | 0.000 |
| | X 19 | -.172 | 0.000 | -1.251 | -2.9E+07 | 0.000 |
| | X 20 | 0.184 | 0.000 | 2.188 | 4.9E+07 | 0.000 |

[a]Dependent Variable : Discriminant Scores from Function 1 for Analysis 1'

Hence, the discriminant function that best discriminates between the two groups of companies having net worth between Rs. 100 Crores and Rs. 200 Crores is as follows:

**$S_2$= .02636X3-.0123X5+3.219X6-2.609X8-1.407X9-1.328X11+.722X12+.01138X17-.172X19+.184X20-3.208**

To find out the cut-off score:

**$D_1$= .484 and $D_2$= -1.193**; hence the cut-off score will be ***–0.354***

**Companies having Net Worth between Rs. 200 Crores and Rs. 300 Crores:** The number of such companies in our sample was 23 with 10 of them in Group 1, i.e., excellent companies and remaining 13 not-so-excellent companies.

The best results for such companies are as follows:

**Table 37: Findings for Companies having Net Worth between Rs. 200 Crores and Rs. 300 Crores**

**Discriminant**

**Analysis Case Processing Summary**

| *Unweighted Cases* | | *N* | *Percent* |
|---|---|---|---|
| Valid | | 23 | 100.0 |
| Excluded | Missing or out-of-range group codes | 0 | 0.0 |
| | At least one missing discriminating variable | 0 | 0.0 |
| | Both missing or out-of-range group codes and at least one missing discriminating variable | 0 | 0.0 |
| | Total | 0 | 0.0 |
| Total | | 23 | 100.0 |

**Group Statistics**

| | | *Valid N (listwise)* | |
|---|---|---|---|
| *Group* | | *Unweighted* | *Weighted* |
| 1 | X 6 | 10 | 10.000 |
| | X 7 | 10 | 10.000 |
| | X 8 | 10 | 10.000 |

| | | | |
|---|---|---|---|
| | X 9 | 10 | 10.000 |
| | X 10 | 10 | 10.000 |
| | X 12 | 10 | 10.000 |
| | X 13 | 10 | 10.000 |
| | X 15 | 10 | 10.000 |
| | X 16 | 10 | 10.000 |
| | X 20 | 10 | 10.000 |
| 2 | X 6 | 13 | 13.000 |
| | X 7 | 13 | 13.000 |
| | X 8 | 13 | 13.000 |
| | X 9 | 13 | 13.000 |
| | X 10 | 13 | 13.000 |
| | X 12 | 13 | 13.000 |
| | X 13 | 13 | 13.000 |
| | X 15 | 13 | 13.000 |
| | X 16 | 13 | 13.000 |
| | X 20 | 13 | 13.000 |
| Total | X 6 | 23 | 23.000 |
| | X 7 | 23 | 23.000 |
| | X 8 | 23 | 23.000 |
| | X 9 | 23 | 23.000 |
| | X 10 | 23 | 23.000 |
| | X 12 | 23 | 23.000 |
| | X 13 | 23 | 23.000 |
| | X 15 | 23 | 23.000 |
| | X 16 | 23 | 23.000 |
| | X 20 | 23 | 23.000 |

## Analysis 1
## Summary of Canonical Discriminant Functions

### Eigenvalues

| *Function* | *Eigenvalue* | *% of Variance* | *Cumulative %* | *Canonical Correlation* |
|---|---|---|---|---|
| 1 | 2.563[a] | 100.0 | 100.0 | 0.848 |

[a] First 1 canonical discriminant functions were used in the analysis.

### Wilks' Lambda

| *Test of Function (s)* | *Wilks' Lambda* | *Chi-square* | *df* | *Sig* |
|---|---|---|---|---|
| 1 | 0.281 | 20.329 | 10 | 0.026 |

**Standardized Canonical Discriminant Function Coefficients**

| | *Function* |
|---|---|
| | *1* |
| X 6 | -1.162 |
| X 7 | -0.327 |
| X 8 | 0.901 |
| X 9 | 3.107 |
| X 10 | -0.883 |
| X 12 | 0.834 |
| X 13 | 0.164 |
| X 15 | -0.805 |
| X 16 | 2.708 |
| X 20 | -2.729 |

**Structure Matrix**

| | *Function* |
|---|---|
| | *1* |
| X 16 | 0.385 |
| X 20 | 0.379 |
| X 6 | 0.371 |
| X 9 | 0.334 |
| X 8 | 0.316 |
| X 13 | -0.257 |
| X 7 | 0.232 |
| X 10 | -0.157 |
| X 12 | 0.088 |
| X 15 | -0.011 |

Pooled within-groups correlations between discriminating variables and standardized canonical discriminant functions Variables ordered by absolute size of correlation within function.

**Functions at Group Centroids**

| *Group* | *Function* |
|---|---|
| | *1* |
| 1 | 1.744 |
| 2 | -1.342 |

Unstandardized canonical discriminant functions evaluated at group means.

**Classification Statistics**

### Classification Processing Summary

| | | |
|---|---|---|
| Processed | | 23 |
| Excluded | Missing or out-of-range group codes | 0 |
| | At least one missing discriminating variable | 0 |
| Used in Output | | 23 |

### Prior Probabilities for Groups

| | | *Cases Used in Analysis* | |
|---|---|---|---|
| *Group* | *Prior* | *Unweighted* | *Weighted* |
| 1 | 0.435 | 10 | 10.000 |
| 2 | 0.565 | 13 | 13.000 |
| Total | 1.000 | 23 | 23.000 |

### Classification Results[a]

| | | | *Predicted Group Membership* | | |
|---|---|---|---|---|---|
| | | *Group* | *1* | *2* | *Total* |
| Original | Count | 1 | 10 | 0 | 10 |
| | | 2 | 0 | 13 | 13 |
| | % | 1 | 100.0 | 0.0 | 100.0 |
| | | 2 | 0.0 | 100.0 | 100.0 |

[a] 100.0% of original grouped cases correctly classified.

Thus, the above set of ratios is classifying all the companies of this slab correctly. Now, to find out the discriminant function and cut-off score:

## Table 38: Regression Analysis for Companies having Net Worth between Rs. 200 Crores and Rs. 300 Crores

### Regression

**Variables Entered / Removed[b]**

| *Model* | *Variables Entered* | *Variables Removed* | *Method* |
|---|---|---|---|
| 1 | X 20, X 10, X 7, X 15, X 13, X 6, X 8, X 12, X 9, X 16[a] | | Enter |

[a] All requested variables entered.
[b] Dependent Variable : Discriminant Scores from Function 1 for Analysis 1

**Model Summary**

| *Model* | *R* | *R Square* | *Adjusted R Square* | *Std. Error of the Estimate* |
|---|---|---|---|---|
| 1 | 1.000[a] | 1.000 | 1.000 | 6.4446E-08 |

[a] Predictors : (Constant), X 20, X 10, X 7, X 15, X 13, X 6, X 8, X 12, X 9, X 16.

**Coefficients[a]**

| Model | | Unstandardized Coefficients | | Standardized Coefficients | t | Sig. |
|---|---|---|---|---|---|---|
| | | B | Std. Error | Beta | | |
| 1 | (Constant) | -0.890 | 0.000 | | -5311930 | 0.000 |
| | X 6 | -3.075 | 0.000 | -716 | -2.7E+07 | 0.000 |
| | X 7 | -1.048 | 0.000 | -0.186 | -1.4E+07 | 0.000 |
| | X 8 | 4.775 | 0.000 | 0.535 | 2.8E+07 | 0.000 |
| | X 9 | 3.196 | 0.000 | 1.868 | 5.1E+07 | 0.000 |
| | X 10 | -3.111 | 0.000 | -0.482 | -4.7E+07 | 0.000 |
| | X 12 | 0.965 | 0.000 | 0.446 | 2.1E+07 | 0.000 |
| | X 13 | 0.106 | 0.000 | 0.094 | 7544014 | 0.000 |
| | X 15 | -3.71E-02 | 0.000 | -0.426 | -4.1E+07 | 0.000 |
| | X 16 | 0.348 | 0.000 | 1.685 | 3.7E+07 | 0.000 |
| | X 20 | -0.242 | 0.000 | -1.691 | -3.7E+07 | 0.000 |

[a]Dependent Variable : Discriminant Scores from Function 1 for Analysis 1

Thus, the discriminant function which best classifies the companies of this slab into the two required groups is as follows:

**$S_3$= -3.075X6-1.048X7+4.775X8+3.196X9-3.111X10+.965X12+.106X13-.0371X15+.348X16-.242X20-.890**

To find out the cut-off score:

**$D_1$= 1.744 and $D_2$= -1.342**; hence the cut-off score will be –0.201.

**Companies having Net Worth between Rs. 300 Crores and Rs. 500 Crores:** The number of such companies in our sample was 38 with 26 of them in Group 1, i.e., excellent companies and remaining 12 not-so-excellent companies.

The best results for such companies are as follows:

**Table 39: Findings for Companies having Net Worth between Rs. 300 Crores and Rs. 500 Crores**

**Discriminant**

**Analysis Case Processing Summary**

| *Unweighted Cases* | | *N* | *Percent* |
|---|---|---|---|
| Valid | | 38 | 100.0 |
| Excluded | Missing or out-of-range group codes | 0 | 0.0 |
| | At least one missing discriminating variable | 0 | 0.0 |
| | Both missing or out-of-range group codes and at least one missing discriminating variable | 0 | 0.0 |
| | Total | 0 | 0.0 |
| Total | | 38 | 100.0 |

**Group Statistics**

| | | *Valid N (listwise)* | |
|---|---|---|---|
| *Group* | | *Unweighted* | *Weighted* |
| 1 | X 1 | 26 | 26.000 |
| | X 2 | 26 | 26.000 |
| | X 3 | 26 | 26.000 |
| | X 4 | 26 | 26.000 |

| | | | |
|---|---|---|---|
| | X 6 | 26 | 26.000 |
| | X 7 | 26 | 26.000 |
| | X 8 | 26 | 26.000 |
| | X 9 | 26 | 26.000 |
| | X 10 | 26 | 26.000 |
| | X 11 | 26 | 26.000 |
| | X 12 | 26 | 26.000 |
| | X 14 | 26 | 26.000 |
| | X 15 | 26 | 26.000 |
| | X 16 | 26 | 26.000 |
| | X 18 | 26 | 26.000 |
| | X 19 | 26 | 26.000 |
| 2 | X 1 | 12 | 12.000 |
| | X 2 | 12 | 12.000 |
| | X 3 | 12 | 12.000 |
| | X 4 | 12 | 12.000 |
| | X 6 | 12 | 12.000 |
| | X 7 | 12 | 12.000 |
| | X 8 | 12 | 12.000 |
| | X 9 | 12 | 12.000 |
| | X 10 | 12 | 12.000 |
| | X 11 | 12 | 12.000 |
| | X 12 | 12 | 12.000 |
| | X 14 | 12 | 12.000 |
| | X 15 | 12 | 12.000 |
| | X 16 | 12 | 12.000 |
| | X 18 | 12 | 12.000 |
| | X 19 | 12 | 12.000 |
| Total | X 1 | 38 | 38.000 |
| | X 2 | 38 | 38.000 |
| | X 3 | 38 | 38.000 |
| | X 4 | 38 | 38.000 |
| | X 6 | 38 | 38.000 |
| | X 7 | 38 | 38.000 |
| | X 8 | 38 | 38.000 |
| | X 9 | 38 | 38.000 |
| | X 10 | 38 | 38.000 |
| | X 11 | 38 | 38.000 |
| | X 12 | 38 | 38.000 |
| | X 14 | 38 | 38.000 |
| | X 15 | 38 | 38.000 |
| | X 16 | 38 | 38.000 |
| | X 18 | 38 | 38.000 |
| | X 19 | 38 | 38.000 |

## Analysis 1
## Summary of Canonical Discriminant Functions

### Eigenvalues

| *Function* | *Eigenvalue* | *% of Variance* | *Cumulative %* | *Canonical Correlation* |
|---|---|---|---|---|
| 1 | 1.379[a] | 100.0 | 100.0 | 0.761 |

(a) First 1 canonical discriminant functions were used in the analysis.

### Wilks' Lambda

| *Test of Funcation (s)* | *Wilks' Lambda* | *Chi-square* | *df* | *Sig* |
|---|---|---|---|---|
| 1 | 0.420 | 24.271 | 16 | 0.084 |

### Standardized Canonical Discriminant Function Coefficients

| | *Function* |
|---|---|
| | *1* |
| X 1 | 3.414 |
| X 2 | 2.984 |
| X 3 | 0.998 |
| X 4 | 0.902 |
| X 6 | 8.213 |
| X 7 | 2.061 |
| X 8 | -2.467 |
| X 9 | -9.254 |
| X 10 | -1.437 |
| X 11 | 1.700 |
| X 12 | -1.942 |
| X 14 | 0.764 |
| X 15 | -0.336 |
| X 16 | -8.085 |
| X 18 | 1.082 |
| X 19 | 2.180 |

### Structure Matrix

| | *Function* |
|---|---|
| | *1* |
| X 7 | -0.420 |
| X 9 | -0.385 |

| | |
|---|---|
| X 6 | -0.351 |
| X 16 | -0.315 |
| X 1 | -0.300 |
| X 19 | -0.249 |
| X 8 | -0.207 |
| X 18 | -0.200 |
| X 15 | 0.173 |
| X 14 | -0.156 |
| X 11 | -0.116 |
| X 4 | 0.104 |
| X 3 | 0.087 |
| X 12 | -0.052 |
| X 10 | -0.016 |
| X 2 | -0.006 |

Pooled within-groups correlations between discriminating variables and standardized canonical discriminant functions Variables ordered by absolute size of correlation within function.

**Functions at Group Centroids**

| *Group* | *Function* |
|---|---|
| | *1* |
| 1 | -0.777 |
| 2 | 1.683 |

Unstandardized canonical discriminant functions evaluated at group means.

**Classification Statistics**

**Classification Processing Summary**

| | | |
|---|---|---|
| Processed | | 38 |
| Excluded | Missing or out-of-range group codes | 0 |
| | At least one missing discriminating variable | 0 |
| Used in Output | | 38 |

**Prior Probabilities for Groups**

| | | *Cases Used in Analysis* | |
|---|---|---|---|
| *Group* | *Prior* | *Unweighted* | *Weighted* |
| 1 | 0.684 | 26 | 26.000 |
| 2 | 0.316 | 12 | 12.000 |
| Total | 1.000 | 38 | 38.000 |

**Classification Results**[a]

| | | Group | Predicted Group Membership 1 | 2 | Total |
|---|---|---|---|---|---|
| Original | Count | 1 | 26 | 0 | 26 |
| | | 2 | 2 | 10 | 12 |
| | % | 1 | 100.0 | .0 | 100.0 |
| | | 2 | 16.7 | 83.3 | 100.0 |

[a]94.7% of original grouped cases correctly classified.

Thus, the above set of ratios is classifying 94.7% of the companies of this slab correctly. Now, to find out the discriminant function and cut-off score:

**Table 40 : Regression Analysis for Companies having Net Worth between Rs. 300 Crores and Rs. 500 Crores**

**Regression**

**Variables Entered / Removed**[b]

| *Variables Model* | *Variables Entered* | *Removed* | *Method* |
|---|---|---|---|
| 1 | X 19, X 4, X 10, X 14, X 15, X 3, X 2, X 12, X 18, X 9, X 8, X 7, X 11, X 1 X 16, X 6[a] | | Enter |

[a]All requested variables entered.
[b]Dependent Variable : Discriminant Scores from Function 1 for Analysis 1.

**Model Summary**

| *Model* | *R* | *R Square* | *Adjusted R Square* | *Std. Error of the Estimate* |
|---|---|---|---|---|
| 1 | 1.000[a] | 1.000 | 1.000 | 0.0000000 |

[a] Predictors : (Constant), X 19, X 4, X 10, X 14, X 15, X 3, X 2, X 12, X 18, X 9, X 8, X 7, X 11, X 1, X 16, X 6

**Coefficients**

| Model | | Unstandardized Coefficients | | Standardized Coefficients | t | Sig. |
|---|---|---|---|---|---|---|
| | | B | Std. Error | Beta | | |
| 1 | (Constant) | -0.924 | 0.000 | | - | - |
| | X 1 | 0.222 | 0.000 | 2.347 | - | - |
| | X 2 | 0.202 | 0.000 | 1.934 | - | - |
| | X 3 | 0.142 | 0.000 | 0.650 | - | - |
| | X 4 | 0.124 | 0.000 | 0.589 | - | - |
| | X 6 | 14.191 | 0.000 | 5.759 | - | - |
| | X 7 | 6.899 | 0.000 | 1.490 | - | - |
| | X 8 | -11.095 | 0.000 | -1.646 | - | - |
| | X 9 | -9.346 | 0.000 | -6.584 | - | - |
| | X 10 | -6.582 | 0.000 | -0.932 | - | - |
| | X 11 | 5.781 | 0.000 | 1.112 | - | - |
| | X 12 | -3.542 | 0.000 | -1.261 | - | - |
| | X 14 | 1.075E-02 | 0.000 | 0.503 | - | - |
| | X 15 | -2.20E-02 | 0.000 | -0.223 | - | - |
| | X 16 | -0.743 | 0.000 | -5.588 | - | - |
| | X 18 | 0.179 | 0.000 | 0.720 | - | - |
| | X 19 | 0.218 | 0.000 | 1.472 | - | - |

(a) Dependent Variable : Discriminant Scores from Function 1 for Analysis 1.

Hence, the discriminant function which best discriminates the companies of this slab into excellent and not-so-excellent companies can be represented as:

$$S_4 = .222X1+.202X2+.142X3+.124X4+14.191X6+6.899X7-11.095X8-9.346X9-6.582X10+5.781X11-3.542X12+.01075X14-.022X15-.743X16+.179X18+.218X19-.924$$

To find out the cut-off score:

**$D_1$ = -0.777 and $D_2$ = 1.683**; hence the cut-off score will be 0.450.

**Companies having Net Worth more than Rs. 500 Crores:** The number of such companies in our sample was 39 with 35 of them in Group 1, i.e., excellent companies and remaining 4 not-so-excellent companies.

The best results for companies having net worth more than Rs. 500 Crores are as follows:

**Table 41: Findings for Companies having Net Worth more than Rs. 500 Crores**

**Discriminant**

**Analysis Case Processing Summary**

| *Unweighted Cases* | | *N* | *Percent* |
|---|---|---|---|
| Valid | | 39 | 100.0 |
| Excluded | Missing or out-of-range group codes | 0 | .0 |
| | At least one missing discriminating variable | 0 | .0 |
| | Both missing or out-of-range group codes and at least one missing discriminating variable | 0 | .0 |
| | Total | 0 | .0 |
| Total | | 39 | 100.0 |

**Group Statistics**

| | | *Valid N (listwise)* | |
|---|---|---|---|
| *Group* | | *Unweighted* | *Weighted* |
| 1 | X 9 | 35 | 35.000 |
| | X 13 | 35 | 35.000 |
| | X 16 | 35 | 35.000 |
| | X 17 | 35 | 35.000 |
| 2 | X 9 | 4 | 4.000 |
| | X 13 | 4 | 4.000 |
| | X 16 | 4 | 4.000 |
| | X 17 | 4 | 4.000 |
| Total | X 9 | 39 | 39.000 |
| | X 13 | 39 | 39.000 |
| | X 16 | 39 | 39.000 |
| | X 17 | 39 | 39.000 |

## Analysis 1
## Summary of Canonical Discriminant Functions

### Eigenvalues

| *Function* | *Eigenvalue* | *% of Variance* | *Cumulative %* | *Canonical Correlation* |
|---|---|---|---|---|
| 1 | .549[a] | 100.0 | 100.0 | 0.595 |

[a]First 1 canonical discriminant functions were used in the analysis

### Wilks' Lambda

| *Test of Funcation (s)* | *Wilks' Lambda* | *Chi-square* | *df* | *Sig* |
|---|---|---|---|---|
| 1 | 0.646 | 15.313 | 4 | 0.004 |

### Standardized Canonical Discriminant Function Coefficients

| | *Function* |
|---|---|
| | *1* |
| X 9 | 0.462 |
| X 13 | 0.927 |
| X 16 | -0.396 |
| X 17 | -0.552 |

### Structure Matrix

| | *Function* |
|---|---|
| | *1* |
| X 9 | 0.831 |
| X 13 | -0.385 |
| X 16 | -0.103 |
| X 17 | 0.043 |

Pooled within-groups correlations between discriminating variables and standardized canonical discriminant functions Variables ordered by absolute size of correlation within function.

**Functions at Group Centroids**

| *Group* | *Function* |
|---|---|
| | *1* |
| 1 | -0.244 |
| 2 | 2.135 |

Unstandardized canonical discriminant functions evaluated at group means.

## Classification Statistics

**Classification Processing Summary**

| | | |
|---|---|---|
| Processed | | 39 |
| Excluded | Missing or out-of-range group codes | 0 |
| | At least one missing discriminating variable | 0 |
| Used in Output | | 39 |

**Prior Probabilities for Groups**

| *Group* | *Prior* | *Cases Used in Analysis* | |
|---|---|---|---|
| | | *Unweighted* | *Weighted* |
| 1 | .897 | 35 | 35.000 |
| 2 | .103 | 4 | 4.000 |
| Total | 1.000 | 39 | 39.000 |

**Classification Results[a]**

| | | | *Predicted Group Membership* | | |
|---|---|---|---|---|---|
| | | *Group* | *1* | *2* | *Total* |
| Original | Count | 1 | 35 | 0 | 35 |
| | | 2 | 1 | 3 | 4 |
| | % | 1 | 100.0 | .0 | 100.0 |
| | | 2 | 25.0 | 75.0 | 100.0 |

[a]97.4% of original grouped cases correctly classified.

Thus a combination of four ratios, i.e., X9, X13, X16, and X17 classifies 97.4 % of the companies with net worth more than Rs. 500 Crores correctly. To find out the discriminant function and cut-off score :

**Table 42 : Regression Analysis for Companies having Net Worth more than Rs. 500 Crores**

**Regression**

**Variables Entered / Removed**[b]

| *Model* | *Variables Entered* | *Variables Removed* | *Method* |
|---|---|---|---|
| 1 | X 17, X 9, X 13, X 16[a] | | Enter |

[a]All requested variables entered.
[b]Dependent Variable : Discriminant Scores from Function 1 for Analysis 1.

**Model Summary**

| *Model* | *R* | *R Square* | *Adjusted R Square* | *Std. Error of the Estimate* |
|---|---|---|---|---|
| 1 | 1.000[a] | 1.000 | 1.000 | 0.0000000 |

[a]Predictors : (Constant), X 17, X 9, X 13, X 16.

**Coefficients**[a]

| Model | | Unstandardized Coefficients | | Standardized Coefficients | t | Sig. |
|---|---|---|---|---|---|---|
| | | B | Std. Error | Beta | | |
| 1 | (Constant) | -0.728 | 0.000 | | - | 0.000 |
| | X 9 | 0.510 | 0.000 | 0.372 | - | 0.000 |
| | X 13 | 1.547 | 0.000 | 0.875 | - | 0.000 |
| | X 16 | -4.82E-02 | 0.000 | -0.331 | - | 0.000 |
| | X 17 | -1.93E-02 | 0.000 | -0.445 | - | 0.000 |

[a]Dependent Variable : Discriminant Scores from Function 1 for Analysis 1.

Hence, the function which best discriminates the companies of this slab into excellent and not-so-excellent is as follows:

**S5= 0.510X9+1.547X13-0.0482X16-0.0193X17-0.728**

To find out the cut-off score:

**D1= -0.244 and D2= 2.135**; hence the cut-off score comes to be 0.945.

To summarize the size wise results, following table is very helpful:

**Table 43: Results Summary for Size wise Classification**

| *Net Worth (in Rs. Crores)* | *Number of Companies* | *Correct Classif- -ication* | *Eigen Value* | *Canonical Correlation* | *Wilks' Lambda* | *Significance Test* |
|---|---|---|---|---|---|---|
| <100 | 29 | 96.6 % | 2.997 | 0.866 | 0.250 | 0.004 |
| 100-200 | 45 | 88.9 % | 0.605 | 0.614 | 0.623 | 0.055 |
| 200-300 | 23 | 100 % | 2.563 | 0.848 | 0.281 | 0.026 |
| 300-500 | 38 | 94.7 % | 1.379 | 0.761 | 0.420 | 0.084 |
| >500 | 39 | 97.4 % | 0.549 | 0.595 | 0.646 | 0.004 |

From the above analysis it is clear that the set of 20 ratios taken for analysis classify more than 78 % cases correctly whether we look at the year wise analysis, industry wise analysis or size wise analysis. Also these ratios are more discriminatory for Group 1, i.e., excellent companies than for Group 2. One of the major reasons for this may be the fact that the sample is drawn from the BT-500 companies. Hence, even the companies in Group 2 cannot be called as non-excellent companies.

To find out the discriminatory power of each of the 20 ratios, let us find out the frequency of occurrence of each ratio in the discriminant functions. It can be represented in the form of following table:

**Table 44 : Ratios in all the Analysis**

| *Ratio* | *Name of the Ratio* | *Year Wise* | *Industry Wise* | *Size Wise* | *Total* |
|---|---|---|---|---|---|
| X1 | Return on Investment | 2 | 1 | 1 | 4 |
| X2 | Debtors Turnover | 2 | 2 | 2 | 6 |
| X3 | Creditors Turnover | 3 | 1 | 2 | 6 |
| X4 | Raw Material Turnover | 4 | 2 | 1 | 7 |
| X5 | Finished Goods Turnover | 3 | 2 | 0 | 5 |
| X6 | Net Sales / Total Assets | 2 | 1 | 4 | 7 |
| X7 | Fixed Assets Productivity | 3 | 5 | 3 | 11 |

| | | | | | |
|---|---|---|---|---|---|
| X8 | Current Assets Productivity | 1 | 4 | 3 | 8 |
| X9 | Net Sales / Capital Employed | 3 | 1 | 5 | 9 |
| X10 | Cash to Current Liabilities | 1 | 2 | 3 | 6 |
| X11 | Quick Ratio | 3 | 3 | 3 | 9 |
| X12 | Current Ratio | 3 | 3 | 4 | 10 |
| X13 | Debt Equity Ratio | 2 | 2 | 2 | 6 |
| X14 | PBIT / Interest | 0 | 2 | 2 | 4 |
| X15 | Sales Growth | 4 | 2 | 2 | 8 |
| X16 | PBT (NNRT) / Total Assets | 5 | 5 | 3 | 13 |
| X17 | Equity Dividends / PAT | 1 | 2 | 3 | 6 |
| X18 | PAT (NNRT) / Net Sales | 2 | 2 | 1 | 5 |
| X19 | PBIT (NNRT)/Total Assets | 3 | 3 | 3 | 9 |
| X20 | PBDIT (NNRT) / Capital Employed | 1 | 1 | 3 | 5 |

Looking at the above table, it is clear that year wise X16 appears in the discriminant function for all the years. Hence, year wise, *PBT (NNRT) / TOTAL ASSETS* has the maximum discriminatory power. Also, X14 appears in none of them. Industry wise X7 and X16 appear in 5 of the 7 discriminant functions obtained. Also, X1, X3, X6, X9, and X20 appear in only 1 discriminant function. Size wise, the ratio X9 appears in maximum number of discriminant functions (all five), hence the ratio *NET SALES / CAPITAL EMPLOYED* has the maximum discriminating power. Overall, X7, X12 and X16 appear in 10 or more discriminant functions. Hence, they can be said to have the maximum discriminating power.

Another factor that we will have to consider is the correlation coefficients among the different variables used in our analysis. For the year 2000, the correlation coefficients were found to be as follows:

**Table 45: Correlation Coefficients for the year 2000**

Pooled within Group Matrices

| | X1 | X3 | X6 | X7 | X8 | X9 | X10 | X13 | X15 | X16 | X17 |
|---|---|---|---|---|---|---|---|---|---|---|---|
| Correl. X1 | 1.000 | 0.249 | 0.626 | 0.672 | 0.660 | 0.567 | 0.085 | -0.232 | 0.269 | 0.900 | 0.056 |
| X3 | 0.249 | 1.000 | 0.117 | 0.072 | 0.329 | -0.53 | 0.194 | -0.157 | 0.193 | 0.387 | -0.42 |
| X6 | 0.626 | 0.117 | 1.000 | 0.482 | 0.445 | 0.889 | -0.125 | -0.220 | 0.126 | 0.537 | -0.019 |
| X7 | 0.672 | 0.072 | 0.482 | 1.000 | 0.275 | 0.455 | 0.261 | -0.256 | -0.022 | 0.640 | 0.021 |
| X8 | 0.660 | 0.329 | 0.445 | 0.275 | 1.000 | 0.273 | 0.032 | -0.200 | 0.316 | 0.696 | 0.010 |
| X9 | 0.567 | -0.53 | 0.889 | 0.455 | 0.273 | 1.000 | -0.146 | -0.141 | 0.068 | 0.353 | 0.003 |
| X10 | 0.085 | 0.194 | -0.125 | 0.261 | 0.032 | -0.146 | 1.000 | -0.156 | -0.109 | 0.217 | -0.080 |
| X13 | -0.232 | -0.157 | -0.220 | -0.256 | -0.200 | -0.141 | -0.156 | 1.000 | -0.90 | -0.310 | -0.094 |
| X15 | 0.269 | 0.193 | 0.126 | -0.022 | 0.316 | 0.068 | -0.109 | -0.090 | 1.000 | 0.279 | -0.020 |
| X16 | 0.900 | 0.387 | 0.537 | 0.640 | 0.696 | 0.353 | 0.217 | -0.310 | 0.279 | 1.000 | 0.055 |
| X17 | 0.056 | -0.042 | -0.019 | 0.021 | 0.010 | 0.003 | -0.080 | -0.094 | -0.020 | 0.055 | 1.000 |

From the above table, it is clear that a number of variables have a high correlation (more than 0.5) between them. There are two methods by which the effect of correlation coefficients can be reduced:

1. As most of the ratios have some common base, it is their nature to have some correlation between them. A method to reduce its impact is to reduce the number of variables involved in the discriminant function.
2. Take mean of the ratios having high correlation and see whether the results improve.

For these two purposes, a number of alternatives were tested and it was found that if we take mean of X1, X6, and X16 the result improves a lot in terms of correlation coefficient between variables, although the correct classification percentage gets reduced marginally to 80.5%. Now only one set of variable, i.e., between X8 and X17MEAN there is a high correlation of 0.692. All the other correlation coefficients are below 0.4. Here X17MEAN is a variable, which refers to the mean value of X1, X6, and X16. The result now comes as follows :

**Table 46 : Findings after taking Mean**

**Discriminant**

**Analysis Case Processing Summary**

| *Unweighted Cases* | | *N* | *Percentage* |
|---|---|---|---|
| Valid | | 174 | 100.0 |
| Excluded | Missing or out-of-range group codes | 0 | 0.0 |
| | At least one missing discriminating variable | 0 | 0.0 |
| | Both missing or out-of-range group codes and at least one missing discriminating variable | 0 | 0.0 |
| | Total | 0 | 0.0 |
| Total | | 174 | 100.0 |

**Group Statistics**

| *Group* | | *Mean* | *Std. Deviation* | *Valid N (listwise)* | |
|---|---|---|---|---|---|
| | | | | *Unweighted* | *Weighted* |
| 1. | X 3 | 7.1819469 | 4.7762565 | 113 | 113.000 |
| | X 4 | 9.3246903 | 6.1651469 | 113 | 113.000 |

| | | | | | |
|---|---|---|---|---|---|
| | X 8 | 0.4930088 | 0.2238578 | 113 | 113.000 |
| | X 13 | 0.6753097 | 0.6506591 | 113 | 113.000 |
| | X 15 | 12.95558 | 22.7253962 | 113 | 113.000 |
| | X 17 | 42.34593 | 27.3150815 | 113 | 113.000 |
| | X 17 Mean | 11.96702 | 8.4695618 | 113 | 113.000 |
| 2. | X 3 | 7.1119672 | 5.8442279 | 61 | 61.000 |
| | X 4 | 13.31672 | 22.6117512 | 61 | 61.000 |
| | X 8 | 0.3196721 | 0.2298910 | 61 | 61.000 |
| | X 13 | 1.7711475 | 2.7562536 | 61 | 61.000 |
| | X 15 | 13.16295 | 19.6737505 | 61 | 61.000 |
| | X 17 | 21.99279 | 38.8654458 | 61 | 61.000 |
| | X 17 Mean | 4.8053005 | 7.4089522 | 61 | 61.000 |
| Total | X 3 | 7.1574138 | 5.1590361 | 174 | 174.000 |
| | X 4 | 10.72420 | 14.3381551 | 174 | 174.000 |
| | X 8 | 0.4322414 | 0.2401087 | 174 | 174.000 |
| | X 13 | 1.0594828 | 1.7843314 | 174 | 174.000 |
| | X 15 | 13.02828 | 21.6470343 | 174 | 174.000 |
| | X 17 | 35.21063 | 33.1929558 | 174 | 174.000 |
| | X 17 Mean | 9.4563027 | 8.7876567 | 174 | 174.000 |

**Pooled Within Groups Matrices**

| | | *X3* | *X4* | *X8* | *X13* | *X15* | *X17* | *X 17 mean* |
|---|---|---|---|---|---|---|---|---|
| Correlat. | X 3 | 1.000 | -0.051 | 0.329 | -0.157 | 0.193 | -0.042 | 0.311 |
| | X 4 | -.051 | 1.000 | -0.016 | 0.093 | 0.062 | -0.012 | -0.047 |
| | X 8 | .329 | -0.016 | 1.000 | -0.200 | 0.316 | 0.010 | 0.692 |
| | X 13 | -.157 | 0.093 | -0.200 | 1.000 | -0.090 | -0.094 | -0.272 |
| | X 15 | .193 | 0.062 | 0.316 | -0.090 | 1.000 | -0.020 | 0.279 |
| | X 17 | -.042 | -0.012 | 0.010 | -0.094 | -0.020 | 1.000 | 0.056 |
| | X 17 Mean | .311 | -0.047 | 0.692 | -0.272 | 0.279 | 0.056 | 1.000 |

## Analysis 1
## Summary of Canonical Discriminant Functions

### Eigenvalues

| *Function* | *Eigenvalue* | *Percantage of Variance* | *Cumulative %* | *Canonical Correlation* |
|---|---|---|---|---|
| 1 | 0.352[a] | 100.0 | 100.0 | 0.510 |

[a]First 1 canonical discriminant functions were used in the analysis.

**Wilks' Lambda**

| *Test of Funcation (s)* | *Wilks' Lambda* | *Chi-square* | *df* | *Sig* |
|---|---|---|---|---|
| 1 | 0.739 | 50.874 | 7 | 0.000 |

**Standardized Canonical Discriminant Function Coefficients**

| | *Function* |
|---|---|
| | *1* |
| X 3 | -0.258 |
| X 4 | -0.163 |
| X 8 | 0.372 |
| X 13 | -0.317 |
| X 15 | -0.219 |
| X 17 | 0.440 |
| X 17 Mean | 0.479 |

**Structure Matrix**

| | *Function* |
|---|---|
| | *1* |
| X 3 | 0.713 |
| X 4 | 0.620 |
| X 8 | -0.518 |
| X 13 | 0.517 |
| X 15 | -0.226 |
| X 17 | 0.011 |
| X 17 Mean | -0.008 |

Pooled within-groups correlations between discriminating variables and standardized canonical discriminant functions Variables ordered by absolute size of correlation within function.

**Functions at Group Centroids**

| *Group* | *Function* |
|---|---|
| | *1* |
| 1 | 0.434 |
| 2 | -0.803 |

Unstandardized canonical discriminant functions evaluated at group means.

**Classification Statistics**

**Classification Processing Summary**

| | | |
|---|---|---|
| Processed | | 174 |
| Excluded | Missing or out-of-range group codes | 0 |
| | At least one missing discriminating variable | 0 |
| Used in Output | | 174 |

**Prior Probabilities for Groups**

| *Group* | *Prior* | *Cases Used in Analysis* | |
|---|---|---|---|
| | | *Unweighted* | *Weighted* |
| 1 | 0.649 | 113 | 113.000 |
| 2 | 0.351 | 61 | 61.000 |
| Total | 1.000 | 174 | 174.000 |

**Classification Results**[a]

| | | *Group* | *Predicted Group Membership* | | *Total* |
|---|---|---|---|---|---|
| | | | *1* | *2* | |
| Original | Count | 1 | 108 | 5 | 113 |
| | | 2 | 29 | 32 | 61 |
| | % | 1 | 95.6 | 4.4 | 100.0 |
| | | 2 | 47.5 | 52.5 | 100.0 |

[a]80.5% of original grouped cases correctly classified.

Thus 80.5% of the total cases are now correctly classified. Again, 95.6% of the total companies of Group 1 are correctly classified while only 52.5% are classified correctly in Group 2 because the companies in Group 2 are not-so-excellent but not non-excellent.

Now, to find out the discriminant function we will again use regression analysis.

**Table 47: Regression Analysis after taking mean**

**Regression**

**Variables Entered / Removed**

| *Model* | *Variables Entered* | *Variables Removed* | *Method* |
|---|---|---|---|
| 1 | X 17MEAN, X 4, X 17, X 15, X 3 X 13, X8[a] | | Enter |

(a) All requested variables entered.
(b) Dependent Variable : Discriminant Scores from Function 1 for Analysis 1.

**Model Summary**

| *Model* | *R* | *R Square* | *Adjusted R Square* | *Std. Error of the Estimate* |
|---|---|---|---|---|
| 1 | 1.000[a] | 1.000 | 1.000 | 0.0000000 |

(a) Predictors : (Constant), X 17MEAN, X 4, X 17, X 15, X 3, X 13, X 8.

**Coefficients[a]**

| Model | | Unstandardized Coefficients | | Standardized Coefficients | t | Sig. |
|---|---|---|---|---|---|---|
| | | B | Std. Error | Beta | | |
| 1 | (Constant) | -0.949 | 0.000 | | - | - |
| | X 3 | -4.99E-02 | 0.000 | -0.222 | - | - |
| | X 4 | -1.15E-02 | 0.000 | -0.142 | - | - |
| | X 8 | 1.648 | 0.000 | 0.341 | - | - |
| | X 13 | -0.186 | 0.000 | -0.286 | - | - |
| | X 15 | -1.01E-02 | 0.000 | -0.188 | - | - |
| | X 17 | 1.382E-02 | 0.000 | 0.396 | - | - |
| | X 17MEAN | 5.898E-02 | 0.000 | 0.447 | - | - |

[a] Dependent Variable : Discriminant Scores from function 1 for Analysis 1.

Hence, the new discriminant function is found to be:

$$Z = -0.949 - 0.0499X3 - 0.0115X4 + 1.648X8 - 0.186X13$$
$$0.0101X15 + 0.01382X17 + 0.05898X17\ MEAN$$

In this case, Z1= 0.434 and Z2= -0.803, hence the cut-off score will be the mean of the two values, i.e., -0.1845. If the discriminant function score of the company is more than –0.1845, it will be classified as an excellent company otherwise it is not-so-excellent company.

To find out whether any outlier is still remaining in the solution we will again use the method of curve fit.

**Table 48: Curve Fit after taking mean**

**Curve Fit**

MODEL: MOD_1.

Independent: Z

| Dependent | Mth | Rsq | d.f. | Sigf | b0 | bl | |
|---|---|---|---|---|---|---|---|
| X 3 | LIN. | 0.000 | 172 | .03 | 0.868 | 7.1574 | .0566 |
| X 4 | LIN. | 0.068 | 172 | 12.57 | 0.001 | 10.7242 | -3.227 |
| X 8 | LIN. | 0.458 | 172 | 145.30 | 0.000 | 0.4322 | 0.1401 |
| X 13 | LIN. | 0.331 | 172 | 85.26 | 0.000 | 1.0595 | -0.8858 |
| X 15 | LIN. | 0.000 | 172 | .01 | 0.906 | 13.0283 | -0.1676 |
| X 17 | LIN. | 0.330 | 172 | 84.86 | 0.000 | 35.2106 | 16.453 |
| X 17 MEAN | LIN. | 0.584 | 172 | 241.07 | 0.000 | 9.4563 | 5.7894 |

**X 3**

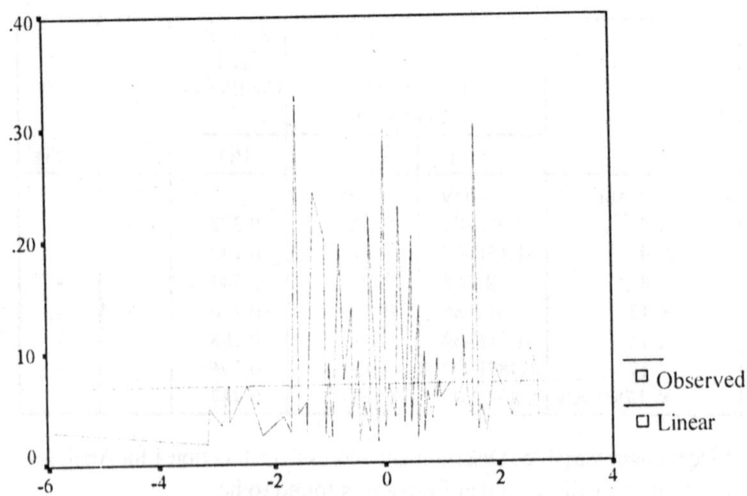


Discriminant Scores from Function 1 for Analysis 1

**X 4**

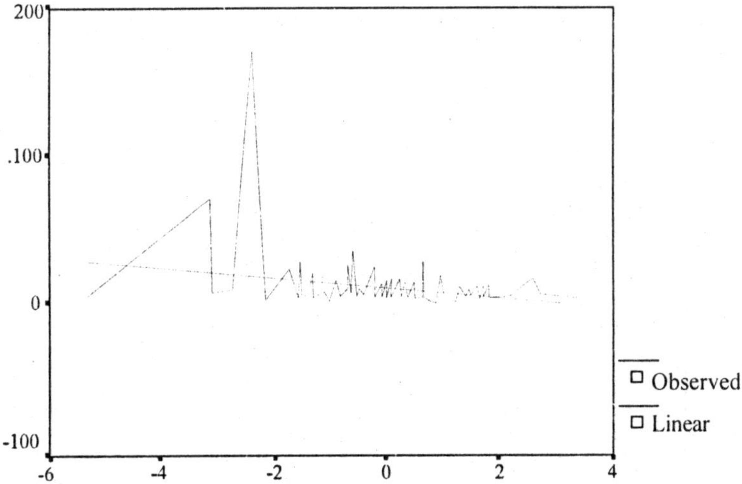


Discriminant Scores from Function 1 for Analysis 1

**X 8**

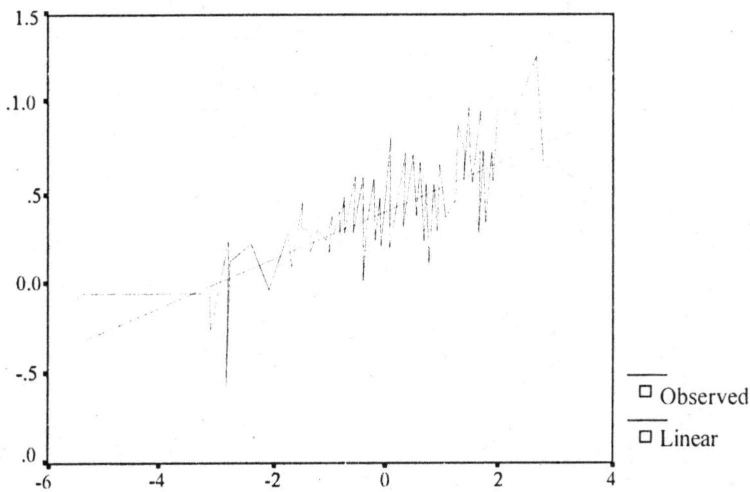


Discriminant Scores from Function 1 for Analysis 1

**X 13**

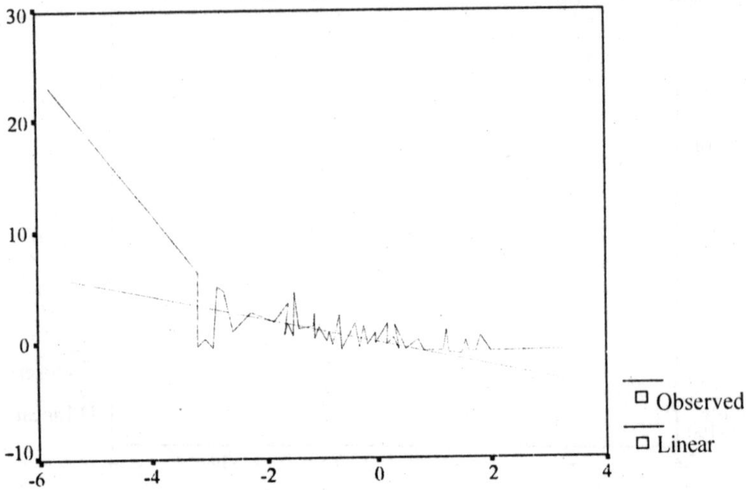


Discriminant Scores from Function 1 for Analysis 1

**X 15**

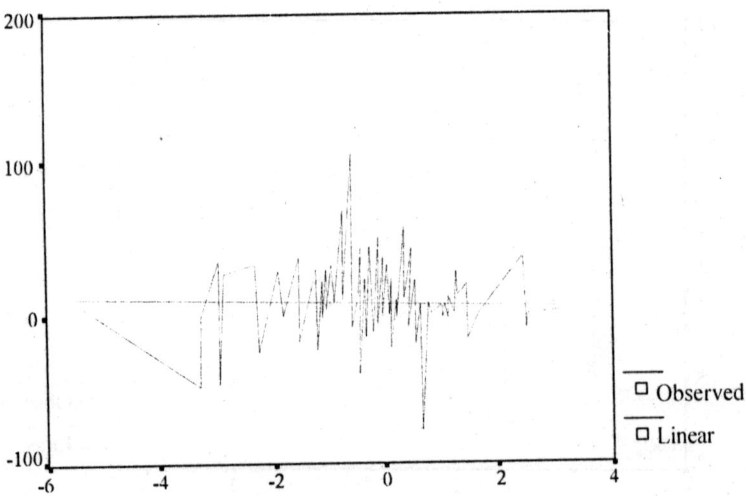


Discriminant Scores from Function 1 for Analysis 1

**X 17**

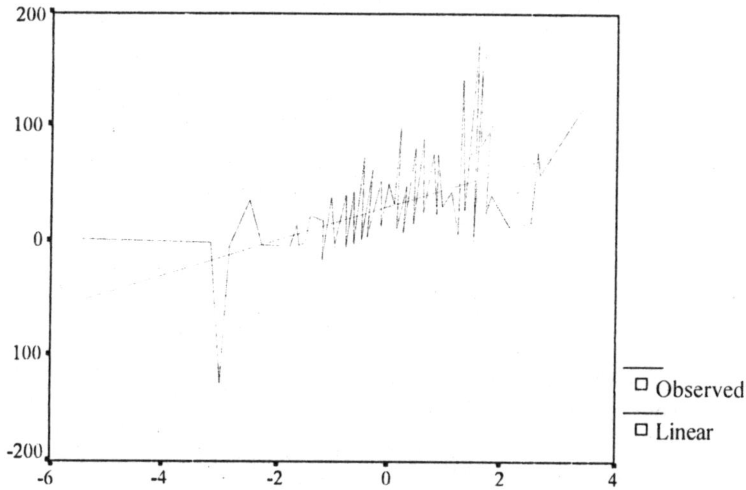


Discriminant Scores from Function 1 for Analysis 1

**X 17 MEAN**

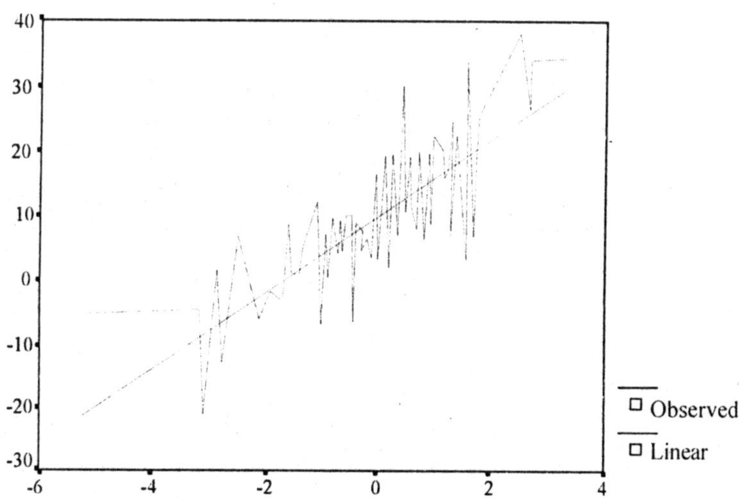


Discriminant Scores from Function 1 for Analysis 1

**Finding out the importance and relative importance of different variables:** Utilizing the coefficients of the discriminant function, we can find out the importance and relative importance of each variable. If the discriminant function is:

$$D = l_1 x_1 + l_2 x_2 + \ldots\ldots + l_n x_n$$

Then the importance value of the i^th^ variable will be $l_i(\hat{x}_{1i} - \hat{x}_{2i})$ where $\hat{x}_{1i}$ and $\hat{x}_{2i}$ are the means of the i^th^ variable for groups 1 and 2 respectively. A relative importance value shows the importance value of a particular variable relative to the sum of the importance values of all variables. Thus, the relative importance of the i^th^ variable is given by

$$R_i = e_i / \sum_{i=1}^{p} e$$

where $R_i$ is the relative importance of the variable i and $e_i$ is the importance value of i^th^ variable. Thus to calculate the relative importance of a particular variable, we divide the importance of that variable by the sum of the importance values of all the variables. The relative importance of the variables is a better measure than the $l_i$'s due to disparity in units of measurements of different variables. The $R_i$'s are however unit free and thus are more reliable.

For calculating importance and relative importance values of different variables, we will require the mean values of different variables for both the groups.

**Table 49: Group Statistics after taking mean**

**Group Statistics**

| Group | | Mean | Std. Deviation | Valid N (listwise) | |
|---|---|---|---|---|---|
| | | | | *Unweighted* | *Weighted* |
| 1 | X 3 | 7.189469 | 4.7762565 | 113 | 113.000 |
| | X 4 | 9.3246903 | 6.1651469 | 113 | 113.000 |
| | X 8 | 0.4930088 | 0.2238578 | 113 | 113.000 |
| | X 13 | 0.6753097 | 0.6506591 | 113 | 113.000 |
| | X 15 | 12.95558 | 22.7253962 | 113 | 113.000 |
| | X 17 | 42.34593 | 27.3150815 | 113 | 113.000 |
| | X 17 MEAN | 11.96702 | 8.4695618 | 113 | 113.000 |
| 2 | X 3 | 7.1119672 | 5.8442279 | 61 | 61.000 |
| | X 4 | 13.31672 | 22.6117512 | 61 | 61.000 |
| | X 8 | 0.3196721 | 0.2298910 | 61 | 61.000 |
| | X 13 | 1.7711475 | 2.7562536 | 61 | 61.000 |
| | X 15 | 13.16295 | 19.6737505 | 61 | 61.000 |
| | X 17 | 21.99279 | 38.8654458 | 61 | 61.000 |
| | X 17 MEAN | 4.8053005 | 7.4089522 | 61 | 61.000 |

| | | | | |
|---|---|---|---|---|
| Total X 3 | 7.1574138 | 5.1590361 | 174 | 174.000 |
| X 4 | 10.72420 | 14.3381551 | 174 | 174.000 |
| X 8 | 0.4322414 | 0.2401087 | 174 | 174.000 |
| X 13 | 1.0594828 | 1.7843314 | 174 | 174.000 |
| X 15 | 13.02828 | 21.6470343 | 174 | 174.000 |
| X 17 | 35.21063 | 33.1929558 | 174 | 174.000 |
| X 17 MEAN | 9.4563027 | 8.7876567 | 174 | 174.000 |

Now, the importance and relative importance values of different variables in the discriminant function can be found out using thefollowing formula

$$R_i = e_i / \sum_{i=1}^{p} e$$

where e is the importance value of each variable.

The importance value is calculated using following formula:

$$\mathbf{e = |cxd|}$$

where c represents the spread of means of a variable, i.e., the difference between the mean values of a variable for two groups and d is the discriminant function coefficient of that variable.

For the above analysis, the importance and relative importance values of different variables can be found out as follows:

**Table 50: Importance and Relative Importance of different ratios**

| | | *a* | *b* | *c* | *d* |
|---|---|---|---|---|---|
| **Creditors Turnover** | **X3** | 7.1819 | 7.112 | 0.0699 | -0.0499 |
| **Raw Materials Turnover** | X4 | **9.32469** | **13.31672** | **-3.99203** | **-0.0115** |
| **Current Assets Productivity** | **X8** | 0.493 | 0.3197 | 0.1733 | 1.648 |
| **Debt-Equity Ratio** | **X13** | 0.6753 | 1.7711 | -1.0958 | -0.186 |
| **Sales Growth** | **X15** | 12.9556 | 13.163 | -0.2074 | -0.0101 |
| **Equity Dividends/Pat** | **X17** | 42.3459 | 21.9928 | 20.3531 | 0.01382 |
| **Roi, Net Sales/Total Assets & PBT(NNRT)/Total Assets Mean** | **X17 Mean** | 11.96702 | 4.8053005 | 7.1617195 | 0.05898 |

| | *e* | *f* | *Rank* |
|---|---|---|---|
| **X3** | 0.003488 | 0.2802546 | 6 |
| **X4** | 0.045908 | 3.6886428 | 5 |
| **X8** | 0.285598 | 22.947255 | 2 |
| **X13** | 0.203819 | 16.376429 | 4 |
| **X15** | 0.002095 | 0.1683081 | 7 |
| **X17** | 0.28128 | 22.600267 | 3 |
| **X17MEAN** | 0.422398 | 33.938844 | 1 |
| **SUM** | 1.244586 | | |

Hence, we find that out of 7 variables used in our analysis the following variables are more important:

| Name of the Variable | Meaning of the Variable | Relative Importance |
|---|---|---|
| X17Mean | Mean of X1, X6 & X16 | 33.9388 |
| X8 | Current Assets Productivity | 22.9473 |
| X17 | Equity Dividends / PAT | 22.6003 |
| X13 | Debt – Equity Ratio | 16.3764 |

The above analysis clearly shows that these 4 variables have more than 95% of the total relative importance of all the variables. So, while examining corporate excellence, the analyst should concentrate on these ratios. This also provides guidance to corporate managers that they should give more attention in maintaining and improving these ratios for maintaining the rank of the company. The investors on the other hand would like to give more weight to these four ratios in their investment decision-making.

# 7

# Findings, Conclusions and Areas for Further Research

**Main Findings:** The present study seeks:

- To define various forms of excellence,
- To discuss the use of ratios for measuring corporate excellence,
- To find out ratios that are more significant for determining corporate excellence of a company.

An attempt has also been made to systematically analyze the role of financial ratios and to develop a multi-ratio model for the measurement of corporate excellence.

The major points of the study are summarized below:

Excellence is not a one-time affair. It is a continuous process of improvement and innovation. In the present competitive environment, it is more difficult to remain excellent than to become excellent. Corporate excellence is just one of the many forms of excellence. It is related to achieving excellence in the organization. It helps an organization to face the intense competition prevailing in the present business environment. Achieving corporate excellence involves lots of efforts and hard work. Commitment of top management is an essential requirement in this respect. The latest developments in the concept of corporate excellence focus on maximizing the value of shareholders' wealth. Shareholders are one of the most important interest groups of the organization as they are the owners of the firm. That is why in present period the concepts of EVA and MVA are gaining so much importance.

So, for the purpose of measuring corporate excellence, twenty financial ratios have been tested empirically in this study on a sample of 180 companies. These companies were classified into excellent and non-excellent companies based on their ranks in BT-500. The technique of discriminant analysis was used to test the usefulness of these ratios in measuring corporate excellence. The discriminant function for the measurement of corporate excellence was found out to be:

$$Z = -0.949 - 0.0499X3 - 0.0115X4 + 1.648X8 - 0.186X13 - 0.0101X15 + 0.01382X17 + 0.05898X17\ MEAN$$

where

| | | |
|---|---|---|
| Z | = | Overall discriminant score |
| X3 | = | Creditors Turnover |
| X4 | = | Raw Materials Turnover |
| X8 | = | Current Assets Productivity |
| X13 | = | Debt Equity Ratio |
| X15 | = | Sales growth |
| X17 | = | Equity Dividends/PAT |
| X17 MEAN | = | Mean of X1, X6, and X16 |
| Where, X1 | = | ROI |
| X6 | = | Net Sales/ Total Assets |
| X16 | = | PBT (NNRT)/ Total Assets |

The discriminant model so developed is not always optimal since the process is iterative, it, however, does the best job among the possible alternatives which involves numerous computer runs and analysis of various ratio profiles.

The discriminant score Z= -0.1845 has been found out as the optimum value to classify the firms into excellent and not-so-excellent firms. If Z for a particular company is found to be more than –0.1845, it is classified as an excellent company and if Z for a company is below –0.1845, it is classified as not-so-excellent company. This score classified more than 80% of the companies of our sample correctly.

GROUP Discriminant Scores from Function 1 for Analysis 1

| | | |
|---|---|---|
| 1 | Mean | .43368 |
| | Minimum | -1.64378 |
| | Maximum | 3.47427 |
| 2 | Mean | -.80337 |
| | Minimum | -5.34176 |
| | *Maximum* | *1.65023* |
| Grand Total | | |
| | Minimum | -5.34176 |
| | Maximum | 3.47427 |

Another important finding about the discriminant scores was that all companies having a discriminant score above 1.65023 are classified into group 1, i.e., excellent companies, while those having scores below –1.64378 are clearly in group 2, i.e., not so excellent companies. So, we can now safely say that the companies having discriminant scores above

1.65023 are excellent while the companies having discriminant scores below −1.64378 are not-so-excellent companies. The area falling between discriminant scores of −1.64378 and 1.65023 is defined as the 'Zone of Ignorance' or 'Area of Uncertainty'. This area is highly susceptible to misclassification.

**Conclusion:** From the above analysis, following conclusions can be drawn about the hypothesis:

1. There are certain ratios that discriminate between excellent and non-excellent companies. Hence, our first hypothesis is true and it is accepted.
2. Some of these ratios are relatively more important than the other ratios in discriminating between excellent and non-excellent companies. Out of the ratios supposed to be excellent, it is found that current assets productivity, equity dividends / PAT, and debt – equity ratio are relatively more important than others. The mean of ratios ROI, NET SALES/TOTAL ASSETS and & PBT(NNRT)/ TOTAL ASSETS is also very important. The other ratios taken for analysis in the second hypothesis, i.e.,
   (a) Creditors Turnover
   (b) Raw Materials Turnover
   (c) Current Ratio
   (d) Debt Equity Ratio
   (e) Sales growth

   are not found to be significant from the point of view of their discriminating ability. Hence, the second hypothesis is partly accepted.

**Applications of the Model:** The above model measures the corporate excellence of a company with a tolerably good accuracy. It is very useful for all the interest groups of the company. The management of the company can find out whether the company is operating to the optimum extent or not. Then it can easily locate the problems in the company. The shareholders want to invest only in an excellent company where they can earn high returns either in terms of dividends or capital gains. The prospective investors will also like to invest in an excellent company. Using this model they can easily find out whether the company in which they want to invest is excellent or not. This model is also helpful for the financial analyst as this model explains the overall performance of the company. The customers also think that an excellent company will provide better goods at a fair rate. Hence, customers are also attracted towards excellent companies. The creditors also test the company for excellence before providing credit to confirm whether the firm will be able to pay back the amount along with interest in time. The government also looks towards excellent companies for the revenue and also it expects them to perform their social responsibilities in a better way. The general public also looks towards the excellent companies as an employment opportunity as they feel that these companies are more likely to survive even in the toughest competition. Hence, this model is useful for all the interest groups of the company.

**Areas for Further Research:** Although this model shows a high degree of accuracy, there is still a lot which can be done on this model:

1. This model excludes the financial companies because the ratios involved in financial companies will be different from those of the manufacturing companies, e.g., financial companies do not involve inventory hence no ratio involving inventory can be calculated for these companies although inventory is one of the most important components in case of manufacturing companies. On the other hand, ratios related to reserves are more important for these companies. Hence, a separate model can be developed for measuring the excellence of financial companies.
2. This model also excludes service sector units due to the same reason. A separate model can be developed for the service sector units too.
3. This model tries to measure the corporate excellence of a company for a particular period. An attempt can be made to develop a model for predicting the excellence of the company.
4. This model is totally based on quantitative factors. An attempt can be made to develop a model, which also includes qualitative factors that are important for measuring corporate excellence.

## APPENDIX-1

**Name and Rank of the Companies in the Sample**

| S.NO. | NAME OF THE COMPANY | 95-96 | 96-97 | 97-98 | 98-99 | 99-00 | SECTION |
|---|---|---|---|---|---|---|---|
| 1. | SESA GOA LTD. | 65 | 76 | 102 | 120 | 240 | 18 |
| 2. | DALMIA CEMENT (BHARAT) | 260 | 198 | 230 | 274 | 273 | 19 |
| 3. | GUJARAT AMBUJA CEMENTS | 20 | 24 | 24 | 25 | 27 | 19 |
| 4. | GUJARAT SIDHEE CEMENT | 350 | 393 | 465 | 428 | 426 | 19 |
| 5. | INDIA CEMENTS | 55 | 54 | 84 | 125 | 85 | 19 |
| 6. | MADRAS CEMENTS | 41 | 40 | 59 | 88 | 105 | 19 |
| 7. | MYSORE CEMENTS | 309 | 346 | 396 | 377 | 438 | 19 |
| 8. | NARMADA CEMENT CO. | 387 | 423 | 391 | 329 | 298 | 19 |
| 9. | SHREE CEMENT | 326 | 372 | 394 | 349 | 307 | 19 |
| 10. | ASAHI INDIA SAFETY GLASS | 406 | 269 | 216 | 295 | 281 | 20 |
| 11. | FLOATGLASS INDIA | 208 | 242 | 291 | 334 | 457 | 20 |
| 12. | KAJARIA CERAMICS | 253 | 223 | 264 | 374 | 455 | 20 |
| 13. | FORBES GOKAK | 190 | 190 | 215 | 316 | 460 | 21 |
| 14. | MAHAVIR SPINNING MILLS | 168 | 206 | 224 | 245 | 330 | 21 |
| 15. | NAHAR SPINNING MILLS | 220 | 220 | 199 | 261 | 383 | 21 |
| 16. | VARDHMAN SPINNING & GENERAL MILLS | 278 | 293 | 271 | 287 | 391 | 21 |
| 17. | BOMBAY DYEING & MANUFACTURING CO. | 49 | 68 | 103 | 151 | 242 | 22 |
| 18. | CENTURY TEXTILES & INDUSTRIES | 19 | 26 | 57 | 108 | 142 | 22 |
| 19. | KESORAM INDUSTRIES | 269 | 182 | 253 | 356 | 271 | 22 |
| 20. | BIRLA VXL | 283 | 307 | 325 | 340 | 480 | 24 |
| 21. | CENTURY ENKA | 137 | 119 | 163 | 264 | 285 | 24 |

| *S.NO.* | *NAME OF THE COMPANY* | *95-96* | *96-97* | *97-98* | *98-99* | *99-00* | *SECTION* |
|---|---|---|---|---|---|---|---|
| 22. | GRASIM INDUSTRIES | 10 | 13 | 25 | 41 | 34 | 24 |
| 23. | HIMATSINGKA SIEDE | 209 | 210 | 251 | 256 | 174 | 24 |
| 24. | INDO RAMA SYNTHETICS (INDIA) | 88 | 85 | 166 | 278 | 295 | 24 |
| 25. | RAYMOND | 37 | 43 | 85 | 72 | 128 | 24 |
| 26. | RELIANCE INDUSTRIES | 3 | 3 | 2 | 3 | 6 | 24 |
| 27. | SRF LTD. | 219 | 217 | 305 | 311 | 235 | 24 |
| 28. | ITC BHADRACHALAM PAPERBOARDS | 76 | 79 | 124 | 184 | 177 | 25 |
| 29. | RAMA NEWSPRINT & PAPERS | 380 | 488 | 501 | 491 | 384 | 25 |
| 30. | ASEA BROWN BOVERI | 28 | 23 | 20 | 21 | 62 | 26 |
| 31. | BHARTI TELECOM | 290 | 272 | 210 | 226 | 277 | 26 |
| 32. | BIRLA ERICSSON OPTICAL | 485 | 491 | 493 | 392 | 270 | 26 |
| 33. | BLUE STAR | 287 | 291 | 285 | 212 | 220 | 26 |
| 34. | BPL | 271 | 317 | 169 | 85 | 77 | 26 |
| 35. | CARRIER AIRCON | 131 | 90 | 79 | 82 | 168 | 26 |
| 36. | CROMPTON GREAVES | 48 | 50 | 137 | 188 | 212 | 26 |
| 37. | DIGITAL EQUIPMENT (INDIA) | 177 | 157 | 89 | 70 | 42 | 26 |
| 38. | ESAB INDIA | 418 | 311 | 206 | 237 | 373 | 26 |
| 39. | EXIDE INDUSTRIES | 345 | 184 | 97 | 84 | 97 | 26 |
| 40. | HEG LTD. | 351 | 370 | 373 | 307 | 419 | 26 |
| 41. | HIMACHAL FUTURISTIC COMMUNICATIONS | 229 | 270 | 273 | 159 | 29 | 26 |
| 42. | INDO NATIONAL | 470 | 359 | 244 | 251 | 328 | 26 |
| 43. | OTIS ELEVATOR CO. (INDIA) | 146 | 115 | 95 | 110 | 144 | 26 |
| 44. | PHILIPS INDIA | 84 | 93 | 116 | 73 | 131 | 26 |
| 45. | ROLTA INDIA | 394 | 465 | 306 | 112 | 60 | 26 |
| 46. | SIEMENS | 32 | 31 | 68 | 69 | 75 | 26 |

| S.NO. | NAME OF THE COMPANY | 95-96 | 96-97 | 97-98 | 98-99 | 99-00 | SECTION |
|---|---|---|---|---|---|---|---|
| 47. | STERLITE INDUSTRIES | 39 | 41 | 50 | 61 | 47 | 26 |
| 48. | USHA BELTRON | 330 | 416 | 475 | 238 | 143 | 26 |
| 49. | VINDHYA TELELINKS | 438 | 422 | 425 | 366 | 305 | 26 |
| 50. | TISCO | 5 | 6 | 8 | 11 | 17 | 27 |
| 51. | HINDALCO INDUSTRIES | 9 | 9 | 6 | 12 | 14 | 28 |
| 52. | INDIAN ALUMINIUM CO. | 35 | 39 | 60 | 79 | 107 | 28 |
| 53. | BALAJi INDUSTRIAL CORP. | 87 | 133 | 146 | 174 | 266 | 29 |
| 54. | BHARAT FORGE | 98 | 97 | 140 | 149 | 110 | 29 |
| 55. | BHUSHAN STEEL & STRIPS | 238 | 274 | 313 | 352 | 439 | 29 |
| 56. | FOSECO INDIA | 318 | 250 | 201 | 280 | 310 | 29 |
| 57. | GOETZE (INDIA) | 313 | 296 | 262 | 315 | 454 | 29 |
| 58. | ITW SIGNODE | 272 | 286 | 192 | 205 | 263 | 29 |
| 59. | JINDAL STRIPS | 126 | 168 | 191 | 219 | 282 | 29 |
| 60. | KEC INTERNATIONAL | 150 | 136 | 226 | 281 | 290 | 29 |
| 61. | LLOYDS STEEL INDUSTRIES | 160 | 142 | 243 | 358 | 481 | 29 |
| 62. | MUKAND LTD. | 120 | 151 | 239 | 292 | 374 | 29 |
| 63. | SAW PIPES | 85 | 128 | 207 | 260 | 338 | 29 |
| 64. | SUNFLAG IRON & STEEL CO. | 306 | 404 | 354 | 388 | 500 | 29 |
| 65. | SURYA ROSHNI | 366 | 417 | 452 | 486 | 496 | 29 |
| 66. | TUBE INVESTMENTS OF INDIA | 154 | 192 | 281 | 312 | 239 | 29 |
| 67. | USHA ISPAT | 61 | 67 | 134 | 200 | 326 | 29 |
| 68. | ALFA LAVAL (INDIA) | 135 | 130 | 194 | 153 | 182 | 30 |
| 69. | ASHOK LEYLAND | 33 | 33 | 83 | 129 | 73 | 30 |
| 70. | ATLAS COPCO | 334 | 251 | 221 | 283 | 336 | 30 |
| 71. | AUTOMOTIVE AXLES | 413 | 313 | 432 | 516 | 429 | 30 |

| S.NO. | NAME OF THE COMPANY | 95-96 | 96-97 | 97-98 | 98-99 | 99-00 | SECTION |
|---|---|---|---|---|---|---|---|
| 72. | BAJAJ AUTO LTD. | 6 | 5 | 5 | 5 | 16 | 30 |
| 73. | BAJAJ TEMPO | 119 | 99 | 133 | 183 | 228 | 30 |
| 74. | ESCORTS | 75 | 77 | 81 | 81 | 82 | 30 |
| 75. | HERO HONDA MOTORS | 94 | 80 | 38 | 20 | 21 | 30 |
| 76. | HINDUSTAN MOTORS | 163 | 178 | 232 | 270 | 288 | 30 |
| 77. | MALANPUR STEEL | 191 | 199 | 321 | 337 | 442 | 30 |
| 78. | INGERSOLL RAND (INDIA) | 59 | 44 | 44 | 37 | 65 | 30 |
| 79. | KIRLOSKAR OIL ENGINES | 235 | 314 | 318 | 375 | 479 | 30 |
| 80. | KSB PUMPS | 183 | 155 | 112 | 145 | 204 | 30 |
| 81. | LAKSHMI MACHINE WORKS | 301 | 112 | 122 | 178 | 276 | 30 |
| 82. | LARSEN & TOUBRO | 7 | 8 | 9 | 10 | 12 | 30 |
| 83. | LML | 78 | 181 | 125 | 122 | 241 | 30 |
| 84. | MAHINDRA & MAHINDRA | 21 | 12 | 14 | 22 | 23 | 30 |
| 85. | MOTOR INDUSTRIES CO. (MICQ) | 23 | 20 | 23 | 35 | 53 | 30 |
| 86. | MUNJAL SHOWA | 362 | 323 | 288 | 271 | 313 | 30 |
| 87. | PUNJAB TRACTORS | 110 | 60 | 40 | 29 | 45 | 30 |
| 88. | SANDVIK ASIA | 145 | 124 | 132 | 169 | 258 | 30 |
| 89. | SKF BEARINGS INDIA | 67 | 62 | 94 | 172 | 222 | 30 |
| 90. | TELCO | 1 | 2 | 4 | 7 | 15 | 30 |
| 91. | TVS SUZUKI | 90 | 56 | 51 | 44 | 67 | 30 |
| 92. | VOLTAS | 213 | 268 | 317 | 168 | 217 | 30 |
| 93. | WARTSILA NSD INDIA | 175 | 122 | 123 | 161 | 189 | 30 |
| 94. | WIDIA (INDIA) | 184 | 135 | 115 | 132 | 236 | 30 |
| 95. | BASF INDIA | 141 | 141 | 113 | 107 | 164 | 31 |
| 96. | BAYER (INDIA) | 195 | 145 | 141 | 142 | 215 | 31 |

| S.NO. | NAME OF THE COMPANY | 95-96 | 96-97 | 97-98 | 98-99 | 99-00 | SECTION |
|---|---|---|---|---|---|---|---|
| 97. | BURROUGHS WELLCOME (INDIA) | 471 | 231 | 126 | 89 | 132 | 31 |
| 98. | CHAMBAL FERTILIZERS & CHEMICALS | 89 | 95 | 104 | 98 | 134 | 31 |
| 99. | CHEMINOR DRUGS | 234 | 257 | 219 | 157 | 109 | 31 |
| 100. | CIPLA | 64 | 46 | 39 | 27 | 13 | 31 |
| 101. | CLARIANT (INDIA) | 180 | 240 | 229 | 187 | 207 | 31 |
| 102. | COLOUR CHEM | 140 | 140 | 118 | 152 | 208 | 31 |
| 103. | CORE HEALTHCARE | 164 | 183 | 365 | 402 | 466 | 31 |
| 104. | DABUR INDIA | 73 | 66 | 72 | 50 | 40 | 31 |
| 105. | DR. REDDY'S LABORATORIES | 79 | 72 | 56 | 39 | 31 | 31 |
| 106. | EID- PARRY | 248 | 279 | 198 | 232 | 265 | 31 |
| 107. | E-MERCK (INDIA) | 166 | 150 | 114 | 77 | 83 | 31 |
| 108. | EVEREADY INDUSTRIES | 102 | 96 | 96 | 130 | 237 | 31 |
| 109. | EXCEL INDUSTRIES | 178 | 167 | 152 | 206 | 200 | 31 |
| 110. | GERMAN REMEDIES | 458 | 305 | 182 | 99 | 100 | 31 |
| 111. | GLAXO INDIA | 38 | 30 | 21 | 17 | 22 | 31 |
| 112. | GODREJ SOAPS | 136 | 162 | 171 | 186 | 205 | 31 |
| 113. | GUJARAT ALKALIES AND CHEMICALS | 115 | 114 | 153 | 269 | 377 | 31 |
| 114. | GUJARAT HEAVY CHEMICALS | 347 | 280 | 204 | 228 | 364 | 31 |
| 115. | GUJARAT NARMADA VALLEY FERTILIZERS | 66 | 92 | 135 | 163 | 167 | 31 |
| 116. | HINDUSTAN LEVER LTD. | 2 | 1 | 1 | 1 | 1 | 31 |
| 117. | ICI INDIA | 70 | 69 | 58 | 60 | 94 | 31 |
| 118. | INDO GULF CORP. | 54 | 61 | 74 | 68 | 72 | 31 |
| 119. | IPCA LABORATORIES | 261 | 282 | 234 | 216 | 243 | 31 |
| 120. | KNOLL PHARMACEUTICALS | 103 | 84 | 86 | 67 | 89 | 31 |
| 121. | KOPRAN | 112 | 117 | 164 | 240 | 262 | 31 |

| S.NO. | NAME OF THE COMPANY | 95-96 | 96-97 | 97-98 | 98-99 | 99-00 | SECTION |
|---|---|---|---|---|---|---|---|
| 122. | LUPIN LABORATORIES | 152 | 148 | 145 | 124 | 92 | 31 |
| 123. | MAX INDIA | 216 | 191 | 237 | 203 | 186 | 31 |
| 124. | MONSANTO INDIA | 419 | 366 | 249 | 202 | 201 | 31 |
| 125. | MOREPEN LABORATORIES | 398 | 258 | 142 | 173 | 78 | 31 |
| 126. | NAGARJUNA FERTILISERS & CHÈMICALS | 86 | 82 | 88 | 78 | 129 | 31 |
| 127. | NATIONAL ORGANIC CHEMICAL INDS. (NOCIL) | 121 | 116 | 106 | 116 | 230 | 31 |
| 128. | NICHOLAS PIRAMAL INDIA | 108 | 144 | 61 | 56 | 61 | 31 |
| 129. | NIRMA | 72 | 73 | 41 | 48 | 46 | 31 |
| 130. | NOVARTIS INDIA | 68 | 59 | 52 | 23 | 28 | 31 |
| 131. | PARKE DAVIS (INDIA) | 346 | 233 | 148 | 115 | 156 | 31 |
| 132. | PFIZER | 218 | 163 | 99 | 62 | 71 | 31 |
| 133. | PIDILITE | 242 | 203 | 170 | 138 | 98 | 31 |
| 134. | RALLIS INDIA | 179 | 153 | 205 | 225 | 284 | 31 |
| 135. | RANBAXY LABORATORIES | 17 | 16 | 15 | 14 | 10 | 31 |
| 136. | RECKITT BENCKISER (INDIA) | 69 | 64 | 48 | 46 | 69 | 31 |
| 137. | RHONE- POULENC (INDIA) | 239 | 166 | 160 | 133 | 124 | 31 |
| 138. | SILTAP CHEMICALS | 359 | 318 | 312 | 525 | 421 | 31 |
| 139. | SKB PHARMA (INDIA) | 117 | 105 | 71 | 43 | 81 | 31 |
| 140. | SOUTHERN PETROCHEMICAL INDUSTRIES CORP | 124 | 131 | 167 | 177 | 269 | 31 |
| 141. | TAMILNADU PETROPRODUCTS | 224 | 207 | 213 | 235 | 267 | 31 |
| 142. | TATA CHEMICALS | 13 | 10 | 16 | 24 | 74 | 31 |
| 143. | UNITED PHOSPHORUS | 74 | 75 | 107 | 135 | 184 | 31 |
| 144. | VIKAS WSP | 336 | 298 | 265 | 239 | 101 | 31 |
| 145. | WOCKHARDT | 60 | 53 | 64 | 57 | 199 | 31 |
| 146. | BALRAMPUR CHINI MILLS | 324 | 281 | 179 | 175 | 283 | 32 |

| S.NO. | NAME OF THE COMPANY | 95-96 | 96-97 | 97-98 | 98-99 | 99-00 | SECTION |
|---|---|---|---|---|---|---|---|
| 147. | DCM SHRIRAM CONSOLDATED | 197 | 224 | 328 | 641 | 382 | 32 |
| 148. | Mc. DOWELL & CO. | 436 | 411 | 357 | 266 | 96 | 32 |
| 149. | OSWAL AGRO MILLS | 266 | 222 | 188 | 211 | 331 | 32 |
| 150. | UNITED BREWERIES | 391 | 380 | 329 | 317 | 155 | 32 |
| 151. | BRITANNIA INDUSTRIES | 142 | 107 | 75 | 36 | 43 | 33 |
| 152. | CADBURY INDIA | 123 | 78 | 70 | 53 | 52 | 33 |
| 153. | NESTLE INDIA | 27 | 22 | 17 | 8 | 18 | 33 |
| 154. | WIPRO LTD. | 80 | 70 | 27 | 4 | 2 | 33 |
| 155. | TATA TEA | 40 | 38 | 28 | 31 | 44 | 34 |
| 156. | APOLLO TYRES | 109 | 103 | 138 | 167 | 146 | 36 |
| 157. | ASIAN PAINTS (INDIA) | 36 | 32 | 43 | 47 | 63 | 36 |
| 158. | BATA INDIA | 299 | 193 | 69 | 54 | 90 | 36 |
| 159. | CASTROL INDIA | 22 | 17 | 12 | 13 | 20 | 36 |
| 160. | CEAT | 185 | 169 | 292 | 324 | 287 | 36 |
| 161. | COLGATE- PALMOLIVE (INDIA) | 14 | 11 | 11 | 18 | 33 | 36 |
| 162. | ESSEL PACKAGING | 167 | 196 | 185 | 134 | 103 | 36 |
| 163. | ETERNIT EVEREST | 222 | 213 | 267 | 351 | 445 | 36 |
| 164. | FINOLEX CABLES | 118 | 129 | 156 | 126 | 93 | 36 |
| 165. | GODFREY PHILIPS INDIA | 315 | 285 | 168 | 104 | 113 | 36 |
| 166. | GOODLASS NEROLAC PAINTS | 189 | 147 | 130 | 162 | 232 | 36 |
| 167. | GOODYEAR INDIA | 358 | 252 | 211 | 231 | 229 | 36 |
| 168. | GRINDWELL NORTON | 450 | 211 | 175 | 227 | 308 | 36 |
| 169. | INDIAN SHAVING PRODUCTS | 196 | 109 | 66 | 45 | 50 | 36 |
| 170. | ITC LTD. | 8 | 4 | 3 | 2 | 5 | 36 |
| 171. | JINDAL PHOTO FILMS | 251 | 287 | 260 | 249 | 259 | 36 |

| S.NO. | NAME OF THE COMPANY | 95-96 | 96-97 | 97-98 | 98-99 | 99-00 | SECTION |
|---|---|---|---|---|---|---|---|
| 172. | JK INDUSTRIES | 226 | 244 | 309 | 322 | 349 | 36 |
| 173. | LAKHANI INDIA | 379 | 331 | 323 | 373 | 494 | 36 |
| 174. | MODI RUBBER | 312 | 241 | 276 | 355 | 311 | 36 |
| 175. | MRF | 44 | 35 | 45 | 64 | 88 | 36 |
| 176. | SUPREME INDUSTRIES | 161 | 173 | 196 | 191 | 234 | 36 |
| 177. | THERMAX | 63 | 51 | 78 | 106 | 169 | 36 |
| 178. | TIMEX WATCHES | 233 | 221 | 274 | 363 | 443 | 36 |
| 179. | TITAN INDUSTRIES | 113 | 102 | 136 | 156 | 157 | 36 |
| 180. | VST INDUSTRIES | 212 | 212 | 217 | 196 | 346 | 36 |

Here, the 95-96 column contains the ranks of the respective companies for the year 1995-96 as given in the Business Today issue of 7 September, 1996. Similarly, 96-97, 97-98, 98-99, and 99-00 columns represent the ranks of the respective companies as given in the Business Today issue of 22 September 1997, 7 September 1998, 7 September 1999 and 6 October 2000 respectively. The SECTION column represents the classification of different companies in the sample into different industries.

## APPENDIX-2
**Ratios for all the Companies in the Sample**
**(Before considering the Correlation Coefficients**
**For the Year 1999-2000**

**GROUP - 1**

| *Rank* | *X1* | *X3* | *X6* | *X7* | *X8* | *X9* | *X10* | *X13* | *X15* | *X16* | *X17* | *Z* |
|---|---|---|---|---|---|---|---|---|---|---|---|---|
| 1. | 70.02 | 4.31 | 2.12 | 1.57 | 0.68 | 4.99 | 0.41 | 0.08 | 6.98 | 29.3 | 66.2 | 2.317 |
| 2. | 61.01 | 9.15 | 2.00 | 1.28 | 0.94 | 3.71 | 0.16 | 0.09 | 28.9 | 30.4 | 3.26 | 1.344 |
| 5. | 43.39 | 2.49 | 0.78 | 1.00 | 0.74 | 1.20 | 0.02 | 0.24 | 4.90 | 24.8 | 28.3 | 1.794 |
| 6. | 16.29 | 5.24 | 0.68 | 0.21 | 0.55 | 0.84 | 0.30 | 1.03 | 49.2 | 9.28 | 17.9 | -0.155 |
| 10. | 19.04 | 8.24 | 0.86 | 0.52 | 0.34 | 1.17 | 0.13 | 0.23 | 47.5 | 10.1 | 49.8 | -0.066 |
| 12. | 12.32 | 5.21 | 0.56 | 0.26 | 0.21 | 1.07 | 0.11 | 1.05 | 1.20 | 2.41 | 52.6 | -0.221 |
| 13. | 33.74 | 8.27 | 1.14 | 0.97 | 0.39 | 1.37 | 0.52 | 0.03 | 23.6 | 27.6 | 14.8 | 0.9881 |
| 14. | 22.77 | 9.30 | 0.47 | 0.30 | 0.74 | 0.49 | 3.32 | 0.15 | 14.9 | 20.4 | 11.3 | 1.133 |
| 15. | 6.12 | 4.32 | 0.83 | 0.22 | 0.34 | 1.43 | 0.03 | 1.01 | 35.8 | -2.2 | 110 | 0.2609 |
| 16. | 20.42 | 6.98 | 0.81 | 0.49 | 0.28 | 0.95 | 0.86 | 0.15 | 4.57 | 17.2 | 20.9 | 0.4128 |
| 17. | 11.10 | 3.66 | 0.57 | 0.21 | 0.59 | 0.79 | 11 | 1.33 | 2.11 | 4.44 | 40.7 | 0.5065 |
| 18. | 48.57 | 8.05 | 1.97 | 0.52 | 0.91 | 3.50 | 0.01 | 0.39 | -3.7 | 23.8 | 87.2 | 1.904 |
| 20. | 61.06 | 5.45 | 1.57 | 1.54 | 0.63 | 2.48 | 0.34 | 0.02 | 10.7 | 38.3 | 134 | 3.404 |
| 21. | 71.98 | 10.41 | 3.19 | 0.97 | 1.33 | 5.60 | 0.03 | 0.12 | 46.7 | 36.8 | 23.1 | 1.760 |
| 22. | 26.13 | 7.64 | 1.72 | 0.82 | 0.55 | 2.47 | 0.30 | 0.06 | 10.9 | 16.1 | 52.1 | 0.9428 |
| 23. | 17.43 | 3.95 | 0.96 | 0.55 | 0.51 | 1.29 | 0.29 | 0.52 | 5.33 | 9.12 | 25.6 | 0.4118 |
| 27. | 15.25 | 9.48 | 0.49 | 0.16 | 0.64 | 0.60 | 0.75 | 0.69 | 9.30 | 6.42 | 38.5 | 0.1968 |
| 28. | 48.90 | 5.74 | 1.59 | 1.19 | 0.60 | 2.59 | 0.13 | 0.05 | 9.74 | 29.6 | 51.3 | 1.859 |
| 29. | 14.98 | 8.41 | 0.50 | 0.88 | 0.26 | 0.61 | 0.63 | 0.02 | 47.6 | 8.81 | 24.7 | -0.080 |

| RANK | X1 | X3 | X6 | X7 | X8 | X9 | X10 | X13 | X15 | X16 | X17 | Z |
|---|---|---|---|---|---|---|---|---|---|---|---|---|
| 31. | 18.97 | 6.27 | 0.76 | 0.60 | 0.42 | 0.99 | 0.61 | 0.46 | 15.8 | 11.7 | 14.9 | 0.2010 |
| 33. | 30.45 | 5.63 | 1.88 | 0.66 | 0.57 | 3.42 | 0.33 | 0.02 | 9.03 | 16.7 | 87.5 | 1.748 |
| 34. | 11.08 | 8.34 | 0.75 | 0.17 | 0.51 | 0.95 | 0.08 | 0.82 | 19.1 | 4.28 | 31.0 | -0.252 |
| 40. | 19.81 | 11.46 | 1.42 | 0.47 | 0.41 | 2.11 | 0.65 | 0.90 | 13.9 | 8.75 | 40.8 | -0.395 |
| 42. | 23.63 | 9.44 | 0.35 | 2.06 | 0.28 | 0.63 | 3.27 | 0.00 | -75 | 13.2 | 28.7 | 1.786 |
| 43. | 36.22 | 5.33 | 2.32 | 0.85 | 0.67 | 5.28 | 0.35 | 0.63 | 4.91 | 14.4 | 27.3 | 1.526 |
| 44. | 22.16 | 5.53 | 0.81 | 0.92 | 0.86 | 1.06 | 0.20 | 0.32 | 4.27 | 14.0 | 44.2 | 1.963 |
| 45. | 56.00 | 30.67 | 2.40 | 1.07 | 0.97 | 3.02 | 0.30 | 0.03 | 8.28 | 43.6 | 45.0 | 1.663 |
| 46. | 21.08 | 5.03 | 0.76 | 0.32 | 0.76 | 0.94 | 0.03 | 1.36 | 17.0 | 14.2 | 5.78 | 0.6853 |
| 47. | 12.55 | 3.71 | 0.59 | 0.20 | 0.26 | 0.79 | 0.67 | 1.01 | 23.1 | 5.30 | 31.1 | -0.516 |
| 50. | 37.45 | 4.14 | 1.37 | 0.48 | 0.63 | 2.17 | 0.08 | 0.51 | 65.1 | 20.4 | 22.0 | 0.2548 |
| 52. | 30.68 | 6.44 | 1.77 | 0.51 | 0.79 | 2.46 | 0.33 | 0.05 | 19.3 | 20.8 | 47.2 | 1.324 |
| 53. | 33.47 | 4.97 | 1.59 | 0.38 | 0.93 | 2.70 | 0.34 | 0.08 | 16.3 | 18.9 | 10.4 | 1.220 |
| 60. | 35.16 | 22.94 | 0.55 | 1.00 | 0.55 | 0.67 | 0.08 | 0.48 | 47.1 | 24.4 | 25.5 | 0.4891 |
| 61. | 20.82 | 4.98 | 0.77 | 0.64 | 0.58 | 0.92 | 0.49 | 0.30 | 10.9 | 11.3 | 44.9 | 0.8231 |
| 62. | 13.40 | 2.14 | 0.98 | 0.75 | 0.28 | 1.87 | 0.17 | 0.12 | -11 | 6.24 | 62.4 | 1.176 |
| 63. | 35.00 | 23.39 | 1.74 | 0.52 | 0.63 | 2.57 | 0.08 | 0.49 | 19.7 | 20.7 | 45.7 | 0.0134 |
| 65. | 33.97 | 7.57 | 1.25 | 1.26 | 0.46 | 1.86 | 0.38 | 0.00 | 11.1 | 22.8 | 52.5 | 1.617 |
| 67. | 32.58 | 7.59 | 2.16 | 0.39 | 0.75 | 3.42 | 0.07 | 0.65 | 17.4 | 16.9 | 23.9 | .3564 |
| 69. | 13.87 | 5.70 | 2.03 | 0.56 | 0.42 | 3.37 | 0.22 | 0.00 | 15.8 | 7.02 | 92.2 | 1.020 |
| 71. | 60.57 | 4.48 | 1.66 | 1.50 | 0.96 | 3.06 | 0.30 | 0.00 | 25.0 | 31.1 | 21.2 | 2.121 |
| 72. | 16.11 | 14.11 | 0.68 | 0.20 | 0.55 | 0.84 | 0.39 | 0.79 | 44.2 | 7.71 | 24.6 | -0.593 |
| 73. | 13.57 | 6.75 | 0.94 | 0.33 | 0.32 | 1.37 | 0.08 | 0.87 | 27.2 | 3.72 | 58.9 | -0.364 |
| 74. | 14.39 | 7.46 | 0.44 | 0.19 | 0.40 | 0.53 | 0.04 | 0.84 | 3.93 | 5.10 | 85.5 | 0.3783 |
| 75. | 32.04 | 2.02 | 1.16 | 0.41 | 0.33 | 4.99 | 0.32 | 0.15 | 3.95 | 6.56 | 32.5 | 1.674 |

| RANK | X1 | X3 | X6 | X7 | X8 | X9 | X10 | X13 | X15 | X16 | X17 | Z |
|---|---|---|---|---|---|---|---|---|---|---|---|---|
| 77. | 25.58 | 7.05 | 1.43 | 0.45 | 0.38 | 2.57 | 0.07 | 0.88 | 3.86 | 9.33 | 17.0 | -0.391 |
| 81. | 22.74 | 10.35 | 1.60 | 1.46 | 0.52 | 1.95 | 0.73 | 0.00 | 4.26 | 18.1 | 40.0 | 1.342 |
| 82. | 13.64 | 5.24 | 0.72 | 0.53 | 0.35 | 1.02 | 0.11 | 0.93 | 19.2 | 3.73 | 32.1 | -0.315 |
| 83. | 28.31 | 7.42 | 1.68 | 0.80 | 0.80 | 2.48 | 0.04 | 0.12 | 7.27 | 17.2 | 43.7 | 1.466 |
| 85. | 11.50 | 6.65 | 0.47 | 0.19 | 0.57 | 0.62 | 0.09 | 2.18 | 4.36 | 1.81 | 140 | 1.101 |
| 88. | 33.28 | 8.05 | 1.58 | 0.40 | 0.51 | 2.86 | 0.15 | 0.77 | 4.73 | 12.3 | 9.54 | -0.433 |
| 89. | 37.50 | 3.49 | 1.21 | 0.94 | 0.35 | 2.41 | 0.99 | 0.02 | 10.3 | 17.9 | 106 | 1.648 |
| 90. | 28.44 | 9.10 | 2.12 | 1.46 | 0.90 | 3.55 | 0.02 | 0.12 | 4.10 | 14.1 | 30.9 | 1.799 |
| 92. | 12.84 | 3.64 | 0.56 | 0.41 | 0.21 | 0.80 | 0.10 | 1.91 | -21 | 4.18 | 28.4 | -0.331 |
| 93. | 17.83 | 7.11 | 0.61 | 0.64 | 0.32 | 0.76 | 0.18 | 0.22 | 26.9 | 12.0 | 40.5 | 0.4302 |
| 94. | 15.32 | 4.77 | 1.28 | 0.32 | 0.31 | 2.29 | 0.25 | 0.15 | 5.36 | 5.94 | 38.9 | 0.0814 |
| 96. | 20.64 | 5.59 | 1.69 | 0.59 | 0.24 | 2.66 | 0.09 | 0.49 | 20.1 | 8.06 | 64.2 | -0.160 |
| 97. | 19.44 | 6.89 | 0.96 | 0.34 | 0.49 | 1.35 | 0.03 | 1.36 | 15.7 | 6.85 | 29.4 | -0.403 |
| 98. | 47.16 | 7.48 | 1.39 | 0.67 | 0.74 | 2.40 | 0.27 | 0.44 | 17.1 | 25.0 | 23.9 | 0.9400 |
| 100. | 38.47 | 11.99 | 1.20 | 0.75 | 0.89 | 1.77 | 0.29 | 0.05 | 11.3 | 25.2 | 25.9 | 1.607 |
| 101. | 54.01 | 20.78 | 1.11 | 0.80 | 0.62 | 1.63 | 1.11 | 0.38 | 43.8 | 33.3 | 15.3 | 0.1542 |
| 103. | 23.61 | 9.22 | 0.72 | 0.24 | 0.73 | 0.81 | 0.43 | 0.18 | 34.3 | 17.5 | 94.1 | 1.664 |
| 105. | 13.59 | 14.47 | 0.55 | 0.14 | 0.72 | 0.64 | 0.30 | 1.50 | -0.83 | 4.86 | 19.5 | -0.244 |
| 107. | 10.59 | 7.94 | 0.81 | 0.21 | 0.52 | 0.97 | 0.02 | 0.54 | 2.09 | 5.88 | 47.0 | 0.3363 |
| 109. | 20.02 | 3.13 | 0.64 | 0.35 | 0.35 | 0.92 | 0.07 | 1.41 | 2.18 | 7.91 | 20.2 | -0.318 |
| 110. | 17.36 | 2.63 | 0.52 | 0.28 | 0.62 | 0.77 | 0.08 | 1.02 | 22.0 | 7.29 | 45.8 | 0.6200 |
| 113. | 36.70 | 9.39 | 1.71 | 1.53 | 0.56 | 2.56 | 1.19 | 0.21 | 3.39 | 22.8 | 39.8 | 1.439 |
| 124. | 47.46 | 6.40 | 1.65 | 1.64 | 0.59 | 2.59 | 0.09 | 0.13 | 11.4 | 29.3 | 42.3 | 1.981 |
| 128. | 11.52 | 8.03 | 0.77 | 0.21 | 0.41 | 0.98 | 0.18 | 0.95 | 5.15 | 3.16 | 39.4 | -0.409 |
| 129 | 16.71 | 7.31 | 0.49 | 0.21 | 0.50 | 0.57 | 0.43 | 1.30 | 17.7 | 4.85 | 37.0 | -0.418 |

| RANK | X1 | X3 | X6 | X7 | X8 | X9 | X10 | X13 | X15 | X16 | X17 | Z |
|---|---|---|---|---|---|---|---|---|---|---|---|---|
| 131. | 21.67 | 5.09 | 2.42 | 0.49 | 0.35 | 5.70 | 0.31 | 0.83 | 1.65 | 4.46 | 44.9 | 0.7616 |
| 134. | 12.13 | 10.46 | 0.50 | 0.18 | 0.65 | 0.54 | 0.08 | 1.97 | 71.7 | 5.03 | 50.8 | -0.268 |
| 142. | 9.65 | 7.15 | 0.77 | 0.16 | 0.51 | 1.08 | 0.15 | 1.57 | 8.40 | -0.56 | 40.9 | -0.520 |
| 143. | 8.62 | 2.58 | 0.41 | 0.19 | 0.26 | 0.53 | 0.08 | 1.66 | -23 | 1.93 | 19.2 | -0.397 |
| 144. | 41.82 | 3.23 | 0.65 | 1.14 | 0.25 | 4.53 | 0.07 | 0.00 | 57.8 | 5.78 | 69.3 | 1.777 |
| 146. | 23.51 | 4.17 | 1.24 | 0.41 | 0.44 | 1.86 | 0.25 | 0.86 | 17.3 | 9.57 | 27.3 | -0.279 |
| 155. | -11.01 | 2.08 | 0.49 | 0.06 | 0.04 | 0.82 | 0.06 | 0.86 | -7.4 | -13 | 83.6 | -0.540 |
| 156. | 56.18 | 8.94 | 2.21 | 0.93 | 0.99 | 4.27 | 0.07 | 1.49 | 10.4 | 22.9 | 40.3 | 1.167 |
| 157. | 14.87 | 8.20 | 0.83 | 0.40 | 0.38 | 1.26 | 0.23 | 2.09 | 30.7 | 1.64 | 65.6 | -0.621 |
| 164. | 18.93 | 5.42 | 0.97 | 0.33 | 0.39 | 1.35 | 0.03 | 0.42 | 10.9 | 9.92 | 53.7 | 0.2950 |
| 167. | 13.55 | 5.86 | 0.66 | 0.16 | 0.34 | 0.92 | 0.26 | 1.12 | 4.76 | 4.17 | 62.7 | -0.124 |
| 168. | 16.34 | 4.94 | 1.50 | 0.78 | 0.27 | 3.04 | 0.10 | 0.20 | -4.8 | 6.92 | 65.6 | 1.092 |
| 169. | 9.19 | 7.33 | 0.79 | 0.64 | 0.25 | 1.11 | 0.58 | 0.11 | -13 | 5.20 | 28.2 | 0.1628 |
| 174. | 25.94 | 29.98 | 0.62 | 0.34 | 0.86 | 0.68 | 1.19 | 0.01 | 34.1 | 22.3 | 28.7 | 0.7044 |
| 177. | 4.34 | 5.80 | 0.44 | 0.07 | 0.32 | 0.53 | 0.00 | 1.10 | 42.1 | -4.5 | .00 | -1.69 |
| 182. | 19.70 | 3.24 | 0.88 | 0.59 | 0.31 | 1.47 | 0.72 | 0.03 | 47.6 | 10.9 | 85.1 | 0.8439 |
| 184. | 12.79 | 4.82 | 0.57 | 0.34 | 0.27 | 0.84 | 0.24 | 0.92 | 2.27 | 4.79 | 31.9 | -0.227 |
| 186. | 2.55 | 2.86 | 0.16 | 0.19 | 0.12 | 0.18 | 0.63 | 0.17 | -23 | .72 | 99.0 | 0.8032 |
| 189. | 29.35 | 4.20 | 1.20 | 0.70 | 0.18 | 2.52 | 0.16 | 0.15 | 36.4 | 6.78 | 46.9 | -0.519 |
| 199. | 18.75 | 9.11 | 0.85 | 0.50 | 0.66 | 1.06 | 0.07 | 0.43 | 112 | 11.6 | 38.0 | 0.0440 |
| 200. | 19.99 | 4.45 | 1.03 | 0.57 | 0.37 | 1.67 | 0.23 | 1.04 | 6.08 | 6.54 | 44.7 | 0.000 |
| 201. | 36.89 | 2.64 | 1.30 | 1.45 | 0.23 | 2.72 | 0.02 | 0.05 | -7.9 | 14.6 | 23.1 | 0.7518 |
| 204. | 4.17 | 4.23 | 0.98 | 0.42 | 0.34 | 1.73 | 0.25 | 0.45 | -8.6 | 0.37 | 39.4 | 0.3885 |
| 205. | 14.21 | 4.99 | 0.79 | 0.34 | 0.52 | 1.11 | 0.07 | 1.32 | -21 | 2.46 | 29.0 | -0.101 |
| 207. | 42.29 | 6.08 | 2.18 | 1.05 | 0.38 | 3.94 | 0.45 | 0.10 | 7.55 | 22.0 | 34.2 | 0.7580 |

| RANK | X1 | X3 | X6 | X7 | X8 | X9 | X10 | X13 | X15 | X16 | X17 | Z |
|---|---|---|---|---|---|---|---|---|---|---|---|---|
| 208. | 18.82 | 5.10 | 1.17 | 0.44 | 0.49 | 1.60 | 0.28 | 0.40 | -1.2 | 10.8 | 40.0 | 0.5185 |
| 212. | -3.19 | 2.65 | 0.87 | 0.29 | 0.17 | 1.80 | 0.01 | 2.36 | .56 | -8.8 | 0.00 | -1.18 |
| 215. | 25.59 | 8.29 | 1.51 | 0.61 | 0.42 | 3.12 | 0.34 | 2.41 | 13.6 | 2.12 | 89.3 | -0.168 |
| 217. | 13.23 | 3.85 | 1.12 | 0.70 | 0.35 | 2.99 | 0.08 | 1.27 | -20 | 0.66 | 80.2 | 1.419 |
| 220. | 22.35 | 10.25 | 1.52 | 0.72 | 0.41 | 3.10 | 0.07 | 0.57 | .69 | 7.58 | 49.0 | 0.5111 |
| 222. | 9.59 | 7.20 | 0.60 | 0.16 | 0.33 | 0.84 | 0.15 | 1.76 | -21 | 1.57 | 32.0 | -0.495 |
| 228. | 1.74 | 3.19 | 1.42 | 0.17 | 0.29 | 3.31 | 0.06 | 0.73 | 24.0 | -4.0 | 0.00 | -0.352 |
| 229. | 22.38 | 3.76 | 1.57 | 0.43 | 0.33 | 3.30 | 0.08 | 0.44 | 23.4 | 5.93 | 40.6 | 0.0360 |
| 230. | 5.38 | 4.41 | 0.76 | 0.22 | 0.24 | 1.29 | 0.18 | 0.94 | -4.5 | -0.02 | 0.00 | -0.721 |
| 232. | 24.34 | 5.77 | 1.67 | 0.82 | 0.43 | 2.51 | 0.08 | 0.31 | 15.3 | 12.7 | 36.8 | 0.3528 |
| 234. | 20.21 | 6.10 | 0.99 | 0.24 | 0.42 | 1.46 | 0.09 | 1.65 | 15.2 | 3.66 | 43.6 | -0.848 |
| 235. | 20.34 | 3.60 | 0.75 | 0.28 | 0.60 | 0.96 | 0.11 | 1.27 | 16.2 | 4.64 | 38.5 | -0.274 |
| 236. | 28.41 | 6.10 | 0.95 | 0.71 | 0.56 | 1.31 | 0.11 | 0.18 | 9.92 | 16.7 | 13.2 | 0.6365 |
| 237. | 12.40 | 7.05 | 0.87 | 0.27 | 0.48 | 1.09 | 0.20 | 3.43 | 4.72 | -.07 | 94.5 | -0.324 |
| 239. | 14.03 | 8.60 | 1.43 | 0.34 | 0.36 | 2.20 | 0.14 | 0.51 | 43.5 | 5.79 | 33.3 | -0.609 |
| 240. | 4.27 | 9.52 | 0.59 | 0.18 | 0.39 | 0.67 | 0.05 | 0.77 | -12 | 0.80 | 45.4 | -0.079 |
| 241. | 9.67 | 3.47 | 1.03 | 0.26 | 0.30 | 1.93 | 0.32 | 1.31 | -41 | 0.16 | 0.00 | -0.454 |
| 242. | 8.93 | 8.75 | 0.64 | 0.22 | 0.29 | 0.86 | 0.07 | 0.95 | 9.63 | 1.61 | 31.6 | -0.723 |
| 243. | 22.04 | 9.54 | 1.12 | 0.53 | 0.45 | 1.72 | 0.09 | 0.70 | 8.24 | 9.06 | 36.6 | -0.80 |

**GROUP - 2**

| RANK | X1 | X3 | X6 | X7 | X8 | X9 | X10 | X13 | X15 | X16 | X17 | Z |
|---|---|---|---|---|---|---|---|---|---|---|---|---|
| 258. | 40.16 | 6.66 | 1.23 | 0.56 | 0.48 | 2.10 | 0.14 | 0.74 | 16.0 | 17.2 | 31.8 | -0.062 |
| 259. | 16.56 | 5.41 | 0.83 | 0.93 | 0.28 | 1.06 | 0.40 | 0.05 | 18.7 | 11.9 | -3.7 | 0.1316 |
| 262. | 10.75 | 2.65 | 0.36 | 0.26 | 0.23 | 0.52 | 0.13 | 0.93 | -14 | 2.61 | 157 | 1.356 |
| 263. | 5.94 | 6.71 | 1.26 | 0.38 | 0.38 | 1.56 | 0.58 | 0.00 | 7.60 | 2.07 | 0.00 | -0.748 |
| 265. | 15.22 | 5.75 | 1.06 | 0.26 | 0.35 | 1.46 | 0.05 | 1.04 | 14.0 | 5.10 | 26.2 | -0.696 |
| 266. | 12.37 | 2.94 | 0.52 | 0.40 | 0.11 | 0.80 | -0.02 | 5.20 | -15 | 1.81 | 26.1 | -1.22 |
| 267. | 17.73 | 5.78 | 0.61 | 0.17 | 0.38 | 0.74 | 1.04 | 1.01 | 27.6 | 10.4 | 48.3 | -0.023 |
| 269. | 14.73 | 3.47 | 0.76 | 0.21 | 0.29 | 1.40 | 0.00 | 3.33 | 12.3 | 0.89 | 47.4 | -0.835 |
| 270. | 16.94 | 18.14 | 1.01 | 0.31 | 0.23 | 1.22 | 0.52 | 0.66 | 30.1 | 10.6 | 47.8 | -0.879 |
| 271. | 11.58 | 6.92 | 0.72 | 0.16 | 0.66 | 0.88 | 0.10 | 1.29 | -1.0 | 1.48 | 39.0 | -0.072 |
| 273. | 12.07 | 9.59 | 0.61 | 0.19 | 0.31 | 0.73 | 0.68 | 1.17 | 14.6 | 4.07 | 18.2 | -1.00 |
| 276. | 13.38 | 4.88 | 0.84 | 0.15 | 0.38 | 1.38 | 0.41 | 0.44 | 5.21 | 4.86 | 19.7 | -0.267 |
| 277. | 1.93 | 3.96 | 0.38 | 0.26 | 0.22 | 0.48 | 0.17 | 0.09 | 23.9 | 0.11 | 190 | 1.734 |
| 281. | 42.54 | 8.05 | 1.62 | 0.27 | 0.66 | 3.51 | 0.03 | 2.81 | 42.3 | 12.0 | 22.0 | -0.772 |
| 282. | 17.10 | 3.65 | 0.68 | 0.24 | 0.34 | 1.08 | 0.11 | 1.63 | 19.6 | 3.60 | 12.9 | -0.957 |
| 283. | 15.32 | 7.08 | 0.68 | 0.21 | 0.27 | 1.06 | 0.02 | 1.23 | 33.5 | 4.35 | 36.2 | -0.843 |
| 284. | 25.29 | 5.05 | 1.91 | 0.68 | 0.28 | 3.96 | 0.04 | 2.31 | 13.9 | 3.43 | 33.5 | -0.679 |
| 285. | 11.94 | 11.84 | 0.87 | 0.11 | 0.52 | 0.98 | 0.16 | 0.64 | 23.9 | 6.69 | 25.6 | -0.450 |
| 287. | 20.21 | 4.34 | 0.94 | 0.64 | 0.34 | 1.70 | 0.23 | 1.65 | 15.6 | 1.70 | 35.0 | -0.712 |
| 288. | 7.04 | 4.20 | 1.25 | 0.26 | 0.30 | 2.34 | 0.10 | 3.41 | 25.0 | -5.3 | 0.00 | -1.73 |
| 290. | 17.57 | 1.94 | 0.69 | 0.87 | 0.23 | 1.34 | 0.05 | 2.12 | -8.8 | 0.11 | 40.7 | -0.383 |
| 295. | 11.19 | 5.17 | 0.75 | 0.11 | 0.52 | 1.01 | 0.05 | 4.51 | 23.0 | -0.43 | 0.00 | -1.57 |
| 305. | 19.26 | 19.83 | 0.75 | 0.56 | 0.27 | 0.85 | 1.17 | 0.56 | 36.3 | 14.7 | 20.2 | -0.671 |

| RANK | X1 | X3 | X6 | X7 | X8 | X9 | X10 | X13 | X15 | X16 | X17 | Z |
|---|---|---|---|---|---|---|---|---|---|---|---|---|
| 307. | 13.16 | 7.42 | 0.69 | 0.15 | 0.50 | 0.86 | 0.07 | 1.54 | 9.24 | 2.20 | 0.00 | -1.03 |
| 308. | 16.52 | 4.60 | 0.96 | 0.49 | 0.51 | 1.24 | 0.18 | 0.24 | 10.8 | 10.7 | 38.7 | 0.7172 |
| 310. | 4.70 | 3.60 | 0.94 | 0.71 | 0.30 | 1.27 | 0.73 | 0.58 | 39.8 | -1.3 | -125 | -2.48 |
| 311. | 23.29 | 5.60 | 1.61 | 0.45 | 0.42 | 3.91 | 0.27 | 0.91 | 11.5 | 1.46 | 0.00 | -0.484 |
| 313. | 25.47 | 5.22 | 2.00 | 0.39 | 0.38 | 2.94 | 0.04 | 0.16 | 30.2 | 16.6 | 23.8 | -0.075 |
| 326. | 2.14 | 9.38 | 0.46 | 0.12 | 0.42 | 0.54 | 0.02 | 2.18 | -7.0 | 0.13 | 0.00 | -0.691 |
| 328. | 32.40 | 14.82 | 2.18 | 0.48 | 0.65 | 2.92 | 0.20 | 0.03 | 14.0 | 23.5 | 21.5 | 0.3163 |
| 330. | 18.41 | 33.84 | 0.89 | 0.33 | 0.38 | 1.16 | 0.16 | 0.95 | 18.3 | 8.40 | 21.2 | -1.73 |
| 336. | 24.11 | 3.48 | 1.24 | 0.89 | 0.33 | 2.18 | 0.12 | 0.01 | 26.9 | 13.4 | 41.3 | 0.7997 |
| 338. | 20.85 | 4.34 | 0.56 | 0.40 | 0.37 | 0.82 | 0.70 | 1.09 | 13.2 | 5.20 | 16.1 | -0.773 |
| 346. | 32.11 | 5.35 | 1.35 | 0.80 | 0.51 | 2.64 | 0.57 | 1.75 | 5.81 | 9.09 | 12.6 | -0.273 |
| 349. | 12.74 | 3.89 | 0.64 | 0.22 | 0.44 | 0.97 | 0.05 | 1.09 | 3.84 | 1.94 | 44.8 | -0.114 |
| 364. | 13.85 | 9.62 | 0.65 | 0.17 | 0.44 | 0.78 | 0.32 | 0.81 | -4.8 | 4.84 | 58.2 | -0.060 |
| 373. | -14.78 | 2.71 | 1.13 | 0.26 | 0.26 | 2.65 | 0.14 | 0.53 | -21 | -8.1 | 0.00 | 0.5459 |
| 374. | 18.85 | 2.26 | 0.45 | 0.35 | 0.29 | 0.86 | 0.06 | 2.34 | 21.8 | -.59 | 0.32 | -1.63 |
| 377. | 5.23 | 4.62 | 0.47 | 0.06 | 0.29 | 0.68 | 0.37 | 2.59 | 30.5 | -5.0 | 0.00 | -1.89 |
| 382. | 14.79 | 10.24 | 1.01 | 0.28 | 0.58 | 1.31 | 0.17 | 1.39 | 38.6 | 5.02 | 22.8 | -0.700 |
| 383. | 9.41 | 9.45 | 0.58 | 0.27 | 0.25 | 0.76 | 0.29 | 0.35 | 9.53 | 4.25 | -10 | -0.966 |
| 384. | 0.28 | 3.49 | 0.15 | 0.02 | 0.12 | 0.20 | 0.02 | 2.97 | 0.73 | -3.6 | 0.00 | -1.44 |
| 391. | 13.96 | 24.90 | 0.68 | 0.22 | 0.33 | 0.93 | 0.22 | 1.39 | 6.39 | 4.54 | 23.6 | -1.49 |
| 419. | 17.78 | 20.43 | 0.81 | 0.24 | 0.42 | 1.15 | 0.10 | 1.14 | 9.18 | 5.40 | 27.0 | -1.19 |
| 421. | 18.45 | 5.07 | 0.77 | 0.25 | 0.48 | 0.92 | 0.34 | 0.58 | 37.4 | 12.3 | 44.8 | 0.3658 |
| 426. | -32.97 | 5.43 | 0.82 | -0.11 | -0.31 | 1.48 | 0.19 | 0.00 | -0.57 | -34 | 0.00 | -3.54 |
| 429. | 18.40 | 6.11 | 1.26 | 0.26 | 0.44 | 1.84 | 0.03 | 0.64 | 61.3 | 9.30 | 58.3 | -0.118 |
| 438. | -7.28 | 3.44 | 0.53 | -0.01 | -0.03 | 0.80 | 0.03 | 3.30 | -26 | -13 | 0.00 | -2.36 |

| RANK | X1 | X3 | X6 | X7 | X8 | X9 | X10 | X13 | X15 | X16 | X17 | Z |
|---|---|---|---|---|---|---|---|---|---|---|---|---|
| 439. | 14.57 | 7.75 | 0.78 | 0.18 | 0.34 | 1.02 | 0.11 | 1.26 | 27.2 | 4.43 | 8.21 | -1.19 |
| 443. | -2.61 | 2.81 | 0.59 | 0.08 | 0.10 | 0.91 | 0.07 | 3.37 | 36.0 | -10 | 0.00 | -2.42 |
| 445. | -1.97 | 3.05 | 0.96 | 0.19 | 0.25 | 1.50 | 0.19 | 0.25 | 2.23 | -2.5 | 0.00 | -.574 |
| 454. | 13.84 | 7.68 | 0.61 | 0.31 | 1.05 | 0.85 | 0.11 | 0.72 | 16.0 | 3.70 | 69.8 | 1.446 |
| 455. | 17.02 | 13.86 | 0.63 | 0.23 | 0.47 | 0.77 | 0.21 | 1.68 | 23.6 | 3.86 | 16.3 | -1.29 |
| 457. | -8.41 | 2.82 | 0.38 | -0.01 | -0.06 | 0.95 | 0.05 | 19.8 | 9.35 | -9.6 | 0.00 | -4.00 |
| 460. | -12.78 | 6.20 | 0.93 | 0.11 | 0.14 | 1.50 | 0.11 | 0.50 | -6.5 | -11 | 44.4 | -0.719 |
| 466. | -17.82 | 7.26 | 0.15 | -0.09 | -0.57 | 0.28 | 0.02 | 0.00 | -48 | -25 | 0.00 | -3.67 |
| 479. | 14.45 | 3.47 | 1.03 | 0.41 | 0.31 | 1.67 | 0.09 | 0.45 | 8.93 | 2.68 | 9.09 | -0.682 |
| 480. | -3.92 | 3.75 | 0.45 | 0.07 | 0.14 | 0.66 | 0.02 | 5.38 | 31.0 | -18 | 0.00 | -3.43 |
| 481. | -3.80 | 1.70 | 0.20 | -0.01 | -0.04 | 0.40 | 0.01 | 7.23 | -45 | -11 | 0.00 | -2.49 |
| 494. | 9.52 | 4.19 | 0.66 | 0.21 | 0.16 | 0.96 | 0.02 | 0.60 | 23.9 | 1.16 | 0.00 | -1.30 |
| 500. | 13.52 | 5.97 | 0.73 | 0.13 | 0.41 | 0.95 | 0.04 | 1.46 | 19.9 | 1.78 | 0.00 | -1.30 |

# APPENDIX 3
## NUMBER OF OCCURENCES OF VARIOUS RATIOS IN THE DISCRIMINANT FUNCTION

| | YEAR WISE | | | | | | SIZE WISE | | | | | | INDUSTRY WISE | | | | | | | | TOTAL |
|---|---|---|---|---|---|---|---|---|---|---|---|---|---|---|---|---|---|---|---|---|---|
| | *95-96* | *96-97* | *97-98* | *98-99* | *99-00* | *Y* | *<100* | *100-200* | *200-300* | *300-500* | *>500* | *Y* | *19* | *24* | *26* | *29* | *30* | *31* | *36* | *Y* | **Y** |
| X1 | N | Y | N | N | Y | 2 | N | N | N | Y | N | 1 | N | N | N | N | N | Y | N | 1 | **4** |
| X2 | N | Y | Y | N | N | 2 | Y | N | N | Y | N | 2 | N | N | Y | N | N | Y | N | 2 | **6** |
| X3 | Y | Y | N | N | Y | 3 | Y | Y | N | Y | N | 3 | N | N | N | N | N | N | Y | 1 | **7** |
| X4 | Y | Y | Y | Y | Y | 5 | N | N | N | Y | N | 1 | Y | N | N | N | N | N | Y | 2 | **8** |
| X5 | Y | Y | Y | N | N | 3 | N | Y | N | N | N | 1 | N | N | Y | N | N | N | Y | 2 | **6** |
| X6 | Y | N | N | N | Y | 2 | Y | Y | Y | Y | N | 4 | N | N | N | N | N | N | Y | 1 | **7** |
| X7 | N | N | Y | Y | Y | 3 | Y | N | Y | Y | N | 3 | Y | Y | Y | N | Y | N | Y | 5 | **11** |
| X8 | N | N | N | N | Y | 1 | N | Y | Y | Y | N | 3 | Y | N | Y | N | Y | N | Y | 4 | **8** |
| X9 | Y | N | N | Y | Y | 3 | Y | Y | Y | Y | Y | 5 | N | N | N | N | N | N | Y | 1 | **9** |
| X10 | N | N | N | N | Y | 1 | Y | N | Y | Y | N | 3 | N | N | N | N | Y | N | Y | 2 | **6** |
| X11 | Y | N | Y | Y | N | 3 | Y | Y | N | Y | N | 3 | N | N | Y | N | Y | N | Y | 3 | **9** |
| X12 | Y | Y | Y | N | N | 3 | Y | Y | Y | Y | N | 4 | N | N | Y | N | Y | N | Y | 3 | **10** |
| X13 | N | Y | N | N | Y | 2 | N | N | Y | N | Y | 2 | N | N | Y | N | N | N | Y | 2 | **6** |
| X14 | N | N | N | N | N | 0 | Y | N | N | Y | N | 2 | N | N | Y | N | N | N | Y | 2 | **4** |
| X15 | Y | N | Y | Y | Y | 4 | N | N | Y | Y | N | 2 | N | N | N | N | Y | N | Y | 2 | **8** |
| X16 | Y | Y | Y | Y | Y | 5 | N | N | Y | Y | Y | 3 | N | N | Y | Y | Y | Y | Y | 5 | **13** |
| X17 | N | N | N | N | Y | 1 | Y | Y | N | N | Y | 3 | N | N | N | N | Y | N | Y | 2 | **6** |
| X18 | Y | Y | N | N | Y | 3 | N | N | N | Y | N | 1 | N | N | N | Y | N | N | Y | 2 | **6** |
| X19 | Y | N | Y | Y | N | 3 | Y | Y | N | Y | N | 3 | Y | N | N | N | Y | N | Y | 3 | **9** |
| X20 | Y | N | N | N | N | 1 | Y | Y | Y | N | N | 3 | N | N | N | N | N | N | Y | 1 | **5** |

# APPENDIX 4

## Ratios and Discriminant Scores for all the Companies after taking Mean

| RANK | X3 | X4 | X8 | X13 | X15 | X17 | X17MEAN* | GROUP | Z |
|---|---|---|---|---|---|---|---|---|---|
| 1. | 4.31 | 7.16 | 0.68 | 0.08 | 6.98 | 66.23 | 33.82667 | 1 | 2.69999 |
| 2. | 9.15 | 9.31 | 0.94 | 0.09 | 28.88 | 3.26 | 31.14667 | 1 | 1.61150 |
| 5. | 2.49 | 1.91 | 0.74 | 0.24 | 4.90 | 28.34 | 23.00000 | 1 | 1.77897 |
| 6. | 5.24 | 36.34 | 0.55 | 1.03 | 49.16 | 17.93 | 8.75000 | 1 | -0.64268 |
| 10. | 8.24 | 5.71 | 0.34 | 0.23 | 47.47 | 49.84 | 9.98667 | 1 | -0.10820 |
| 12. | 5.21 | 7.97 | 0.21 | 1.05 | 1.20 | 52.58 | 5.09667 | 1 | -0.13370 |
| 13. | 8.27 | 3.71 | 0.39 | 0.03 | 23.64 | 14.84 | 20.82000 | 1 | 0.42797 |
| 14. | 9.30 | 5.37 | 0.74 | 0.15 | 14.87 | 11.28 | 14.53000 | 1 | 0.58036 |
| 15. | 4.32 | 22.15 | 0.34 | 1.01 | 35.75 | 109.59 | 1.57667 | 1 | 0.20225 |
| 16. | 6.98 | 17.47 | 0.28 | 0.15 | 4.57 | 20.88 | 12.80000 | 1 | -0.06627 |
| 17. | 3.66 | 6.62 | 0.59 | 1.33 | 2.11 | 40.68 | 5.37000 | 1 | 0.37602 |
| 18. | 8.05 | 8.19 | 0.91 | 0.39 | -3.71 | 87.15 | 24.76667 | 1 | 2.68560 |
| 20. | 5.45 | 6.11 | 0.63 | 0.02 | 10.68 | 134.15 | 33.64000 | 1 | 3.47427 |
| 21. | 10.41 | 17.32 | 1.33 | 0.12 | 46.68 | 23.08 | 37.33000 | 1 | 2.55339 |
| 22. | 7.64 | 6.68 | 0.55 | 0.06 | 10.85 | 52.05 | 14.64000 | 1 | 0.96220 |
| 23. | 3.95 | 13.11 | 0.51 | 0.52 | 5.33 | 25.60 | 9.17000 | 1 | 0.28887 |
| 27. | 9.48 | 17.47 | 0.64 | 0.69 | 9.30 | 38.53 | 7.38667 | 1 | 0.17916 |
| 28. | 5.74 | 6.53 | 0.60 | 0.05 | 9.74 | 51.30 | 26.69000 | 1 | 1.85450 |
| 29. | 8.41 | 7.10 | 0.26 | 0.02 | 47.57 | 24.68 | 8.09667 | 1 | -0.68571 |
| 31. | 6.27 | 7.24 | 0.42 | 0.46 | 15.77 | 14.87 | 10.49000 | 1 | -0.07251 |
| 33. | 5.63 | 8.00 | 0.57 | 0.02 | 9.03 | 87.45 | 16.33667 | 1 | 1.69545 |

| RANK | X3 | X4 | X8 | X13 | X15 | X17 | X17MEAN* | GROUP | Z |
|---|---|---|---|---|---|---|---|---|---|
| 34. | 8.34 | 6.59 | .51 | .82 | 19.13 | 30.99 | 5.37000 | 1 | -0.19985 |
| 40. | 11.46 | 9.89 | .41 | .90 | 13.94 | 40.76 | 9.99333 | 1 | -0.11309 |
| 42. | 9.44 | 3.14 | .28 | .00 | -75.19 | 28.72 | 12.37667 | 1 | 0.88983 |
| 43. | 5.33 | 21.36 | .67 | .63 | 4.91 | 27.26 | 17.63667 | 1 | 0.89529 |
| 44. | 5.53 | 4.91 | .86 | .32 | 4.27 | 44.17 | 12.30667 | 1 | 1.37029 |
| 45. | 30.67 | 8.85 | .97 | .03 | 8.28 | 44.95 | 33.98667 | 1 | 1.55439 |
| 46. | 5.03 | 10.80 | .76 | 1.36 | 17.03 | 5.78 | 12.00000 | 1 | 0.29275 |
| 47. | 3.71 | 55.75 | .26 | 1.01 | 23.13 | 31.11 | 6.14667 | 1 | -0.62842 |
| 50. | 4.14 | 9.17 | .63 | .51 | 65.11 | 22.04 | 19.73333 | 1 | 0.49575 |
| 52. | 6.44 | 8.84 | .79 | .05 | 19.32 | 47.17 | 17.73333 | 1 | 1.42446 |
| 53. | 4.97 | 9.20 | .93 | .08 | 16.29 | 10.38 | 17.97000 | 1 | 1.25491 |
| 60. | 22.94 | 8.89 | .55 | .48 | 47.12 | 25.48 | 20.02333 | 1 | -0.31986 |
| 61. | 4.98 | 5.01 | .58 | .30 | 10.92 | 44.91 | 10.96000 | 1 | 0.80261 |
| 62. | 2.14 | 5.52 | .28 | .12 | -10.98 | 62.37 | 6.87333 | 1 | 0.69835 |
| 63. | 23.39 | 11.82 | .63 | .49 | 19.70 | 45.70 | 19.14000 | 1 | 0.25770 |
| 65. | 7.57 | 2.76 | .46 | .00 | 11.13 | 52.52 | 19.33667 | 1 | 1.15406 |
| 67. | 7.59 | 31.01 | .75 | .65 | 17.42 | 23.92 | 17.20667 | 1 | 0.60252 |
| 69. | 5.70 | 8.52 | .42 | .00 | 15.82 | 92.15 | 7.64000 | 1 | 0.92613 |
| 71. | 4.48 | 7.11 | .96 | .00 | 24.96 | 21.18 | 31.11333 | 1 | 2.20467 |
| 72. | 14.11 | 10.06 | .55 | .79 | 44.17 | 24.62 | 8.16667 | 1 | -0.63147 |
| 73. | 6.75 | 7.06 | .32 | .87 | 27.16 | 58.87 | 6.07667 | 1 | -0.10221 |
| 74. | 7.46 | 6.62 | .40 | .84 | 3.93 | 85.48 | 6.64333 | 1 | 0.64003 |
| 75. | 2.02 | 6.89 | .33 | .15 | 3.9 | 32.50 | 13.25333 | 1 | 0.57852 |
| 77. | 7.05 | 16.78 | .38 | .88 | 3.86 | 16.96 | 12.11333 | 1 | -0.12001 |

| RANK | X3 | X4 | X8 | X13 | X15 | X17 | X17MEAN* | GROUP | Z |
|---|---|---|---|---|---|---|---|---|---|
| 81. | 10.35 | 4.06 | 0.52 | 0.00 | 4.26 | 39.97 | 14.14667 | 1 | 0.68897 |
| 82. | 5.24 | 11.55 | 0.35 | 0.93 | 19.15 | 32.11 | 6.03000 | 1 | -0.33188 |
| 83. | 7.42 | 5.53 | 0.80 | 0.12 | 7.27 | 43.68 | 15.71333 | 1 | 1.37098 |
| 85. | 6.65 | 11.03 | 0.57 | 2.18 | 4.36 | 140.24 | 4.59333 | 1 | 1.29309 |
| 88. | 8.05 | 18.42 | 0.51 | 0.77 | 4.73 | 9.54 | 15.72000 | 1 | 0.14737 |
| 89. | 3.49 | 13.38 | 0.35 | 0.02 | 10.29 | 106.45 | 18.87000 | 1 | 1.77731 |
| 90. | 9.10 | 10.40 | 0.90 | 0.12 | 4.10 | 30.89 | 14.87000 | 1 | 1.20158 |
| 92. | 3.64 | 6.26 | 0.21 | 1.91 | -21.46 | 28.41 | 5.86000 | 1 | -0.25608 |
| 93. | 7.11 | 8.55 | 0.32 | 0.22 | 26.92 | 40.47 | 10.13667 | 1 | -0.02909 |
| 94. | 4.77 | 12.47 | 0.31 | 0.15 | 5.36 | 38.89 | 7.51333 | 1 | 0.07995 |
| 96. | 5.59 | 9.67 | 0.24 | 0.49 | 20.06 | 64.24 | 10.13000 | 1 | 0.24922 |
| 97. | 6.89 | 4.26 | 0.49 | 1.36 | 15.70 | 29.41 | 9.08333 | 1 | -0.00223 |
| 98. | 7.48 | 8.45 | 0.74 | 0.44 | 17.10 | 23.85 | 24.52000 | 1 | 1.32254 |
| 100. | 11.99 | 4.14 | 0.89 | 0.05 | 11.32 | 25.92 | 21.61000 | 1 | 1.38163 |
| 101. | 20.78 | 3.06 | 0.62 | 0.38 | 43.77 | 15.32 | 29.45667 | 1 | 0.43835 |
| 103. | 9.22 | 12.60 | 0.73 | 0.18 | 34.27 | 94.05 | 13.95000 | 1 | 1.39379 |
| 105. | 14.47 | 17.19 | 0.72 | 1.50 | -0.83 | 19.50 | 6.33333 | 1 | -0.30823 |
| 107. | 7.94 | 18.47 | 0.52 | 0.54 | 2.09 | 47.01 | 5.76000 | 1 | 0.16851 |
| 109. | 3.13 | 4.52 | 0.35 | 1.41 | 2.18 | 20.15 | 9.52333 | 1 | -0.02340 |
| 110. | 2.63 | 15.38 | 0.62 | 1.02 | 21.96 | 45.82 | 8.39000 | 1 | 0.48322 |
| 113. | 9.39 | 1.17 | 0.56 | 0.21 | 3.39 | 39.76 | 20.39333 | 1 | 1.17122 |
| 124. | 6.40 | 4.41 | 0.59 | 0.13 | 11.39 | 42.28 | 26.12000 | 1 | 1.63961 |
| 128. | 8.03 | 7.30 | 0.41 | 0.95 | 5.15 | 39.42 | 5.15000 | 1 | -0.13709 |
| 129. | 7.31 | 30.30 | 0.50 | 1.30 | 17.65 | 37.02 | 7.35000 | 1 | -0.31062 |

| RANK | X3 | X4 | X8 | X13 | X15 | X17 | X17MEAN* | GROUP | Z |
|---|---|---|---|---|---|---|---|---|---|
| 131. | 5.09 | 5.86 | 0.35 | 0.83 | 1.65 | 44.90 | 9.51667 | 1 | 0.31805 |
| 134. | 10.46 | 17.19 | 0.65 | 1.97 | 71.74 | 50.84 | 5.88667 | 1 | -0.63491 |
| 142. | 7.15 | 5.49 | 0.51 | 1.57 | 8.40 | 40.93 | 3.28667 | 1 | -0.14441 |
| 143. | 2.58 | 5.50 | 0.26 | 1.66 | -22.68 | 19.21 | 3.65333 | 1 | -0.31066 |
| 144. | 3.23 | 5.08 | 0.25 | 0.00 | 57.78 | 69.25 | 16.08333 | 1 | 0.56738 |
| 146. | 4.17 | 10.24 | 0.44 | 0.86 | 17.28 | 27.31 | 11.44000 | 1 | 0.16943 |
| 155. | 2.08 | 5.23 | 0.04 | 0.86 | -7.44 | 83.64 | -7.87333 | 1 | -0.43962 |
| 156. | 8.94 | 5.81 | 0.99 | 1.49 | 10.37 | 40.28 | 27.10000 | 1 | 1.94418 |
| 157. | 8.20 | 6.47 | 0.38 | 2.09 | 30.73 | 65.61 | 5.78000 | 1 | -0.25562 |
| 164. | 5.42 | 6.79 | 0.39 | 0.42 | 10.93 | 53.65 | 9.94000 | 1 | 0.48534 |
| 167. | 5.86 | 10.01 | 0.34 | 1.12 | 4.76 | 62.70 | 6.12667 | 1 | 0.17652 |
| 168. | 4.94 | 5.39 | 0.27 | 0.20 | -4.84 | 65.61 | 8.25333 | 1 | 0.59306 |
| 169. | 7.33 | 8.27 | 0.25 | 0.11 | -12.68 | 28.23 | 5.06000 | 1 | -0.20147 |
| 174. | 29.98 | 2.15 | 0.86 | 0.01 | 34.14 | 28.68 | 16.28333 | 1 | -0.04145 |
| 177. | 5.80 | 6.31 | 0.32 | 1.10 | 42.07 | 0.00 | .10333 | 1 | -1.40499 |
| 182. | 3.24 | 4.82 | 0.31 | 0.03 | 47.58 | 85.10 | 10.48667 | 1 | 0.65494 |
| 184. | 4.82 | 6.92 | 0.27 | 0.92 | 2.27 | 31.94 | 6.05000 | 1 | -0.21900 |
| 186. | 2.86 | 6.30 | 0.12 | 0.17 | -23.02 | 98.95 | 1.14333 | 1 | 0.66939 |
| 189. | 4.20 | 13.04 | 0.18 | 0.15 | 36.36 | 46.86 | 12.44333 | 1 | -0.02379 |
| 199. | 9.11 | 8.38 | 0.66 | 0.43 | 112.16 | 37.97 | 10.41333 | 1 | -0.48244 |
| 200. | 4.45 | 6.04 | 0.37 | 1.04 | 6.08 | 44.66 | 9.18667 | 1 | 0.27452 |
| 201. | 2.64 | 1.72 | 0.23 | 0.05 | -7.93 | 23.11 | 17.60667 | 1 | 0.70717 |
| 204. | 4.23 | 4.43 | 0.34 | 0.45 | -8.61 | 39.36 | 1.84000 | 1 | 0.00544 |
| 205. | 4.99 | 10.02 | 0.52 | 1.32 | -20.61 | 28.97 | 5.82000 | 1 | 0.25073 |

| RANK | X3 | X4 | X8 | X13 | X15 | X17 | X17MEAN* | GROUP | Z |
|---|---|---|---|---|---|---|---|---|---|
| 207. | 6.08 | 5.93 | 0.38 | 0.10 | 7.55 | 34.17 | 22.14667 | 1 | 0.98986 |
| 208. | 5.10 | 9.12 | 0.49 | 0.40 | -1.19 | 39.98 | 10.26333 | 1 | 0.59539 |
| 212. | 2.65 | 15.86 | 0.17 | 2.36 | 0.56 | 0.00 | -3.69000 | 1 | -1.64378 |
| 215. | 8.29 | 8.98 | 0.42 | 2.41 | 13.56 | 89.29 | 9.74000 | 1 | 0.45147 |
| 217. | 3.85 | .00 | 0.35 | 1.27 | -20.41 | 80.18 | 5.00333 | 1 | 0.80909 |
| 220. | 10.25 | 11.30 | 0.41 | 0.57 | 0.69 | 49.01 | 10.48333 | 1 | 0.26878 |
| 222. | 7.20 | 3.79 | 0.33 | 1.76 | -21.17 | 31.98 | 3.92000 | 1 | -0.24784 |
| 228. | 3.19 | 3.43 | 0.29 | 0.73 | 23.96 | 0.00 | -.27667 | 1 | -1.06248 |
| 229. | 3.76 | 14.48 | 0.33 | 0.44 | 23.43 | 40.57 | 9.96000 | 1 | 0.07197 |
| 230. | 4.41 | 15.92 | 0.24 | 0.94 | -4.53 | 0.00 | 2.04000 | 1 | -0.96424 |
| 232. | 5.77 | 8.48 | 0.43 | 0.31 | 15.29 | 36.82 | 12.90000 | 1 | 0.43290 |
| 234. | 6.10 | 16.62 | 0.42 | 1.65 | 15.15 | 43.61 | 8.28667 | 1 | -0.11879 |
| 235. | 3.60 | 13.94 | 0.60 | 1.27 | 16.17 | 38.54 | 8.57667 | 1 | 0.34066 |
| 236. | 6.10 | 6.04 | 0.56 | 0.18 | 9.92 | 13.16 | 15.36000 | 1 | 0.55495 |
| 237. | 7.05 | 10.80 | 0.48 | 3.43 | 4.72 | 94.48 | 4.40000 | 1 | 0.24800 |
| 239. | 8.60 | 12.10 | 0.36 | 0.51 | 43.49 | 33.28 | 7.08333 | 1 | -0.57838 |
| 240. | 9.52 | 2.59 | 0.39 | 0.77 | -12.46 | 45.37 | 1.88667 | 1 | -0.08989 |
| 241. | 3.47 | 5.88 | 0.30 | 1.31 | -41.44 | 0.00 | 3.62000 | 1 | -0.30704 |
| 242. | 8.75 | 6.07 | 0.29 | 0.95 | 9.63 | 31.63 | 3.72667 | 1 | -0.59347 |
| 243. | 9.54 | 4.31 | 0.45 | 0.70 | 8.24 | 36.56 | 10.74000 | 1 | 0.19313 |
| 258. | 6.66 | 5.14 | 0.48 | 0.74 | 15.98 | 31.79 | 19.54000 | 2 | 0.74449 |
| 259. | 5.41 | 10.68 | 0.28 | 0.05 | 18.74 | -3.66 | 9.74667 | 2 | -0.55353 |
| 262. | 2.65 | 5.20 | 0.23 | 0.93 | -14.18 | 157.14 | 4.57333 | 2 | 1.65023 |
| 263. | 6.71 | 12.75 | 0.38 | 0.00 | 7.60 | 0.00 | 3.09000 | 2 | -0.69781 |

| RANK | X3 | X4 | X8 | X13 | X15 | X17 | X17MEAN* | GROUP | Z |
|---|---|---|---|---|---|---|---|---|---|
| 265. | 5.75 | 12.41 | 0.35 | 1.04 | 14.02 | 26.20 | 7.12667 | 2 | -0.35292 |
| 266. | 2.94 | 24.62 | 0.11 | 5.20 | -14.67 | 26.09 | 4.90000 | 2 | -1.36389 |
| 267. | 5.78 | 10.09 | 0.38 | 1.01 | 27.56 | 48.33 | 9.58000 | 2 | 0.04132 |
| 269. | 3.47 | 15.64 | 0.29 | 3.33 | 12.25 | 47.44 | 5.46000 | 2 | -0.58685 |
| 270. | 18.14 | 8.12 | 0.23 | 0.66 | 30.11 | 47.80 | 9.52000 | 2 | -0.77191 |
| 271. | 6.92 | 11.47 | 0.66 | 1.29 | -1.02 | 38.99 | 4.59333 | 2 | 0.24290 |
| 273. | 9.59 | 8.67 | 0.31 | 1.17 | 14.64 | 18.15 | 5.58333 | 2 | -0.80032 |
| 276. | 4.88 | 4.93 | 0.38 | 0.44 | 5.21 | 19.70 | 6.36000 | 2 | -0.10931 |
| 277. | 3.96 | 7.41 | 0.22 | 0.09 | 23.86 | 190.36 | .80667 | 2 | 1.55269 |
| 281. | 8.05 | 5.53 | 0.66 | 2.81 | 42.29 | 21.97 | 18.70667 | 2 | 0.13332 |
| 282. | 3.65 | 8.49 | 0.34 | 1.63 | 19.61 | 12.87 | 7.12667 | 2 | -0.56969 |
| 283. | 7.08 | 167.59 | 0.27 | 1.23 | 33.47 | 36.16 | 6.78333 | 2 | -2.44291 |
| 284. | 5.05 | 6.26 | 0.28 | 2.31 | 13.92 | 33.48 | 10.21000 | 2 | -0.31509 |
| 285. | 11.84 | 29.20 | 0.52 | 0.64 | 23.93 | 25.62 | 6.50000 | 2 | -0.63965 |
| 287. | 4.34 | 16.56 | 0.34 | 1.65 | 15.59 | 35.01 | 7.61667 | 2 | -0.32492 |
| 288. | 4.20 | 4.12 | 0.30 | 3.41 | 25.00 | 0.00 | 1.00333 | 2 | -1.53660 |
| 290. | 1.94 | 9.50 | 0.23 | 2.12 | -8.78 | 40.67 | 6.12333 | 2 | -0.15711 |
| 295. | 5.17 | 31.20 | 0.52 | 4.51 | 23.01 | 0.00 | 3.83667 | 2 | -1.54963 |
| 305. | 19.83 | 7.69 | 0.27 | 0.56 | 36.34 | 20.19 | 11.56333 | 2 | -1.09070 |
| 307. | 7.42 | 3.33 | 0.50 | 1.54 | 9.24 | 0.00 | 5.35000 | 2 | -0.59652 |
| 308. | 4.60 | 4.97 | 0.51 | 0.24 | 10.80 | 38.74 | 9.39667 | 2 | 0.54152 |
| 310. | 3.60 | 6.30 | 0.30 | 0.58 | 39.81 | -125.00 | 1.45000 | 2 | -2.85696 |
| 311. | 5.60 | 9.32 | 0.42 | 0.91 | 11.53 | 0.00 | 8.78667 | 2 | -0.40965 |
| 313. | 5.22 | 9.94 | 0.38 | 0.16 | 30.16 | 23.79 | 14.68333 | 2 | 0.16433 |

| RANK | X3 | X4 | X8 | X13 | X15 | X17 | X17MEAN* | GROUP | Z |
|---|---|---|---|---|---|---|---|---|---|
| 326. | 9.38 | 2.36 | 0.42 | 2.18 | -7.04 | 0.00 | 0.91000 | 2 | -1.03171 |
| 328. | 14.82 | 12.56 | 0.65 | 0.03 | 13.96 | 21.47 | 19.36667 | 2 | 0.53162 |
| 330. | 33.84 | 3.47 | 0.38 | 0.95 | 18.32 | 21.16 | 9.23333 | 2 | -1.57519 |
| 336. | 3.48 | 4.79 | 0.33 | 0.01 | 26.90 | 41.29 | 12.90333 | 2 | 0.42534 |
| 338. | 4.34 | 12.22 | 0.37 | 1.09 | 13.15 | 16.13 | 8.87000 | 2 | -0.28428 |
| 346. | 5.35 | 3.26 | 0.51 | 1.75 | 5.81 | 12.55 | 14.18333 | 2 | 0.21408 |
| 349. | 3.89 | 11.23 | 0.44 | 1.09 | 3.84 | 44.77 | 5.10667 | 2 | 0.13258 |
| 364. | 9.62 | 5.68 | 0.44 | 0.81 | -4.83 | 58.17 | 6.44667 | 2 | 0.31368 |
| 373. | 2.71 | 9.36 | 0.26 | 0.53 | -21.44 | 0.00 | -7.23667 | 2 | -1.07193 |
| 374. | 2.26 | 7.53 | 0.29 | 2.34 | 21.77 | 0.32 | 6.23667 | 2 | -0.95117 |
| 377. | 4.62 | 24.42 | 0.29 | 2.59 | 30.49 | 0.00 | 0.24667 | 2 | -1.75441 |
| 382. | 10.24 | 28.68 | 0.58 | 1.39 | 38.56 | 22.84 | 6.94000 | 2 | -0.75395 |
| 383. | 9.45 | 3.65 | 0.25 | 0.35 | 9.53 | -10.38 | 4.74667 | 2 | -1.07474 |
| 384. | 3.49 | 7.57 | 0.12 | 2.97 | 0.73 | 0.00 | -1.06333 | 2 | -1.63313 |
| 391. | 24.90 | 3.71 | 0.33 | 1.39 | 6.39 | 23.60 | 6.39333 | 2 | -1.30935 |
| 419. | 20.43 | 8.49 | 0.42 | 1.14 | 9.18 | 26.95 | 7.99667 | 2 | -0.83351 |
| 421. | 5.07 | 7.67 | 0.48 | 0.58 | 37.40 | 44.82 | 10.52000 | 2 | 0.25691 |
| 426. | 5.43 | 7.50 | -0.31 | 0.00 | -0.57 | 0.00 | -21.8933 | 2 | -3.10219 |
| 429. | 6.11 | 9.72 | 0.44 | 0.64 | 61.29 | 58.26 | 9.65333 | 2 | -0.00158 |
| 438. | 3.44 | 12.89 | -0.03 | 3.30 | -25.54 | 0.00 | -6.59667 | 2 | -2.06176 |
| 439. | 7.75 | 13.43 | 0.34 | 1.26 | 27.18 | 8.21 | 6.59333 | 2 | -0.93441 |
| 443. | 2.81 | 2.69 | 0.10 | 3.37 | 36.02 | 0.00 | -4.04000 | 2 | -2.18152 |
| 445. | 3.05 | 4.47 | 0.25 | 0.25 | 2.23 | 0.00 | -1.17667 | 2 | -0.87845 |
| 454. | 7.68 | 7.71 | 1.05 | 0.72 | 16.04 | 69.78 | 6.05000 | 2 | 1.33624 |

| RANK | X3 | X4 | X8 | X13 | X15 | X17 | X17MEAN* | GROUP | Z |
|---|---|---|---|---|---|---|---|---|---|
| 455. | 13.86 | 8.57 | 0.47 | 1.68 | 23.63 | 16.26 | 7.17000 | 2 | -0.86633 |
| 457. | 2.82 | 3.99 | -0.06 | 19.76 | 9.35 | 0.00 | -5.88000 | 2 | -5.34176 |
| 460. | 6.20 | 8.66 | 0.14 | 0.50 | -6.53 | 44.44 | -7.73333 | 2 | -0.99563 |
| 466. | 7.26 | 13.41 | -0.57 | 0.00 | -47.50 | 0.00 | -14.0667 | 2 | -2.75546 |
| 479. | 3.47 | 7.87 | 0.31 | 0.45 | 8.93 | 9.09 | 6.05333 | 2 | -0.39205 |
| 480. | 3.75 | 7.85 | 0.14 | 5.38 | 31.02 | 0.00 | -7.05000 | 2 | -2.72174 |
| 481. | 1.70 | 73.28 | -0.04 | 7.23 | -45.07 | 0.00 | -4.90000 | 2 | -3.11574 |
| 494. | 4.19 | 1.27 | 0.16 | 0.60 | 23.86 | 0.00 | 3.78000 | 2 | -1.03756 |
| 500. | 5.97 | 15.23 | 0.41 | 1.46 | 19.86 | 0.00 | 5.34333 | 2 | -0.90136 |

Here X17MEAN* is a variable representing the mean value of X1, X6 and X16.

# Index

### D



### E



### F



### G



### H

I



K



L



M



N



O



P